ESSAYS ON
PRIMITIVISM AND RELATED IDEAS IN THE
MIDDLE AGES

CONTRIBUTIONS TO THE HISTORY OF PRIMITIVISM

ESSAYS ON PRIMITIVISM AND RELATED IDEAS IN THE MIDDLE AGES

BY

GEORGE BOAS

BALTIMORE

THE JOHNS HOPKINS PRESS

1948

PRINTED IN THE UNITED STATES OF AMERICA
BY J. H. FURST COMPANY, BALTIMORE, MARYLAND

ACKNOWLEDGMENTS

The author desires to express his thanks to the Council of Learned Societies, to Dr. Panos Morphopoulos, to Miss Margaret Boehm, to Dr. Grace Frank, and to Professor Harold Cherniss for aid in the preparation of this volume.

ABBREVIATIONS

CSEL — *Corpus scriptorum ecclesiasticorum Latinorum*

EETS — Early English Text Society

MGH — *Monumenta Germaniae historica*

MPG — Migne's *Patrologia Graeca*

MPL — Migne's *Patrologia Latina*

PIA   — Lovejoy and Boas, *Primitivism and Related Ideas in Antiquity*

CONTENTS

PREFACE

In 1935 the author of the essays which compose this book published in collaboration with Professor A. O. Lovejoy the first of what was to have been a series of four volumes, covering the history of primitivism and related ideas. This first volume, *Primitivism and Related Ideas in Antiquity*, was based upon an exhaustive reading of all the texts which remain of classical literature. A documentary history, it presented side by side the Greek and Latin originals and English translations. It was hoped that after a reasonable interval it might be possible to publish a second volume which would cover medieval literature in the same fashion. To do so would have required the services of collaborators skilled in Byzantine and Western European theological and philosophical writings, in liturgy, in secular literature, and all this not only in the ancient tongues but also in the vernaculars. A few months of preliminary survey sufficed to convince the authors that they would have to be much more modest in their program. For the field was too rich and the possible collaborators too busy with their own affairs to undertake so distracting a task.

Accordingly, the authors decided to limit the second volume to the Patristic Period and work was begun on that basis. But though their files grew steadily and enough material was in time available to make up a volume, the second World War broke out and they found themselves so involved in it that all writing of this sort had to be abandoned. The author of these essays spent over two years in the United States Navy and, though Professor Lovejoy was not in uniform, he too gave all his energies and time to the cause for which we were presumably fighting.

When the War closed and release from national service was secured, the two collaborators again surveyed the work and it was decided that the junior partner publish a series of essays on *Primitivism and Related Ideas in the Middle Ages*. These essays cannot be considered to be a satisfactory substitute for the volume which was originally planned. They are neither complete nor exhaustive, nor do they exhibit that detailed analysis of ideas which characterised the first volume. Though they make passing reference to secular and sometimes to vernacular literatures, they make no serious attempt to do more than glance at them. But to give these essays a title which would indicate their contents with exactitude would produce something so cumbersome that a short title would have been necessitated for purposes of reference, to say nothing of printing. Their author is now too old and too ignorant to venture upon as complete an analysis of medieval literature as would be desirable. He may be wrong in offering the public a work so admittedly far from perfect. But he has the feeling that younger men may be interested in

completing a study which he still believes to have importance for an understanding of intellectual history. These essays then are suggestions for
further research. At a minimum they demonstrate the continuity of ideas
between pagan and Christian civilizations in one field as well as the peculiar
modifications which the latter introduced into a group of favorite classical
topoi. They may also be said to drive the piles for a bridge between the
Renaissance and Classical Antiquity, although the superstructure itself
remains to be constructed.

In writing these essays, their author had the advantage of access to notes
and comments by Professor Lovejoy. In certain sections, such as that on the
Biblical sources, Lactantius, Tertullian, Saint Ambrose, the *Clementina*,
whole paragraphs have been lifted bodily from such notes. In the very nature
of the case this was inevitable. For frequently the first draft had been written
by the author of these essays; it was then rewritten by Professor Lovejoy; it
was then reviewed by its original author and after consultation either revised
once more or accepted as it stood. Just who is responsible for what is no
longer determinable. At the same time, the version as printed here must be
attributed solely to the author whose name appears on the title page. If
there are errors, he alone committed them. If there are omissions, he alone
failed to fill them. None of the short-comings of this volume must be laid
to his colleague's door, except in the sense that he generously gave his permission to use the material, part of which he prepared, as might be seen fit.
Thus a very heavy debt is owing him. It is too bad that it cannot be more
adequately repaid.

G. B.

The Johns Hopkins University
1946

PRIMITIVISM AND RELATED IDEAS IN PHILO-JUDAEUS

Philo-Judaeus is of peculiar importance in this study as the earliest writer to attempt a fusion of pagan and Hebraic ideas. His work, as we see it now, was the systematization and restatement of the religion of Judaism in the language of the various philosophic schools influential in Alexandria in the first century B. C. His technical vocabulary is Peripatetic, but he is likely to use it as Plotinus did two centuries later,[1] to express ideas which would have been repugnant to Aristotle and which are commonly called Platonistic to-day. Along with much of the number-symbolism of the Neo-Pythagoreans Philo retains many of the ethical notions of the Cynics and Stoics, and has justly been described as a " Stoicising Platonist." [2] But wherever possible, such elements in his thinking serve to elucidate what he believes to be the truths of Judaism and if, for instance, he makes the young Moses appear as half Stoic-Sage and half Philosopher-King, it is not as an apologist for Stoicism and Platonism but to point out that the Jewish tradition contained all the truth of the pagan philosophies and contained it before it had appeared in literary form. One would scarcely be able to tell whether certain passages of Philo, lifted out of their context, were not written by a late Stoic; their general ideas, as well as their rhetoric, recall the *topoi* of writers like Cicero and Seneca. Some, such as the *De ebrietate*, are actually such *topoi*, and in at least one passage his argument is almost word for word like a passage of Seneca.[3]

Not only is the fusion of Hebrew and Pagan ideas characteristic of Philo, but he was, if not the inventor, at least the most influential exponent of a method for bringing about this fusion. This method is the interpretation of Scripture as allegory. The Pagans had been accustomed from at least the time of Plato to consider the poetry of Homer and Hesiod as disguised philosophy, but such poetry had not the authority in their thinking which the Scriptures had in that of the Jews and Christians. Philo's *Legum*

---

[1] Henri Guyot in *Les reminiscences de Philon le juif chez Plotin*, Paris, 1906, argues that Plotinus actually read Philo.

[2] See Helmut Schmidt, *Die Anthropologie Philons von Alexandreia*, Wuerzburg, 1933. Cf. P. Wendland, " Philo und die Kynisch-stoische Diatribe," in P. Wendland and O. Kern, *Beitr. z. Gesch. d. Griech. Phil. u. Relig.*, Berlin, 1895, pp. 17, 26 ff.; H. von Arnim, " Quellenstudien zu Philo von Alexandria," Berlin, 1888, in *Philologische Untersuchungen*, Vol. XI, esp. pp. 101 ff. and 108; D. W. Bosset, *Juedisch-Christlicher Schulbetrieb in Alexandria und Rom*, Goettingen, 1915, esp. pp. 26, 84-98; Isaak Heinemann, *Philons griechische und juedische Bildung*, Breslau, 1932.

[3] *De posteritate Caini*, xlvi (160-161). Cf. Seneca, *Ep. mor.*, XX, vii, 124. See *PIA*, p. 397.

Allegoria is the formulation of this exegetical technique. But it not only established a technique, it also established a tradition based upon the results of that technique. Thus Philo's interpretation of the story of the Garden of Eden was to be continued with only slight changes throughout the Middle Ages.

On some points it was inevitable that Philo's interpretation of the Scriptures should differ from that of the early Fathers. These were, of course, the points in which Christianity differed from Judaism. Philo was not under the necessity of interpreting the New Testament and, as a matter of fact, never went beyond the Pentateuch. But the Fathers had not only to harmonize the Gospels with one another and with the rest of the New Testament, but also to reconcile the whole of the latter with the Old Testament. The allegorical method was just what was required for that purpose. Philo had recourse to it presumably because a literal interpretation of the Scriptures would simply not make sense; and by making sense he meant, naturally, what was conceived as sense in that strange eclectic philosophy which he inherited from the Pagans. Thus when Moses says that God completed creation on the sixth day, Philo maintains that " sixth " as an ordinal number could not be meant, since God's creativity is not temporal, but that Moses simply meant to indicate a " perfect number." [4] It is not so easy to say what " making sense " meant for the Christians, for though they professedly all believed in the same fundamental doctrine, the existence of heresy and error proved that it was not always possible to tell what that doctrine was. The codification of dogma took time and was scarcely completed even with the formulation of the Nicene Creed in the fourth century. Consequently the key to Biblical allegory was always a matter of dispute in the first four or five centuries of Christianity.

In other words, the interpretation of an allegory demands a non-allegorical language. Such a language is naturally sought in philosophy and science. When the early Christians of the West turned to these sources, they found only the Pagan tradition. God to a reader of the Bible was Jehovah; but to an enlightened Pagan was the Prime Mover, or the Creator, or the Universal Spirit, or the One, depending upon whether the reader was educated mainly in Peripateticism, Platonism, Stoicism, or Neo-Platonism. Similar translations had to be made of all the supposed allegories in Scripture, the Creation and the Fall, the Deluge, the Wanderings in the Desert, and so on. Later on, when the concepts of Christianity came to acquire a non-figurative meaning, partly from men's being reared in them from infancy, partly by their lack of intellectual curiosity, and partly from the programmatic anti-intellectualism of some Western theologians, they became a key, strangely replacing that confused body of ideas which had been originally used to explain them.

---

[4] Why 6 is perfect need not concern us here. See *Legum allegoria*, I, ii (3-4).

Chronological primitivism

Adam allegorically is the *Nous*, as contrasted with Eve who is *Aisthesis*,[5] and the story of the Fall is interpreted as the corruption of *Nous* by sensual pleasure. But for Philo there are two Adams, the Adam of the first chapter of *Genesis* and the Adam of the second. The former Adam is the image of God, " a sort of idea or class-concept (*genos*) or pattern (*sphragis*), noetic, incorporeal, neither male nor female, immortal by nature." [6] The second Adam is a composite copy of the first, in part immortal and ideal, in part mortal and sensory. It is the latter who becomes the ancestor of the human race; the former is the original model or archetype—really a Platonic idea.

It is the second Adam who before the Fall is humanly perfect. His character is a model for ours and his body a standard of corporeal beauty. We thus find added to the Biblical account of the first man details which are inferred from philosophical considerations in themselves foreign to the Hebraic tradition. There was nothing in Hebrew thought to suggest that the image of God was a Platonic Idea. Nor was there anything to suggest that corporeal beauty would consist in Pythagorean numerical ratios. And when it was a question of psychic excellence, there was certainly nothing except Greek tradition upon which Philo could argue that Adam was *kalos kai agathos*.

> That first man, the earth-born, the original ancestor of our whole race, seems to me to have been born in the best condition of both soul and body, and to have differed to a great degree from those who succeeded him by his high superiority in both. For that man was in truth really beautiful and good.
>
> One might give evidence of the fair form of his body from three things, of which this is the first. At the moment of the appearance of the newly created earth after its separation from the great water, which was named " sea," it happened that the matter of the things which came into being was unmixed and clean and pure, as well as supple and workable, wherefore the things made from it were, as might be expected, without flaw. In the second place, it was not likely that God, taking clay from some chance part of the earth, would have been willing to fashion this manlike image in haste, but rather that He should have selected from all earth the best, from pure matter the purest and most highly sifted, which was especially adapted to His plan. For a sort of dwelling or sacred temple of the rational soul was being constructed, which was to enshrine the most godlike of images. In the third place—and this is beyond comparison with what has been said—the Creator was good especially in intelligence, so that each part of the body in itself had the numerical proportions fitting to it, and in relation to the entire structure was harmoniously finished. And along with symmetry He clothed it well

[5] This is a commonplace in Philo, but see esp. *Op. mundi*, lix (165) ; *Leg. alleg.*, II, xi (38).

[6] *Op. mundi*, xlvi (134). This may not have been original with Philo. Cf. C. H. Kraeling, *Anthropos and Son of Man*, N. Y., 1927.

with flesh and beautified it with a fine complexion, wishing the first man to appear as beautiful as possible.

And that he was also best in soul is evident. For God seems to have used the pattern of no other generated thing in constructing him, but only, as I have said, His own reason. Wherefore He says that man was created in His image and as a copy of Him when He breathed into his face, wherein is the place of the senses, with which the Creator animated the body; but installing reason as king, He endowed the guiding faculty with a guardian for the apprehension of colors and sounds and tastes and odors and so on, which without sensation, reason by its own power could not grasp. And the copy of an absolutely beautiful model must itself be absolutely beautiful. But God's reason is superior to beauty itself, such as beauty is in nature, since it is not adorned with beauty, but is itself, if the truth be told, the most glorious adornment of beauty.[7]

Adam's condition is further expounded in a later passage, in which a technical and a pacifist state of nature are mentioned. The first man in this passage becomes a cosmopolite of the Stoic type, tempered somewhat by the Biblical story of man's dominion over the animal kingdom.

Should we call that original ancestor [of our race] not only the first man but also the only cosmopolite, we should not be speaking falsely. For the cosmos was both his home and his state, since nothing had been made by the work of hands, created out of stone and wood. In this cosmos, as if in his fatherland, he spent his days in all security, being far from fear, since he had been judged worthy of the rule over the things of earth; and all mortality cowered before him and obeyed him as if taught, or compelled to, and he lived blamelessly in the comfort of a peace uninterrupted by war.[8]

The union of *Nous* and Sense-perception which is the first couple was described in *Genesis* as "naked." The nakedness of Adam and Eve means, according to Philo, a complete absence of both vice and virtue. In that they are like infants.[9] That the condition of Adam was that of an infant occurred to later writers also—possibly because of this remark of Philo's. But the observation could lead to two diverse conclusions: first, that, if the first man was an infant, he was at the beginning of a history which could show only growth and hence improvement; second, that since he was the first man, and the primal is better than that which comes after it, it must be better to be like an infant than to be like an adult. It is easy to develop

---

[7] *De opificio mundi*, xlvii-xlviii (136-139). Ed. Cohn-Wendland, Vol. I, pp. 47-49. All future references are to this edition unless otherwise indicated. In the Middle Ages "the second Adam usually refers to Christ."

[8] *Op. mundi*, xlix (142).

[9] See *Leg. alleg.*, II, xv (53). In the *Quaest. in Gen.*, I, 30, Philo says that their lack of shame was due to the simplicity and sincerity of their way of life and to their natural disposition which had no pride. Ambition, he says, was not yet born. For the evil effects of pride in man's early history, cf. Lucretius in *PIA*, pp. 231 and 241.

the latter conclusion into praise of childlike innocence, especially when certain Biblical verses of both testaments were remembered. The first couple according to Philo were so devoid of vice or virtue that they had not even the feeling of their powers of reason or perception.[10] Philo swears " by the only true God " that he deems nothing so shameful as " to assume that I think or that I perceive." [11] Shame enters with the exercise of mind or perception. But " so long as they are naked, the mind of thinking, sense of sensation, they are in no way shameful." Adam and Eve, therefore, were originally unthinking thought and unperceiving sense; they were in Aristotelian language unexercised potencies, and in this respect were also like children. But Aristotle, of course, would not have found such a condition praiseworthy.

The theory of decline

The notion of Adam's perfection is not merely a deduction from his divine origin. Chronological primitivism in Philo's mind seems to be associated with the Aristotelian principle of the natural prority of the " form." But whereas Aristotle thought the form better than its incorporation, he did not believe that within any species the later incorporations were worse than the earlier. In Philo the decline has a twofold explanation. The children of Adam must be worse than their father, for they were born of men, whereas he was born of God. But there is a general principle of decline running through creation, so that later generations receive " ever dimmer forms and powers." If the words, *morphas* and *dynameis*, in this passage retained their Aristotelian connotation, human degeneration would seem to have consisted in the growing weakness of man's purposes and of his powers of realizing them.

> Such the first man appears to me to have been created in body and soul, surpassing all those who now exist and those who existed before us. For we are born of men, but God created him. And the better the maker is, the better is his creation. For just as that which is in flower is always better than that which is past its prime, either animal or plant or fruit or anything in the natural order, so the first man to be formed seems to have been the flower of our whole race, and those after him never to have bloomed like him, for they, generation after generation, receive ever dimmer forms and powers.
>
> Such I have seen to be the case in sculpture and painting. For the copies fall short of the originals and the things drawn or sculptured after the copies much more so, for they are at a great distance from their source. The magnet produces the same impression. For of the iron rings, the one touching the magnet is held most strongly, but the one touching that one less, and the third hangs down from the second, the fourth from the third, and the fifth from the fourth, and the others from the others in a long row, supported by one attractive force, but not in the same way. For always those hanging farther

---

[10] *Leg. alleg.*, II, xvii (68 f.).   [11] *Ib.*

2

from the beginning are loosened because of the diminution of the attraction which is no longer able to hold them equally. The race of men seems to have suffered much the same sort of thing too, receiving, generation after generation, weaker powers and qualities of body and soul.[12]

A doctrine frequently associated with the theory of human degeneration was that of terrestrial senescence. It was believed by certain of the Pagans that life was produced by the spontaneous fertility of the earth. Why then, since other productive agencies lose their vigor, should not the earth, as in the *Book of Ezra*—and in Lucretius and Stoicism—grow old and barren? Philo, though he believes in a decline of man, does not admit a corresponding decline of the earth, or of its products, i. e., plants and their fruits.

> What then hinders men from sprouting out of the earth as they say they did in ancient times? Has the earth grown so old that it is thought to have become barren with the lapse of time? On the contrary, it remains ever young, unchanged, because it is the fourth part of the whole and for the sake of the permanence of the whole it is bound not to waste away, since its sister elements, water, air, and fire, continue free from senility. And visible proof of the uninterrupted and eternal prime of the earth is the vegetation that grows out of her. For purified either by freshets, as they say Egypt is, or by yearly rains, she is refreshed after the fatigue of her fruitfulness, and relaxed, and then, after resting, she recovers her proper potencies to full strength, and takes up again her generation of similar things, to bestow unstinted food upon all species of living beings.[13]

Cycles

The Stoic was able to retain at least an appearance of preserving both the doctrine of the conservation of matter and the principle of universal degeneration by the assumption of cosmic cycles.[14] For a Jew, even though inclined to Stoicism in his ethics, it was impossible to maintain either the persistent degeneration of the cosmos or its periodic renascence and decay. For Philo particularly, the world was the perfect work of a perfect Creator,

---

[12] *Op. mundi*, xlix (140-141). Cf. lii (148), on the loss of vigor through racial senescence. The metaphor of the magnet comes from Plato's *Ion*, 533 D. Cf. Euripides, frag. 567.

[13] *De aeternitate mundi*, VI (61-62). The doctrine of cosmic senescence had a long and influential history which we shall not attempt to cover in these essays. One of its earliest Christian exponents was Saint Cyprian, Bishop of Carthage, whose letter, *Ad Demetrianum*, 3, 4, contained one of the most widely read versions of the notion. This letter was written to a Roman proconsul in Africa who had maintained that the evils of the times were due to the spread of Christianity and the consequent neglect of the gods. Cyprian replies that the evils follow necessarily from the senility of the world which is, in fact, approaching its death. See *MPL*, IV, pp. 546 ff. That even stones grew was apparently a commonplace in the early Christian period. Cf. Plotinus, *Enneades*, IV, iv, 27, 9.

[14] See *PIA*, pp. 79 ff., 156 ff., 170 ff., 217.

but it was the work of a Creator Who, like Plotinus's One, was always creating.[15] Hence if the flow of His activity did not cease, it would be logically impossible for the world as a whole to decay.

But there was enough of the Greek in Philo to give him a certain respect for the prestige of the theory of cycles in at least one of its forms. The rise and fall of empires was an old topic, part of the general concept of Fortune's ball or wheel.[16] It required no philosophical indoctrination to believe that "what goes up comes down." But Philo, characteristically, generalizes the idea, attributing the reverses of fortune to the cyclical course of the "divine logos."

> If you do not wish to survey the fortunes of particular men, take the changes in whole countries and nations both for better and for worse. Greece was once flourishing, but the Macedonians took away her power. Macedonia was then in flower, but when she was divided she weakened, until she entirely withered away. Before the Macedonians, Persia enjoyed good fortune, but one day laid low her great and mighty kingdom, and now Parthians, who were once the subjects of the Persians, rule over them, their former masters. Egypt shone in splendor and did so for the longest time, but like a cloud her great prosperity has vanished. And what of the Aethiopians and the Carthaginians and the kingdoms near Libya? And what of the kings of Pontus? What of Europe and Asia and, in a word, of the whole inhabited world? Is it not tossed up and down and shaken like a ship at sea, now blown upon by favorable, now by opposing winds? For in a circle turns the divine plan (*logos*), which many men name fortune. Always flowing, it allots in turn, by cities and nations and countries, the things of one to another and to all the things of all, periodically shifting only the possessions of each from hand to hand, so that like a single city the whole inhabited world may enjoy the best of governments, democracy.[17]

Nature as norm

The divine Logos appears as the "law of nature" in Philo's *De Josepho*, standing for a kind of ethical norm antecedent to all political law. This distinctively Stoic conception that there is a way of life which is more deeply rooted in human nature and better than custom or statute, is in essence the doctrine of the Cynics, but whereas the Cynic never brought out its social implications—arguing, for instance, that if men were more "natural," i. e., less warped from their true grain by custom, they would be more alike—the Stoic was never so anti-social. To him the law of nature

---

[15] *Leg. alleg.*, I, iii (5).

[16] The earliest artistic rendition of Fortune's ball, according to Kirby Flower Smith, is in Lycippus's picture of Kairos. See his edition of Tibullus, p. 306, note on *Eleg.* I, v, line 70.

[17] *Quod deus*, xxxvi (173-176). Cf. *De Abrahamo*, xli (242), for this appreciation of democracy. For an almost literal repetition of the passage on the vicissitudes of political supremacy, see *De Josepho*, xxiii (134 ff.).

was a law which bound men together in a Great City, the City of Zeus. This is Philo's language also, in spite of the Jewish tradition of racial and religious peculiarity. In such passages as the following, Jehovah is indistinguishable from the God of Marcus Aurelius: He is now not only the God of the Jews, but also the God of the Gentiles.

> For this cosmos is a Great City (*Megalopolis*) and enjoys one constitution and one law. And this is the law (*logos*) of nature, commanding what should be done and forbidding what should not be done. But these cities variously located are unlimited in number and have different constitutions and not the same laws, for individually they have invented and added new customs and laws. The cause of this is the unwillingness not only of Greeks to mingle and associate with barbarians, and of barbarians with Greeks, but also that of each race in regard to its own stock. Then too, as it seems, they give as causes of these, things which are not the causes, unfavorable seasons, sterility, poor soil, the site, that it is maritime or inland or insular or on the mainland or suchlike things, but the true cause they avoid. And this is covetousness and mistrust of one another, because of which they are not satisfied with the decrees of nature, but they call laws the things which seem to communities of like-thinking people to have general utility. Thus the individual constitutions are rather an addition to the natural constitution. For the laws of the particular cities are additions to the true law (*logos*) of nature, and the political man is an appendage to him who lives in accordance with nature.[18]

The kind of life which the law of nature prescribes is the typical simple life of the Stoic. Philo inveighs against superfluities with all the scorn of a Cynic but seldom becomes as ruthless in his search for *autarky* as the Diogenes of the legend. Thus in his life of Moses, he describes the lawgiver as existing solely for the sake of his people, caring nothing for external pomp.[19] His treasures are temperance, the ability to endure toil, justice, in short, the usual Stoic virtues. Philo's description of the Essences,[20] introduced to show that some good men are still found on earth, is preceded by a discussion of the evil effects of luxury and the search for needless rarities.

A characteristic passage emphasizing the endurance of the Sage is to be found in Philo's interpretation of the story of Jacob's stone pillow.

> He next says, " He took one of the stones of the place and set it under his head, and slept in that place." (*Gen.*, xxviii, 11). One admires not only his symbolical account and his philosophy, but also his literal meaning, guiding us to toil and patience. For he does not consider it worthy of one who is in pursuit of virtue to indulge

---

[18] *De Josepho*, VI (28-31). For similar ideas in Aristotle, see *PIA*, pp. 190 f., and in Cicero, *Ib.*, p. 256.

[19] *Vita Mosis*, I, vi (27-28).

[20] *Quod omnis probus*, x (62-74). The passage is printed in full in *PIA*, pp. 351 ff.

in luxurious living and to live delicately and to esteem highly the aims and ambitions of those who are called happy and who are in truth laden with unhappiness, whose whole life is a sleep and a dream, according to the most holy lawgiver. These men day by day, when they prosecuted their villainy upon others in law-courts and councils and theaters and everywhere, come home to overturn their own dwellings, unhappy beings—not that dwelling made of buildings, but the natural dwelling of the soul, the body—by unceasingly pouring into them unmeasured food and drowning them in much unmixed wine, until the reason is sunk and the passions below the belly, born of excess, are aroused, raging uncontrollably, and until, falling upon and embracing whomever they meet, they assuage their great madness and are relieved; and at night, when it would be proper to go to bed, they recline with excessive softness upon costly couches and em-broidered sheets with which they are well provided, imitating the luxury of women, whom nature has permitted to lead a more relaxed way of living, wherefore the Creator and Maker has made for them a body of softer stamp. Not such are the disciples of the holy *Logos*, but true men, temperate and well-ordered and lovers of modesty, who have laid down a foundation of self-control, limitation of needs, endurance, as the groundwork of their whole life, a safe refuge for the soul, in which it can lie as in a strong harbor free from danger; stronger than money and pleasure and opinion, disdainful of meat and drink and even of necessities, so long as hunger does not begin to overcome them, quite ready to submit to hunger and thirst and heat and cold and whatever other things are difficult for the sake of acquiring virtue; seeking things most easily procured, so that they are never ashamed in a cheap cloak, but, on the contrary, consider the costly as a reproach and a great danger to life—to these men the soft ground is a costly couch, and their bedding is brush, grass, straw, a great heap of leaves, under the head some stones or little mounds of earth rising somewhat above the level. Such a life the luxurious call hardship, but they who live for the good and fair call it the sweetest. For it is in harmony with those who are not merely called men, but who really are men.[21]

A similar argument is given in the second part of *De somniis*.

Behold what I wish to make clear. We are fed on food and drink, even if it is the cheapest barley and river water. Why then does vain opinion add a thousand kinds of milk cakes and honeyed pastry and elaborate and varied blends of countless wines seasoned for the enjoy-ment of pleasure rather than for the taking of nourishment? Again, the relishes needed for foods are leeks and greens, and many of the fruits and cheese also and anything else of that kind; and, if you wish, in the case of flesh-eating men, we will set down fish and meat besides. Would it not then have been enough to broil them and to roast them on the fire in a simple way and then to eat them like real

---

[21] *De somniis*, I, xx (120-125). The general tone of this passage is repeated in the characters of Joseph and Moses in the *De Josepho* and the *De vita Mosis*. The Cynic influence here is obvious and even the expression is closely parallel to that in the *Cynicus* attributed to Lucian. See *PIA*, pp. 136-145.

heroes? But it is not only such things that the gourmand craves, but, taking as his ally vain opinion and exciting his greedy passions, he searches about for cooks and table-dressers renowned for their art. And they, by baiting their hooks for the miserable belly in ways discovered many ages ago, and by preparing peculiar juices and setting them out in fine order, flatter and tame the palate. Then immediately they angle for the gateway to the senses, the sense of taste, by which the banquet-hunter appears in short order as a slave instead of a freeman.

Who does not know that clothing was first made as a protection for the body against the harm done by frost and summer heat? " Windproof," as the poets say somewhere, in winter . . . Who then contrived the costly purple robes, who the transparent and delicate gauzes, who the spiderweb wraps, who the costumes varied in dyes and weaves by the masters of dyeing and weaving and the inventors of imitative painting? Who? Was it not vain opinion?

But now we needed a house for the same reasons, and that we might not be harmed by wild beasts or by the attacks of men with natures worse than the beasts. Why then do we adorn the pavements and the walls with costly stones? Why do we search through Asia and Libya and all Europe and the islands, seeking for columns, chosen according to our family rank, and architraves? And why are we eager to have the glory of Doric and Ionic and Corinthian carvings and whatever those who scorn the established customs have discovered to adorn the capitals of our columns? Why do we build men's and women's apartments with golden ceilings? Is it not through vain opinion?

Surely for sleep the soft ground was enough—for it is said that up to the present time the Gymnosophists in India lie on the ground in accordance with their ancient custom—but if that be not enough, then a mattress of stones gathered at random or a bed of cheap planks.[22] But, on the contrary, bedsteads are provided with ivory feet and couches with costly mother-of-pearl and variegated tortoise-shell, inlaid with much labor and expense and taking much time, and some, all silver and gold and set with precious stones, have been adorned with bedding embroidered with flowers and threaded with gold, as if for show and ceremony, not for daily use. The creator of such things is vain opinion.

And what need was there to seek for other unguents than the oil pressed from the olive? For it softens the skin and relieves the fatigue of the body and creates portliness, and if anything is slack, it tightens it and infuses strength and firmness better than anything else. But a fortress has been reared against these useful things in the sweet unguents of vain opinion, for the making of which the perfume makers toil and great countries pay tribute, Syria, Babylon, India, Scythia, where the spice trees grow.

To drink what was needed more than the cup of nature, the most excellent production of art? Our hands are that cup. Anyone bringing them together and hollowing them, lifting them carefully to his mouth, while another pours the drink, not only procures the

---

[22] Omitting ἤ with MSS.

quenching of his thirst but even untold pleasure. And if a quite
different cup was needed, was not the rustic wooden cup sufficient,
but was it necessary to seek out the arts of other famous craftsmen?
Why make a huge quantity of silver and gold goblets, if not because
of great neighing vanity and vain opinion, swaying as in a hammock?

When some deem it important to be crowned not with laurel or
ivy, not with a sweet smelling wreath of violets or lilies or roses or
olive or of any flower whatsoever, but passing by the gifts of God,
which He gives through the seasons, devoid of shame, they hang gold
over their heads, a most heavy weight, in the middle of the agora
when it is full, what else is to be thought than that they are the slaves
of vain opinion, though they say that they are not only free but even
the leaders of many others?

The day will leave me as I recount the corruptions of human life.
And why need I speak at length about them? For who has not
heard of them, who has not seen them? Who has not rubbed up
against them and grown used to them? So that the Holy Word
named the enemy of modesty and the friend of arrogance " Addition "
[Joseph]. For just as on trees there grow superfluous sprouts, doing
great injury to the true tree, which the farmer gets rid of by cutting
them down with a view to the tree's needs, so there grows up round
about the true and simple life the false and vain, for which up to
this day no farmer has been found who will cut out the ruinous
superfluous growth with its very roots.[23]

The gospel of work

One might expect that Philo's contempt for luxury would pass over into
that form of hard primitivism which is illustratetd by the Cynic gospel of
work;[24] and there is, in fact, praise of toil in Philo as the source of all the
virtues. Yet he thinks of work as one of the consequences of the Fall.
If man had not yielded to pleasure, he would presumably have continued in
a state of virtue. But having fallen, he needed some help to return to virtue.
In Christianity this help would have been faith, works, the vicarious atonement, penance; in Philo it was simply labor. Thus he sees no inherent value
in work; it has simply the instrumental value of being a means to the
inherently good.

> At his very creation man found all preparations made for his life,
> for the instruction of those to come, since nature well nigh cried
> aloud so many words that, imitating the first parent of the race,
> they were to live without toil or suffering, with a bounteous supply
> of the necessities of life. And this will come to pass if the irrational
> pleasures of the soul do not prevail, erecting gluttony and lust into a
> fortress, or if the desires for reputation or money or power do not

---

[23] *De somniis*, II, vii-ix 48-64). The diatribe against luxury is continued in section
xxiii (155 ff.) of the same work. The passage is in part very similar to Seneca's
Ep. mor., XC; see *PIA*, pp. 264-274.

[24] See *PIA*, pp. 131 f.

clutch the strength of life for themselves, or sorrows do not control and twist the mind, or the bad counselor, fear, overthrow the impulses to earnest deeds or folly and cowardice and injustice and the incalculable sum of other evils set upon him. For now when all the things spoken of have won the day and men have poured themselves out wildly into their passions [25] and guilty yearnings of which it is not right to speak, fitting punishment is decreed, vengeance for impious practices. And the punishment is the difficulty of satisfying one's needs. For, always plowing the fields, and irrigating them from springs and rivers, and sowing them and planting and taking up through the years the weary toil of the farmer day and night without ceasing, they gather in their provisions; and there are times when these are poor or utterly insufficient, having been damaged by many causes. For either rainstorms one after the other fell upon them, or the heavy weight of hail falling flattened them out at one blow, or snow froze them, or the force of the wind tore them up by the roots. For in many ways water and air turn fertility into sterility. But if the unmeasured impulses of the passions were lightened by temperence, and zeal for injustice and ambition by a sense of justice, and, to be brief, the vices and aimless practices attendant upon them by virtues and the activities attendant upon the virtues, then, since the war against the soul would be abolished, which is truly the most painful and oppressive of wars, and since peace would prevail and gently and mildly prepare good order for the powers within us, there would be hope that God, inasmuch as He is a lover of virtue and of beauty and moreover of man, would immediately prepare good things spontaneously for the race. For it is clear that it is easier to give the supply of things existing without the art of agriculture than to bring things not already existing into being.[26]

In another passage Philo accentuates the importance of toil for the acquisition of virtue. God alone is without toil; man can achieve nothing except by labor.

. . . toil is the enemy of leisure, the first and greatest good, waging unheralded war against pleasure. For, to tell the truth, God has appointed toil for men as the source of all good and of all virtue, apart from which you will find nothing fair established for the human race. For just as without light it is impossible to see, since neither colors nor eyes are sufficient for visual perception,—for nature created light as a link for the two by which the eye is connected and joined to color, but in darkness the power of each is useless—in the same way also the eye of the soul cannot apprehend virtuous practices unless it makes use of toil, like light, as a co-worker. For established between the mind and the good desired, with one hand it pulls on one side, with the other on the other, and of itself it creates love and harmony, perfect goods.

[25] The metaphor is Philo's.
[26] *Op. mundi*, xxvi (79-81). The argument of this passage is repeated later in ch. xl.

For should you choose any of the goods you wish, you would find this results from toil and is made secure by it. Piety and holiness are goods, but not without the service of God can we reach them and service is yoked to honors in toil. Prudence and courage and justice are all beautiful and perfect goods, but not in leisure are these things found. One must be content if they have been won over by continuous care.[27]

Animalitarianism

Philo's interpretation of the story of Adam and Eve leaves little doubt in one's mind of his intellectualism. The Fall is essentially the corruption of the *Nous* by sensory pleasure. In discussing man's superiority to the other animals,[28] he emphasizes reasoning (*dianoia*) as the differentia. It is man's power of reason which is the basis of his free-will and free-will is found in neither plants nor the lower animals. Similarly in the *De posteritate Caini* (160-162), he admits the physical superiority of the beasts but argues to man's mental superiority.[29] Elsewhere he slips into the traditional praise of animals, but such passages are of little doctrinal importance. In the *De decalogo* (xxiii), for instance, discussing the commandment, "Honor thy father and thy mother," he points to the filial devotion of young storks as a model for men to follow. But such a reference is merely an *a fortiori* argument to the effect that if the irrational beasts can act as if they were obeying the divine commands, how much the more should men do so.

In the treatise translated from the Armenian into Latin by Aucher as the *De animalibus*, one finds a sharply differentiated point of view.[30] If this work is genuine, it is either the source of Plutarch's *Gryllus* or an important item in the literary tradition which led up to the *Gryllus*. It is in dialogue form and tries to prove that the beasts are rational. The proof is a compilation of anecdotes, such as that of Chrysippus's dog,[31] illustrating behavior which in human beings would be called intelligent. The dialogue, however, has so obscure a history and contains so little that was not already in classical literature, that there is no need to reproduce it here. If, as seems improbable, it is a genuine work of Philo's, it shows that its author had his animalitarian moments. These moments were, however, rare and in no way representative of the main body of his thought.

[27] *De sacrificiis Abelis et Caini*, vi, vii (35-37).
[28] *Quod Deus immutabilis sit*, 45 ff.
[29] Cf. *PIA*, pp. 396 f.
[30] This treatise was translated in 1822 and reprinted in Aucher's edition of Philo in 1828 (Vol. VIII, pp. 106 ff.) Its authenticity is discussed by G. Tappe in his *De Philonis libro qui inscribitur Alexandros, etc.*, Goettingen, 1912. Tappe, after making several emendations to render the work consistent with Philo's other writings, decides that it is authentic and concludes that Philo is following some Stoic in the second part of it and in the first some Academic—not Carneades.
[31] See Arnim's *Stoicorum veterum fragmenta*, fragm. 726.

Anti-primitivism

The history of Israel, according to Philo, constitutes a pilgrimage to the Promised Land, which is not merely the physical Canaan, but also Perfect Virtue. Professor J. B. Boughton sees in this the idea of progress and indeed within the history of one people Philo does indicate the working out of a "law" which might be called a law of progress. The conception may have had some influence on Saint Augustine's philosophy of history, but it should be noted that Philo makes no generalizations whatsoever about the history of mankind.[32]

[32] Professor Boughton's thesis may be found in his *The Idea of Progress in Philo Judaeus*, New York, 1932. See esp. pp. 102-104.

THE ORIGINAL CONDITION OF MAN:
PATRISTIC PERIOD

The Apostolic Fathers

The Christians of the late first and the second centuries appear to have taken little interest in the subject of man's original condition or even in the story of the Fall. In all the writings of the Apostolic Fathers, the name of Adam occurs but once and the Earthly Paradise and the fatal tree are not mentioned at all.[1] Not even Justin Martyr seems to have been interested in this topic, if we may judge from his extant writings. It is not until we come to the end of the second century, in the work of Theophilus, that we find the question treated in some detail.

Theophilus

Theophilus, Bishop of Antioch, a Greek by birth, in his *Ad Autolycum* carries on the type of apologetic found in Justin Martyr, with the usual emphasis upon the absurdities of pagan mythology and the immoralities of the pagan gods, on the prophetic foreshadowing of Christianity in the Old Testament, and on the allegorical interpretation of the Scriptures. His account of the condition of the first pair is in part in the tradition of soft primitivism: Adam was created innocent and happy, free from suffering and exempt from toil; the earth yielded him its fruits in richest abundance, and the beauty of Paradise was intermediate between that of this world and heaven. Also "the animals were not evil or injurious in the beginning; for nothing evil was made by God, but all His works were good." [1a] But the idea of progress—a progress intended by the Creator from the outset—is equally insisted upon. Man's original state in Paradise was not meant to be his permanent state; it was to have been but the first stage in a continuous advance. This primarily refers to the religious and moral progress of Adam, the individual, by which he was to be prepared by degrees for the celestial Paradise, for becoming himself a "god." But there is at least the suggestion of a possible corresponding progress of the race; and we thus already find in the second century a foreshadowing of Lessing's conception of a necessary gradualness in the religious education of mankind. Adam in Eden, with all his advantages, represented only the intellectual and spiritual childhood of man—the age of happy innocence but not of moral maturity. And in this consideration Theophilus finds the solution of what to him was evidently a difficulty in the biblical story—the apparent refusal of "knowl-

---

[1] Except in the *Epistle to Diognetus*, xii, which is, however, of later date. Cf. K. Lake, *The Apostolic Fathers*, vol. II, Index.

[1a] *Ad Autolycum*, II, 17.

edge" to man. To an extreme Christian anti-intellectualist this would
hardly have been a difficulty; but in spite of Theophilus's violent attack on
most of the philosophers, the Platonistic spirit was still too strong in him to
permit him to believe that a benevolent Creator could have intended that
man should never possess this good. The idea that the motive of the
prohibition was "envy," a desire of the Deity to retain a monopoly, is
expressly rejected. The "knowledge" forbidden to Adam, therefore, can
only have been knowledge unsuited to his immaturity, and his—or Eve's—
sin consisted, not in desiring knowledge, but in disobedience to the prohibition which was an expression of the divine pedagogic plan.

> God, when He had placed man, as has been said, in Paradise, to work
> it and keep it, bade him eat of all the fruits—manifestly even of the
> tree of life also—and forbade him only to taste of the tree of knowl-
> edge. And God removed him from the earth from which he was
> born to Paradise, giving him a beginning of progress, so that, matur-
> ing and becoming more perfect, and having finally even been declared
> a god, he might thus ascend into heaven, having attained immortality.
> For man was made in an intermediate condition, neither wholly
> mortal, nor entirely immortal, but capable of becoming either. So
> too, the place, Paradise, in respect to its beauty, was intermediate
> between the world and heaven. And the words, " Work it," would
> seem to command no other work than keeping the injunction of God,
> lest by disobeying he destroy himself, as in fact he did, through sin.[2]
> The tree of knowledge itself was good and the fruit of it was good.
> For the tree did not, as some think, have death in it, but the dis-
> obedience did. For nothing else was in the fruit but knowledge; and
> knowledge is good when it is properly used. But Adam was in age
> still an infant, wherefore he was not able to receive knowledge wor-
> thily. For even now, when a child is born, it is not able to eat
> bread, but first is fed on milk, and then with its advance in years it
> proceeds to solid food. So it was also with Adam. Wherefore, not as
> one jealous of him, as some think, did God command him not to eat
> of [the tree of] knowledge. Moreover, He wished to test him, whether
> he was obedient to His commandment; and at the same time He also
> wished that man should remain for a longer time in a state of child-
> like simplicity and purity.[3] For this is holy not only in the sight of
> God, but also in that of men, to be subjected in simplicity and inno-
> cence to one's parents, but how much the more to the God and Father
> of all things? Moreover, it is unseemly that children while infants
> should have thoughts beyond their years; for as one grows in height
> with age, so also in thought. But when a law bids one abstain from

----

[2] *Ad Autolycum*, II, 24 [*MPG*, VI, p. 1089].

[3] Slomkowski in his *l'Etat primitif de l'homme etc.*, 1928, p. 30, remarking that
Theophilus was the first patristic writer to express the interpretation of *Genesis*
which made of Adam *un véritable enfant*, thinks that he was in this probably repeat-
ing an idea already current, on the ground that there is no reason to suppose that
Clement of Alexandria, in his later adoption of the same idea, was dependent on
Theophilus.

something and one has not obeyed, clearly the law does not bring about the punishment, but the violation of it and the disobedience. For a father sometimes commands his own child to abstain from certain things, and if the child does not obey the paternal injunction, he is beaten and meets with a reprimand for his disobedience. It is not the things themselves that are harmful, but it is disobedience that entails punishment for the transgressor. And so for the first-formed man, disobedience entailed his eviction from Paradise. Not, then, as if the tree of knowledge held any evil, but because of his disobedience did man draw upon himself labor, pain, grief, and finally became subject to death.[4]

Tertullian

In a controversial treatise of his Montanist period, *De jejunio*, Tertullian's defence of fasting is based in part on an overt primitivistic premise: "the necessity [or obligatoriness] of an observance will then be acknowledged when the authority of a reason [for it] which is to be dated back to the beginning of things shall have become clearly manifest." Now the first commandment laid upon all men related to a dietetic abstinence; and the first sin was that Adam "yielded more readily to his belly than to God, heeded the meat more than the mandate, and sold salvation for his gullet." [5] Moreover, not only Adam and Eve, but all their descendants to the time of Noah, were vegetarians; from this the Deity's disapproval of flesh-eating is evident. Tertullian's argument, however, encounters a difficulty in the fact that after the Deluge God abrogated the prohibition against eating meat, and extended rather than restricted the scope of man's diet [*Gen.*, ix]. Tertullian meets the difficulty partly by representing the permission to eat flesh as a concession to human weakness, but chiefly by the pregnant consideration—which was to play an important part in the ethics and theodicy of Christianity—that virtue is possible only through the exercise of freedom of choice, which presupposes the opportunity to choose the evil, or the lesser good; man attains moral character only through exposure to temptation.

> This was the rule which was followed by the Providence of God, Who fits all things to their seasons, lest any of our opponents, in order to refute our proposition, should say, "Why then did not God immediately institute some restriction upon eating, instead of enlarging His permission?" For in the beginning He gave men as his food only grains and fruits [quotes *Genesis* i, 29]; but afterwards, when He was declaring to Noah the subjection [to men] of all the

---

[4] *Ad Autolycum*, II, 25 [*MPG* VI, p. 1091]. Though not pertinent to our principal theme, it is worth noting—in view of the subsequent rôle in literature of the story of man's loss of Paradise—that the non-biblical assumption, which was to be an essential presupposition of Milton's epic, that the serpent was "originally an angel" is expressly made by Theophilus [*Op. cit.*, II, 28].

[5] *De jejunio*, III. The translation of the last sentence is that of Holmes, *Ante-Nicene Christian Library*, vol. 18.

beasts of the earth and the winged things of the air, and of things moving upon the earth, and of the fish in the sea, and of every creeping thing, He said, "They will be yours to eat, even as I have given you all green herbs; but flesh with the life thereof, which is the blood thereof, shall ye not eat" [*Gen.*, ix, 3, 4]. For by this very fact, that He prohibited the eating only of that meat whose soul is not poured out with its blood, it is evident that He permitted the use of all other kinds of meat. To this we answer, that it was not fitting to burden man with any additional law of abstinence, since he has not been able to endure so slight a prohibition as the eating of a single apple. And so when the law was relaxed, he was to be strengthened by his very liberty. And similarly after the Deluge, in the rebuilding of the human race, one law decreeing abstention from blood was enough, the use of other foods being permitted. For the Lord had already made manifest His judgment through the Deluge; and He had, moreover, given warning that He would require [their] blood at the hand of every man's brother and at the hand of every beast [*Gen.*, ix, 5]. And so furnishing [proof] of the justice of His whole sentence, He extended the occasions for free will, aiding discipline through indulgence; permitting all things so that some things might be taken away; requiring more, if He granted more; commanding abstinence, when He had first made indulgence possible; so that, as we have said, the primordial sin might be the more fully expiated through the exercise of a greater abstinence in the midst of opportunity for greater licence.[6]

Tertullian does not, however, always identify the primal sin with gluttony; he is, in fact, somewhat disposed to identify it with whatever sin he happens at the moment to be denouncing.[7] In the *De anima* he connects the eating of the tree of the knowledge of good and evil with the attainment of sexual maturity. Adam and Eve before the Fall were, emotionally and, as is clearly implied, physically, like children of the immediately pre-adolescent age.

. . . In accordance with that association of body and soul which we have asserted, we maintain that the puberty of the soul coincides with that of the body, and that the maturity of the one arises through the suggestion of the senses, and of the other by the development of the bodily members, at about the age of fourteen years. We fix this as the age, not because the followers of Aesculapius assign the attainment of full intelligence to that time of life, nor because the civil laws date the capacity to carry on ordinary business from this age, but because this was the rule from the beginning. For as Adam and Eve, upon their acquiring knowledge of good and evil, felt that they must cover their *pudenda*, so we, from the time we experience the same feeling, recognize that we have attained knowledge of good and evil. From this age [of fourteen years] on, sex is more bashful, and

---

[6] *De jejunio*, iv [Ed. Reifferscheid-Wissowa, in *CSEL*, vol. 20, pp. 278 f.].

[7] E. g., in the *De patientia*, iv, where Eve's sin is said to have been fundamentally "impatience." The implication is that in due course "the knowledge of good and evil" would have been granted to man. Cf. Theophilus above.

covers itself, and concupiscence employs the eye as its minister and communicates its desire and understands what these [organs] are, and girds itself against lascivious touch as by the apron of fig-leaves, and it leads man out of the paradise of innocence.[8]

Despite this assertion of the immaturity—mental as well as physical—of the first pair before the Fall, Tertullian elsewhere in the same treatise [9] declares that the soul as originally created was purely rational. Plato's division of the soul into two parts, rational and irrational, holds good of it only as it is now, *non ut naturae deputetur*. " To be regarded as natural to it is that rational element which was implanted in it at the beginning, namely, by its rational Author." The irrational element was added at the time of the Fall, *ex serpentis instinctu*: this element " henceforth became inherent in the soul and grew with its growth, so that it now has the appearance of being natural because this befell at the beginning of nature." This is equally difficult to reconcile with both of Tertullian's other accounts of the nature of the Fall: that a creature of pure rationality should yet have been so dominated by sensual appetite as to " sell his salvation for his gullet " seems as odd as that a condition of pure rationality should be identified with that of a pre-adolescent child. The conflict of primitivistic and anti-primitivistic motives—and, associated with this, of two meanings of " nature "—is evident. Tertullian at times conceives of man's first condition as so perfect that only his highest faculty then existed in him, and this alone, in strictness, is his " natural " state. But this makes it scarcely conceivable that there should have been any Fall; consequently, when explaining the Fall, Tertullian sometimes adopts the opposite theory, that man at the outset was in an undeveloped state, with the latent implication that he was intended to pass from this to some higher stage or stages. But this idea, in turn, is complicated and confused by the identification of the initial stage with sexual immaturity, which, in so far as the consciousness of sex was assumed to be an evil, made the original condition once more superior to all that followed it.

Pseudo-Clementina

The *Homilies* and *Recognitions* once attributed to Clement I of Rome [fl. ca. 96], are now generally recognized by scholars of the patristic writings as Post-Nicene redactions of a common basic writing, a religious romance designed for the instruction and edification of catechumens, probably written between 220-230, which in turn incorporated parts of several earlier writings.[10] At least three accounts of the circumstances and cause of man's fall

[8] *De anima*, ch. 38 [Ed. Reifferscheid-Wissowa, p. 365]. For a similar passage, see *De pallio*, iii.

[9] *De anima*, 16.

[10] For the dates and sources, see Waitz, *Die Pseudoklementinen* in *Texte u. Untersuchungen zur Gesch. der altchristlichen Literatur*, N. F., Bd. X, 1904, esp. pp. 366 ff. Cf. Schmidt, *Studies zu den Pseudoklementinen*, 1929, esp. pp. 240 ff.

from his original innocence and happiness may be distinguished in them, the inconsistencies being perhaps due to the unharmonized utilization of different sources.

(a) Both the *Homilies* and the *Recognitions* agree in omitting any mention of the fall of Adam, and in the *Homilies* it is expressly denied. " I am persuaded," Saint Peter is made to say, " that Adam was not a transgressor " [II, 52]. If Adam was created perfect, " he must have possessed the great and divine spirit of foreknowledge "; that is, if he had sinned, it could not have been through ignorance. And since he was made in God's image, it is blasphemous to say that he sinned at all. " He who insults the image . . . has the sin reckoned as committed against Him in Whose likeness the image was made " [III, 17]. Adam was a " true prophet," divinely inspired; " how then had he still need to eat the fruit of a tree, in order to know what is good and what is evil " [III, 21] ? [11] Eve, however, did not participate in this exalted character. She differed from Adam " as quality from substance, as the moon from the sun, as fire from light " [III, 22]. The author accordingly develops a species of anti-feminist, almost misogynous, dualism. Nothing is said in the principal passage on the subject [12] of Eve's temptation by the serpent; her inferiority is inherent in her sex—the idea being connected with the belief in the catamenial pollution of women by blood [III, 24] —and her initial sin, it is intimated, lay in " wishing to be thought masculine." As the primal embodiment of the feminine principle, however, she has a certain cosmic rôle; for this present world is in some sense female and under the rule of the female; it was through Eve that death and war and false prophecy and the craving for earthly riches came into the world [*Ib.*, 23-4]; and the lapse from Adam's perfection even in the male became apparent in her first-born son, Cain. In all this the author or redactor boldly disregards the story of *Genesis*, ii and iii, in accordance with his general and convenient assumption that, at least if interpreted literally, " some of the Scriptures are true and some false " [II, 51], the latter being given " to try us " [XVI, 13].

(b) The passage here cited at length fuses two other accounts of the cause and time of man's lapses from his initial state. In neither do the sin of Adam or of Eve, or the wiles of the Serpent, or the crime of Cain figure. In the first Adam is once more without blame; he was not only innocent, but in possession of a full understanding of the divine will concerning man's conduct; this he himself followed, and the knowledge of it he imparted to his sons as a " perpetual law for all "; it is the equivalent of the Stoic and

[11] The theory of the immaturity of Adam is thus precisely reversed by the Pseudo-Clementina.

[12] Yet in *Hom.* XI, 18, Peter says that " by the promise of knowledge the serpent first brought sin into the world "; and in *Recog.* II, 45, there is a reference to the seduction of Eve.

Cynic " law of nature," being of universal validity for mankind and capable of being known by every man. Not only Adam but the earlier generations of his posterity lived a life like that of the Golden Age, enjoying the fruits of the earth in abundance without labor, free from pain and disease, long-lived, though not yet assured of immortality. But their good fortune led to their downfall; for having no experience of evil, they come to look upon their unearned boons as automatic gifts of nature, and thus became insensible of divine providence and forgetful of the God who bestowed these blessings upon them. The moral suggested is that the easy and secure life of a Golden Age is not really good for man, at least for his religious character. Under so benign a dispensation men tend to lose the fear of God. For their ingratitude men therefore suffered a punishment which was really beneficial to them; since " good things " had proved " harmful to them, God introduced evil things as advantageous to them." [13] But here, without indicating the nature of the punishment, the author abruptly drops this theme, and passes to yet another story of the way in which men lost their primeval happiness.

(c) This consists in the legend found in *Genesis*, vi and elaborated in *Enoch*, of the mating of the Sons of God with the Daughters of Men. The version of this in the *Homilies*, however, unlike those in *Genesis* and *Enoch*, but similar to that in *Jubilees*, attributes the angels' descent to earth to an originally pious motive; perhaps the explanation of this detail is the redactor's desire to connect his third account of the Fall with his second. With the purpose of showing men the error of their ways, the lowest rank of angels obtained divine permission to " enter into the life of men." But, like some other reformers, they were corrupted by the very evils which they had set out to correct. Since they had become men, they felt the same appetites as men, and fell victim to the love of women. This deprived them of the power to regain their angelic nature but it did not deprive them of their magical powers. Accordingly, they developed the various arts, the better to charm their mistresses, and the original technological state of nature was lost. As in *Enoch* and *Jubilees* their children were giants, intermediate in size between men and angels, but more bestial than men had been, since they became fond of animal food and even cannibalistic. Under their influence or example men also ceased to be vegetarian. The earth, then, defiled by so much blood, gave forth fumes that bred diseases and began to produce carnivorous and destructive beasts. It was with the intention of washing earth clean of these evil breeds that the Deluge was sent, Noah and his family, however, being saved, so that the history of mankind might have a second beginning. Upon the fact that the first plan had ended in a failure and the necessity of a second start the author does not dwell.

[13] There thus appears a form of the doctrine of the indispensability of evil of which other forms will appear below.

In a passage of the *Recognitions* [VIII, 48] we are told that some races of men still remain relatively uncorrupted and still retain something of man's primeval felicity.[14]

> Since God, the uniquely good, having created all things well and having given them to man who was made in His image, (Adam) who had been born breathing in the divinity of his Maker, being a true Prophet and knowing all things, for the honor of the Father Who had given all things to him and for the salvation of the children born of him, like a true father preserving his benevolence towards his own children and wishing them for their own advantage to love God and to be loved by Him, showed them the road leading to His love, teaching them by what kind of human deeds the one God and Lord of all is pleased; and when he had shown them the things that are pleasing to Him, he decreed an eternal law for all, which can neither be destroyed by enemies nor corrupted by the impious; nor is it hidden in one place, but it can be accurately known by all. There was, therefore, for them who obeyed the law, an abundance of all things, the fairest of fruits, the completion of their years without grief or disease, and therewith also a salubrious air, all freely bestowed on them.[15]
> But they, because they had at first no experience of evil and were insensible to the gift of good things, were turned to ingratitude by the abundance of food and luxuries, so that they even thought that Providence does not exist, since they had not by previous labor received these goods as a reward for righteousness. For none of them had fallen victim to any suffering or disease or any other untoward violence, so that—as is usual with men perverted by error—they might look about for a God capable of healing them.[16] But immediately after the disregard (of God) which resulted from their lack of fear and their unneeded luxuries, there was meted out to them, as though in consequence of a certain suitable harmony, a just punishment, which took away the good things as harmful and introduced evil things as helpful.
> For of the spirits inhabiting heaven, the angels who live in the lowest part, grieved because of man's ingratitude to God, begged that they might enter into the life of men, so that by really becoming men and by closer association with them, they might convict those who were ungrateful to Him and might bring each to his fitting punishment here below. When then they obtained what they had sought, they changed themselves into every kind of being, for they are of a more divine substance and able to turn easily into all things. And they became precious stones, pearls admired by all, porphyry of the most beautiful sort, highly esteemed gold, and every valuable

[14] For this idea and its development, see below, the essay on *The Noble Savage*.
[15] In the *Recognitions*, the corresponding passage (IV, 9) states that there was only one worship of God, a pure mind and uncorrupted spirit; that every creature kept the covenant unviolated; that there was no sickness or bodily disorder, and that though men lived to a thousand years, they had no senile infirmities.
[16] The text is corrupt and the rendering uncertain.

substance. And they rained down into the hands of some and into the laps of others, and unprotesting were stolen by them. And they changed themselves also into quadrupeds and into creeping things and into fishes and birds and into whatever they wished. And these things even your poets, because of their fearlessness, sing as they happened, although they attribute the many and various deeds of all to one.

But when they had been changed into these things, they convicted the plunderers of greed; and then they changed themselves into human form, so that, by living piously and showing that a pious life was possible, they might subject the ungrateful to punishment. Yet, since they had become in all respects really men and also felt human lust, under its compulsion they mingled with women.[17] Entangled with them and ensnared in defilement and utterly emptied of their original power, they did not have the strength to purify their members, which had been perverted from their fiery substance, and to restore them to the original purity of their own nature.[18] For since by the weight of their lust for the flesh their fire was extinguished, they trod the impious path downwards. For they were bound by the bonds of flesh and were held fast and strongly tied, wherefore they could no longer go upwards into the heavens.[19]

For after their union with women, when they were asked and were no longer able to show what they had originally been, because they could not do anything else after their defilement, yet wishing to please their mistresses, they exhibited the bowels of the earth in place of themselves; I mean the flower of the metals, gold, bronze, silver, iron, and the life, with all the most highly valued stones. And along with these magic stones they taught the arts appropriate to each, and they showed the arts of magic, and taught astronomy and the powers of roots and whatever could not be discovered by human faculties, and also the smelting of gold and silver and the like, and the dyeing of garments in many colors. And absolutely everything which exists for the adornment and delight of women is the discovery of the daimons bound in flesh.

But from the bastard union bastard men were born, much taller than men, who were later called giants—not that dragon-footed race who made war against God, as the blasphemous myths of the Greeks relate, yet beastlike in their ways and greater than men in size (since they were born of angels) but smaller than angels (since they were born of women). God, then, knowing that they had become as

[17] This, according to the *Recognitions* [I, 29], occurred in the eighth generation of the human race.

[18] The author is employing terms of the Methodic school of medicine. *Metasynkrisis* is the discharge of " peccant humors " through the pores; the fallen angels in order to regain their original fiery substance, would have to discharge from their bodies all the lower matter—earth, water, and air—which they had assumed in order to carry out the experiment of reforming mankind.

[19] The argument here is implicated with the physics of Aristotle, according to which the " natural " motion of fire is upward. Consequently if the fire in the bodies of the fallen angels was extinguished, they were doomed to remain here below.

savage as beasts and that the world did not contain enough to satisfy them—for it had been created on a human scale and for human use— in order that, from want of food they might not turn to the unnatural eating of animals and yet seem guiltless as having been forced thereto, the omnipotent God rained manna down upon them to satisfy their various desires, and they enjoyed all that they wished. But because of their bastard nature, they were displeased with pure food and thirsted for the taste of blood. And thus they were the first to taste of flesh.

And the men who were with them also then first began to desire to do likewise. Thus we are born neither good nor bad, but become so, and after we have become accustomed to a thing we refrain from it with the greatest difficulty. And when irrational animals were insufficient, the bastard men tasted even of human bodies. For it was no great step for them to kill bodies of their own kind after they had already tasted flesh in other forms.

But through the great flow of blood the pure air was defiled by impure fumes and sickened those who breathed it and became un-healthful, so that henceforth men died young. And the earth, greatly defiled by this, brought forth then for the first time poisonous and destructive beasts. Therefore, when all things went from bad to worse because of the beast-like daimons, God resolved to make away with them as an evil leaven, so that the succession of generations, each coming from bad stock and resembling its predecessor and similarly impious, might not finally bring in a future age when no man should be saved. To this end, when He had sent a warning to a certain righteous man to save himself and his three sons with their wives and children in an ark, he poured forth water in a flood, so that when all were wiped out, the purified cosmos might be entrusted to him who had been saved in the ark to begin a second life in purity. And so it happened.[20]

Clement of Alexandria

Clement of Alexandria distinguishes between man's being made in God's image and in His likeness.[21] Every man, in so far as he is rational, is the image of God; but only those whose life is in accordance with God's law are like Him.[22]

One might expect, since the first man was created both in God's image and in His likeness, that he would have been not only innocent but in the fullest sense rational. But when Clement speaks of Adam, he uses terms which indicate that he thinks of him as mentally a child, much in the manner of Theophilus and others. Thus he " played freely " in the garden for he was a " child of God " [23] and like a child succumbed to the charms of pleasure, for the Serpent, says Clement, possibly following Philo, symbolizes pleasure. The biblical account of the motive of the first sin—desire for

[20] *Homilia*, VIII, 10-17 [*MPG*, II, p. 232 ff.]. Cf. *Recognitions*, I, 28 ff.

[21] *Cohortatio ad gentes*, ch. 12 [Ed. Staehlin, I, 86].

[22] See Le Nourry's note on *Paed.* I, xii [*MPG*, VIII, p. 367, n. 17].

[23] *Coh. ad Gent.*, xi [Staehlin, I, 79], ἔπαιζε λελυμένος, παιδίον τοῦ θεοῦ.

forbidden knowledge—is disregarded by Clement. It is therefore not surprising to find that he emphasizes any biblical passages which compare the ideal man with a child. *John*, xxi, 4, 5; *Matthew*, xix, 14; vii, 3; xxi, 16; *Psalms*, vii, 3 [24] and the like, all seem to play upon the innocence and wisdom of infancy. The true Christian, therefore—though Clement does not explicitly draw this inference—in becoming like a child, returns to the state of Adam before the Fall. This state is "communion" with Heaven, which may be interpreted as "direct knowledge" of Heaven, the kind of knowledge which a child in the Platonic myth of reminiscence might be supposed to have and which, for instance, Wordsworth in the *Ode on Intimations of Immortality* attributed to children. A somewhat similar idea had been familiar in certain schools of Greek philosophy, especially the Academic. Cicero had made an interlocutor in his *De finibus* [IV, 55] say that "all the older philosophers" had held that "the will of nature can be most easily discerned in children." [25] That "all the older philosophers" held this idea is a gross exaggeration. Even Plato, whose influence upon this tradition is indubitable, never asserted that the child was wiser than the adult; it is more likely that, if he thought about children at all in this connection, it was as Aristotle was to think about them: they were potential men and nothing more.

Once the idea is launched that the childlike state of mind is the best, the way is open for Christian anti-intellectualism, the *docta ignorantia*, and the pedagogical primitivism of the Eighteenth Century; for though these doctrines are not by any means identical, they are similar in their common depreciation of acquired learning and in the value they set upon the innocence of the childlike mind.

Although Clement found an abundance of texts in the Bible which to his way of thinking justified this attitude, he also had to recognize the force of Saint Paul's, "When I was a child, I spoke as a child. When I became a man, I put away childish things" [I *Cor.*, xiii, 11]. Here, Clement maintains [*Paed.*, I, vi], "children" means "those who live under the law," i. e., the Jews, whereas "man" means "those who live according to the Logos." But even though utilizing the terms in a new metaphor, Saint Paul has not meant to confer a new value on the adult mind as contrasted with the infant mind, for he still speaks of feeding his followers with milk, obviously the food of babes.[26]

Novatian

Novatian, the third century schismatic, in his *De cibis Judaicis*, confines the diet of primitive man not merely to vegetable food, but to the fruit of

---

[24] See *Paed.*, I, v. vi.

[25] See *PIA*, p. 254, no. LX, 2. But cf. Herodotus's story of the discovery of primitive language in *Hist.*, II, 2.

[26] Cf., he says, Homer's name *Galactophagoi* [milk-drinkers] for righteous men. See *PIA*, p. 288.

trees; man's naturally upright posture shows that he was not meant to stoop to the ground for sustenance. The eating of grains, as well as of flesh, came after the Fall. It was then permitted by God because man, now condemned to labor, needed stronger food. After the coming of Christ, the distinction between clean and unclean animals no longer held and Christians could eat all foods.

This looks on the face of it like a curious mixture of dietetic primitivism and anti-primitivism, since the first food was food for the sinless, and the last was food for the redeemed. But, as a matter of fact, the dietetic features of the account are purely symbolic. For no animals, says Novatian, could be inherently unclean, since all were created by God. The unclean animals represent the vices; there was no further need to prohibit their consumption after the Vicarious Atonement.[27]

> To begin at the beginning, as is proper, the first food of men was the produce and fruit of trees alone. For the use of bread was introduced later by man's guilt, the very position of his body in gathering grain indicating the state of his conscience. For innocence raised men upwards, so long as they had a good conscience, towards heaven to pluck their food from trees, but the commission of sin cast men down to earth and the soil to gather grains. After this, the use of flesh was added, since divine grace extended the kinds of food which would satisfy human needs in the proper seasons. For a softer food was required to nourish tender and untried men, and one prepared not without toil for the correction of the sinful, no doubt lest they should be pleased to sin if the necessity of toil did not admonish them to be innocent. And since it was not Paradise that was to be tended but the whole world that was to be cultivated, the stronger food of meat was granted, so that the strength of the human frame might be somewhat increased to the advantage of husbandry. All these things were done by divine grace and arrangement, as I have said, to prevent an insufficient provision for the strong, through which lack they might fail in their labor, or too ample a revision for the weak, which they could not bear, oppressed by it beyond their powers. The law, however, which followed granted the eating of flesh without reservations. For it permitted the use of certain animals as clean; others it forbade as unclean and polluting to those who might eat them.[28]

Origen

Origen's success in interpreting the Scriptures is in his mind dependent upon his use of the allegorical method. He is particularly outspoken about

---

[27] There follows what resembles some of the features of the medieval bestiaries, an interpretation of the various characteristics of the animals, the camel's hump, fishes' scales, and so on, as symbols of virtues and vices. This is probably original with Novatian, although similar in method, if not in content, to the *Physiologus*.

[28] *De cibis Judaicis*, ch. ii [Ed. Landgraf-Weyman, in *Archiv für latein. Lexikographie und Grammatik*, XI, 1900, pp. 228 f.].

what he considers absurdities in the scriptural narrative, and it is curious
to observe what would be ridicule in a sceptic serving the purposes of faith.[29]

One of the items whose literal interpretation Origen denounces is the
story of the Garden of Eden. Whether Paradise was a physical reality or a
symbol was of vastly more than academic importance. Both theories had
supporters in the Middle Ages, and those who believed in its literal existence
believed also in the possibility of finding its site. Among this group there
were two schools, those who located it in the East, those who believed it to
be in the West. It was not difficult for the latter to confuse it with the
Islands of the Blest, and thus to strengthen the belief, which dates back to
pagan times, that out in the Western Ocean lay lands of a marvelous character. How much this confusion of pagan and Christian legend contributed
to the enthusiasm of the explorers who sought for such lands, we shall
probably never know. Yet it is not unlikely that it stimulated the dream
which a love of wealth and power helped to realize.

> Not only did the Spirit plan these things which occurred before the
> coming of Christ, but whatever else happened has come also from
> the one God, and in the same manner did He act in the case of the
> Evangelists and Apostles. For even those narratives which He in-
> spired in them are constructed with His wise art which we have
> expounded above. Wherefore even in them has He inserted not a
> few details in which the historical order of narration, interrupted or
> broken off, by its very impossibility calls the reader's attention to
> an examination of their inner meaning. But to illustrate that of
> which we are speaking, let us examine some places in Scripture.
> Who, at least who in his right mind, will believe that there was a
> first and a second and a third day, in which there was an evening and
> a morning, when there was no sun or moon or stars? Was there even
> a first day without a sky? And who is so foolish as to think that
> God, like some farmer, planted trees in a garden, in Eden in the East,
> and that He planted the tree of life in it, that is, a visible and
> palpable tree, such that whoever ate of it with corporeal teeth would
> receive life from it, and again, eating of another tree would receive
> the knowledge of good and evil? And then too when God is said to
> walk in the garden at evening and Adam to hide behind a tree, I
> cannot think that anyone will doubt that these things are figurative
> in Scripture, and that certain mystic meanings are concealed in them.
> Cain, again, withdrawing from the face of God will obviously force
> the prudent reader to ask what God's face might be, and how anyone
> might be able to withdraw from Him. In fact, lest we extend our
> work too far, it is very easy for anyone so desiring to gather together
> from the Holy Scriptures things which are described as if they
> actually had happened and which nevertheless cannot be believed to
> have really occurred in a rational way. The Gospels too are full of
> such things, as when the Devil is said to have taken Jesus to the top

[29] It may not be without interest to compare Origen's method with that of the
pious sceptics of the seventeenth century, e. g., Huet of Avranches.

of a high mountain to show Him all the kingdoms of the world and their glory from it. How could it have been literally true that Jesus was led to the mountain top by the Devil or that He saw with carnal eyes spread out before Him and around the mountain all the kingdoms of the world, that is, the kingdom of the Persians, the Scythians, the Indians, and how their kings are glorified by men? Yet he who reads attentively finds scores of similar things in the Gospels.[30]

The allegorical method of Origen led him to accentuate the eternal relationship between his God and Man, rather than historical vicissitudes. The Fall of Adam is for him the Fall of Man, an incident which is repeated, as it was for Plotinus, in the life of each individual soul. Consequently in reading those portions of his writings which deal with Adam, it is essential that the "Neoplatonic" background of his thought be kept constantly in mind. He appears to be neutral on the question of chronological primitivism, but that may be simply because chronology is of purely phenomenal importance to him. He appears to be opposed to cultural primitivism, for he maintains that Adam's condition—in so far as his intelligence was concerned—was in need of improvement; yet that may be simply a way of saying that men require education. He writes as if mankind would progress to a condition in which self-dependence would replace their dependence on God, but there is no sure way of knowing whether he was suggesting a pattern for the history of the race or merely indicating what would happen to each individual soul in its eternal history, for it will be recalled that in his opinion each soul would in the long run find redemption, there being no eternal hell.

Gregory of Nyssa

A change comes into chronological primitivism with Gregory of Nyssa, for the pagan elements of his thought were drawn from Stoicism rather than from pagan mythology. Gregory's conception of the perfect man, a man whose perfection is, it goes without saying, largely moral, is the Stoic sage somewhat Christianized. Adam before the Fall was presumably such a being.

To begin with, Gregory points out that when God created the world, it was good; consequently everything in it, as it left the hands of the Creator, was in a state of perfection; among these creations was man. In fact, he argues, man must have been as much better than the rest of creation as his model, God, is better.

This appears very clearly in his commentary on the *Song of Songs*.[31] Resembling his model, according to *Genesis*, man must have been created

---

[30] *De principiis*, II, xvi, of Rufinus's Latin translation [*MPG*, XI, p. 375]. The original Greek of this work has been lost. This passage should be compared with Philo's *Leg. alleg.*, I, *passim*.

[31] *In Cantica cantic.*, Hom. xii [*MPG*, XLIV, p. 1020 C-D].

immortal, "the image and likeness of eternal life." Elsewhere he points out that Adam could have had none of the defects of human frailty now only too well known: no old age nor infancy, no bodily sickness, and above all, no passion; sexual intercourse, conception, parturition, impurities, suckling, feeding, evacuation, gradual growth, disease, like death, being but the accidents of corporeal life, were bound to be absent.[32] Moreover, man must have been created beautiful in form, passionless, frank, and without envy, for thus alone could he have resembled God.[33] Gregory is particularly emphatic in declaring that envy did not exist in Adam's soul. Nevertheless, envy managed to enter Eden in the form of the Serpent and to cause the Fall, as it caused, says Gregory, most of the evils of human history.[34]

The possibility of Adam's entertaining envy, in the absence of all emotion, is not clarified by Gregory. His ability to sin, however, was solved as it had been solved by other Christians, by the doctrine of his free-will. Adam must have had free-will, since he was made in the image of God; but for reasons which are not cited, his will was less able to choose the good unerringly than his Maker's. Hence the Fall.[35] Adam was "enslaved to no outward necessity whatever; his feelings towards that which pleased him depended only on his private judgment; he was free to choose whatever he liked; and so he was a free agent."[36] But why should he have liked to do evil? He had never experienced any; he could have never known its charm. The answer is that he was circumvented by cunning, a cunning inspired by the Serpent's envy. Here it would seem to have been weakness of intellect, rather than a faulty will, which doomed Adam and his progeny to a life of sorrow. Yet it is somewhat difficult to imagine how such a man could have had a weak intellect, since he is described by Gregory in this very passage as gazing without shrinking on God's countenance, which for the author of that metaphor meant that he had intuitive knowledge of all truth. "He did not yet judge of what was lovely by taste or sight; he found in the Lord alone all that was sweet; and he used the helpmeet given him only for this delight . . ."

The consequences of the Fall in Gregory are naturally anything and everything which he happens to believe to be evil. "In the beginning, human nature was golden and radiant with its similarity to undefiled good. But it turned colorless and black after it had been mixed with evil."[37] The lack of color, the blackness, are symbols of what Aristotle would have called "privations," in this case, the absence of the goodness which made

[32] De anima et ressurectione [MPG, XLVI, pp. 148A-149A].

[33] Oratio catechetica, vi [MPG, XLV, pp. 28 f.].

[34] De vita Moysis [MPG, XLIV, p. 409 B-D].

[35] Oratio catechetica, v [MPG, XLV, p. 21 f.].

[36] De virginitate, xii [MPG, XLVI, p. 369].

[37] In cantica cantic., Hom. IV [MPG, XLIV, p. 832, A-B]. Cf. Id., Hom. XV [Ib., pp. 1109, B-C, 1110, B-C].

the first man resemble God: mortality, moral wickedness, and passion which is its source.

Gregory's emphasis upon mortality as one of the results of the Fall is unwavering, but in one place he interprets it as the necessary consequence of Adam's choice of pleasure in this particular life. God had offered Adam the choice between two lives, the terrestrial and the celestial. The terrestrial was by its very nature of limited duration and Adam's choice fell upon it. Here Adam does not sin through blind choice, but through deliberate choice; he was apparently faced with the alternative of a life of limited duration in which the pleasures would be mixed and which would terminate in death, and one of unlimited extent in which the pleasures were unmixed. It is difficult to understand how a soul as gifted as Adam's was held to be in other passages referred to in this essay could have made the decision which he actually made.[38] Nor does Gregory illuminate this problem.[39] The difficulty becomes the greater when one reads certain passages in Gregory in which it is clear that the human reason, even in its present debased condition, easily perceives the evils of a corporeal state; before Adam was condemned to a bodily, and hence short, life, and while he possessed a mind which was unclouded by matter and the evils implicated in it, he would, one might suppose have had no temptation great enough to induce him to choose the horrors which would inevitably ensue from the wrong choice. Only the beasts, says Gregory,[40] are happy in a life of pleasure, and that is precisely because they are irrational. Must we not either conclude that the human reason since the Fall has the power, which it did not have before that event, to see the consequences of Adam's choice, or that Adam deliberately chose evil ?

In spite of the incalculable misery of man's present life, Gregory believes that we are not so vitiated as to be incapable of returning to something similar to the life of Adam. It is here that his primitivism becomes a program, and not simply poetic regret. We can divest ourselves, he says,[41] of the " coat of skins " and become once more like Adam before the Fall, a condition which can presumably be realized fully only after death. But

---

[38] There are several passages in Gregory which assert God's foreknowledge of the Fall, which revives the old problem of how man was free if he was doomed to sin. See *Oratio catechetica*, viii [*MPG*, XLV, p. 37 B-D] and *Adv. Apollinarem*, xii [*Ib.*, p. 1145 B-C]. Gregory does not undertake a solution of this problem, but does insist that God intended the salvation of all sinners from the very beginning—*Orat. catech.*, xxvi [*Ib.*, pp. 68 D–69 C]. Elsewhere he goes to the extent of saying that God " has prepared for the moral infirmities of each generation the physician who is suitable and appropriate." See his *In laudem fratris Basilii*, 3, in Sister J. A. Stein, *The Catholic University Patristic Studies*, XVII, p. 8.

[39] See *De anima et resurrectione* [*MPG*, XLVI, p. 81 B-C].

[40] *De beatitudinibus*, oratio iii [*MPG*, XLIV, pp. 1225 D–1229 A]. Cf. *Id.*, oratio v [*Ib.*, p. 1257 C ff.]; *In ecclesiasten*, Homilia VI [*Ib.*, pp. 708 C–709 A]. The theme is one of his favorites.

[41] *De anima et resurrectione* [*MPG*, XLVI, pp. 148 A–149 A].

we may begin our preparations for that new life here on this earth. We must first begin by renouncing marriage; next we "must retire from all anxious toil upon the land"; then we must renounce the life of sensation, "the wisdom of the flesh," and follow God's commandments alone.[42] The closeness of such a regimen to that advocated by some of the Cynics needs perhaps no comment, but it will be observed that the motivating force in the two programs is quite different. The Christian is striving to attain a return to primitive life as penance for sin; the Cynic, of course, had no such idea whatever. Yet in both there must have been a contempt for civilized life and its pleasures antecedent to the development of the two systems of ethics.

Saint Basil

Saint Basil, like his brother, Gregory, also thought of Adam before the Fall as a Stoic. His moral excellence consisted, that is, of *apathy*. The lack of passion, moreover, is precisely that characteristic of the first man which made him like God and it is, it is easily seen, a trait which may be regained, or at least approached, on this earth by following the path of renunciation. In this respect the Basilian school differed from many other Christian philosophers who maintained that only after death could the primal felicity be recaptured, and in some cases, that only by an unpredictable act of grace on God's part could even the best men be saved.[43] But by emphasizing Man's passionless perfection before the Fall, Saint Basil finds himself in the same predicament as that of Saint Gregory of Nyssa. How could so perfect a being, especially if his perfection consisted in Stoic *apathy*, have fallen?

There is a suggestion in one of Basil's works that man's very perfection rested upon the possibility of sinning; for what merit would a good man achieve who has not the power of slipping from grace? To choose the good without knowledge of evil is not so morally righteous as to choose it in preference to evil. Hence the original beauty of the human soul must have contained a trace of choice and one cannot choose in any real sense of the word without knowing both alternatives.[44] There thus had to be a command given to Adam which he would have the capability of disobeying. The

[42] *De virginitate*, xii [*MPG*, XLVI, pp. 369 B ff.]. The renunciation of marriage would not necessarily imply the end of the human race. For his ideas on reproduction without marriage, such as he says must have taken place to produce the host of angels, see *De hominis opificio*, xvii [*MPG*, XLVI, pp. 188 C–189 B].

[43] See *Ascetic Discourse*, 318 D [Ed. Garnier, vol. II, p. 445]. The authenticity of this short piece traditionally ascribed to Basil and edited among his complete works, is disputed by the consensus of modern scholars. Cf W. K. L. Clerks, *The Ascetic Works of St. Basil*, 1925, p. 11. Its authenticity is not a matter of importance for our purposes since its historical influence depended in part upon what its readers believed to be its authorship, not upon what its authorship really was.

[44] Cf. *Homily on Psalm XXIX*, v [*MPG*, XXIX, p. 317 A, B].

tree was, as Basil describes it, the "bait" which the Devil held out to the original couple, and the bait could have had no efficacy if Adam had been so made that he could not do evil.[45]

When one inquires what bait could be strong enough to tempt a Stoic Sage from his condition of apathy, one finds that it is not knowledge, but gluttony. Nor is gluttony used by Saint Basil in a figurative sense, such as the thirst for hidden wisdom, it is literal gluttony, the "lust of the belly." [46] Why Adam should have been curious about the taste of any real fruit is again somewhat bewildering, since he had been living on an exclusively vegetarian diet,[47] and might have been tempted more by the taste of meat. The difficulty cannot be avoided nor the apparent contradiction resolved, for, as might have been imagined, Saint Basil switched his point of view with the target of his argument. When he is describing the condition of the first man, he is naturally attempting to depict him in as noble a condition as possible. When, however, he is blaming him for the condition of his descendants, he is quick to forget his nobility.

Consequently when he is trying to discover a way of returning to the state of men before the Fall, it is only to be expected that he would follow the traditional road of penance, and fasting was one of the landmarks of that road. Before the Fall, we are told, fasting was the rule, that is, Adam drank no wine, sacrificed no animals, ate no meat. Were we to fast, we should approximate this way of life. "Since we did not fast, we were driven out of Paradise. Let us fast, therefore, in order to return there." [48]

The eating of meat was considered, not only by Saint Basil but also by many other early Christian Fathers, to be in itself an evil, regardless of whether man or beast was carnivorous. In a Basilian work, no longer considered to be by Saint Basil himself, one of the consequences of the Fall was said to be the spread of carnivorousness to the lower animals. Even the lion and the vulture were satisfied with vegetable food before the Fall. Man is urged to return to this way of life, not because he is to spurn any of the gifts of God, but to free himself from the demands of the flesh and make himself more like that Original in Whose image he was made.[49] But there is an additional reason for simplifying our regimen. We have multiplied our pleasures, we have invented curious and complicated luxuries, as a consolation for the loss of "the real luxury of Paradise." There, like the Cynic in his wine-jar, we were free from wants and needed very little. Luxury in this treatise is based upon the creation of unnecessary desires, which are in themselves a kind of enslavement. There was of course nothing

---

[45] Deus non est auctor malorum, ix [MPG, XXXI, p. 348 C-D].

[46] De renuntiatione saeculi, vii [MPG, XXXI, p. 640 C].

[47] De structura hominis, ii, 3, 4 [MPG, XXX, p. 44 D–45 D]—possibly not a genuine work—and De ieiunio, Hom. I, 5 [MPG, XXXI, p. 169 B].

[48] De ieiunio, Hom. 1, 3, 4 [MPG, XXXI, p. 108 A-C].

[49] De structura hominis, ii, 3, 4 [MPG, XXX, p. 44 D–45 D].

essentially Christian, or Jewish, in the doctrine that man's salvation consisted in or could be aided by freedom. After all, one important tradition had insisted upon man's dependence upon God, not only for his creation and existence upon this earth, but also for every good which he might achieve. The Cynic notion of complete self-dependence, therefore, could be held to be a kind of pride as vicious as that which some doctors of the Church saw as the impulse to the Fall.

On the question of whether Adam worked before the Fall, Saint Basil appears to be of two minds. In the *Constitutiones monasticae* [50] he maintains that "when God created man, He did not want him to be idle and lazy," but rather "to attend to his duty," "for in Paradise He ordered Adam to work and watch Him." The amount of work was not apparently very great nor very burdensome, for in the same passage Basil points out that after the Fall, Adam ate his bread "in the sweat of his brow," thus indicating the theory that labor is a punishment for the Fall. But in the *Regulae fusius tractatae* [51] life in Eden before the Fall was free not only from work, but also from effort and pain; it was a state of self-sufficiency and simplicity. Though such a life was not luxurious, it is described in the terms of a soft primitivism, rather than hard. The earth brought forth whatever food was necessary; man needed no clothes, not only because he had no shame in his nakedness, but also because of the clement climate; similarly, he needed no house and enjoyed perfect health. After the Fall, Nature became corrupted, just as man did, and failed to provide him with his needs. [52] The climate became inclement and his sense of shame demanded covering. Then God gave man agriculture, the crafts, and medicine, as an inferior substitute for the deficiencies of nature. Furthermore, as part of the curse put upon him for his sin, technological acquisitions took place slowly and painfully, rather than swiftly and, so to speak, in a block.

Lactantius

In Lactantius three incongruous ways of thinking about the nature and comparative value of man's primeval condition can be distinguished.

1. The first [53] is derived from scriptural sources, and is little more than a *précis* of *Genesis*, ii-iii; but three points in Lactantius's understanding of the Eden-story are to be noted. (a) The first man lived free from toil; he was placed in the garden *ut expers omnium laborum deo patri summa devotione serviret* [that free from all labor he might serve God the Father with the greatest devotion]. (b) If he had obeyed the commandments laid

[50] iv, 1 [*MPG*, XXXI, p. 1348 C].

[51] lv, p. 397 D [Garnier, II, p. 557].

[52] In the *In Hexaemeron homilia*, v. 6 [*MPG*, XXIX, p. 1053 B-C], it is stated that before the Fall the rose had no thorns; thorns were produced afterwards to "let us have sorrow along with enjoyment."

[53] *Divine Institutes*, II, 12 and *Epitome*, 27.

upon him, "he would have remained immortal"; and the object of the
tempter was to deprive him of his immortality. Thus through the eating
of the forbidden fruit, man's life became transitory, though it was still long,
since it extended to a thousand years.[54] (c) After the Last Judgment,
God, "having put an end to death, will bring back righteous men, his wor-
shipers, to the same place," i. e., to the original abode of Adam; this prediction is supported by a vague reference to the "sacred writings," but also
by an express citation of the Erythraean Sibyl, when she said, "They who
honor the true God will inherit eternal life, dwelling together in Paradise,
the beautiful garden, forever." [55]

The fall of man, as here conceived by Lactantius, was not completed with
the eating of the forbidden fruit and its punishment. Even after "the
first born in this world" became the murderer of the second, degeneration
continued: the Devil "did not thereafter cease from infusing the venom of
malice into the breasts of men through successive generations, corrupting
and depraving them, until at last he so overwhelmed them in crimes that
an example of justice became rare, and men lived after the manner of
beasts." [56] When this point was reached, an unsuccessful effort to restore
mankind was made by God; He "sent angels to improve the life of men
and to protect them from all evils" [57]—in particular, to guard them against
the deceits of the Devil. The rescuers, however, proved so incapable of
fulfilling their mission that they themselves were led astray by these same
deceits. Though they had been commanded "to abstain from earthly things,
so that they might not impair the angelic honor by any taint," they were
tempted by the "crafty accuser" to "defile themselves with women." In
consequence, "they both lost the name and the substance of angels," and
became "satellites of the Devil"; "these are the demons of whom the poets
often speak." [58] The state of mankind, naturally, was not improved, and the
Creator, his purpose for man having been twice frustrated, sent the Deluge
to destroy the entire race, except Noah and his family, preserved *ad
multitudinem reparandum*.

2. For Lactantius, however, one of the most learned in classical literature
among the early Fathers, the Jewish Scriptures were not the only source of
information about early history. Greek mythology and legend, interpreted

---

[54] *Div. inst.*, II, 5. Lactantius finds evidence that the tradition of this primeval
longevity was known to Varro. After the Flood, the limit of man's life was
shortened to 120 years [*loc. cit.* and *Epit.*, 27]; the purpose of this was to give men
less time to think up evil things to do. If shorter-lived, the species might prove
less mischievous.

[55] Note that here there is no millenium, but an everlasting Earthly Paradise.

[56] *Epit.*, 27. An influence from Seneca or another Stoic appears in the last clause.
Cf. *PIA*, p. 286.

[57] *Ib.*

[58] *Epit.*, 27; fuller version in *Div. inst.*, II, 15.

in accordance with the method of Euhemerus, was another. Euhemerism, as a theory already current among educated pagans which at once rejected polytheism and also seemed plausibly to account for its genesis, was peculiarly suited to the purposes of both Jewish and Christian polemic.[59] Its adoption created some complications, since it entailed the obligation of fitting the Greek and Roman stories and the biblical narratives into the same historical scheme. For the former must all, on Euhemeristic principles, be regarded as distorted versions of actual events and not as pure fictions. What then was to be done by a Christian Euhemerist with the stories of the Golden Age and the Reign of Saturn? The Golden Age could not be identified with the life of Adam and Eve in Eden before the Fall, nor with any other episode in the early chapters of *Genesis,* for there was no place in these for Saturn conceived as a beneficent human ruler, nor for the conflict between him and Jupiter, nor the triumph of the latter. And in fact a recent Euhemeristic pagan historian had assigned the supposedly historical Saturn to a much later date.

> Thallus writes in his history that Belus, the king of the Assyrians, whom the Babylonians worship and who was the friend and contemporary of Saturn, lived 322 years before the Trojan War, and it is 1470 years from the taking of Troy to the present.[60]

Upon this authority Lactantius concludes that the Golden Age under King Saturn must have given place to the degenerate age of Jupiter "not more than 1800 years" before his own time, i. e., about 1500 B. C. This, according to a synchronism of sacred and profane history which was already being worked out, was a little before the time of Abraham.[61] Lactantius, however, does not mention this fact, nor does he unequivocally tell us where Saturn reigned or whether the conditions of the Golden Age prevailed universally or only among a single people. In the *Epitome,* 22, there is a suggestion that Saturn was king of Latium, which was in accordance with a great part of pagan opinion, but in the following chapter he assimilates him to a Carthaginian god, presumably Moloch, a confusion which also

---

[59] For Lactantius's account of the life, writings, and theories of Euhemerus, see *Epit.,* 13.

[60] *Epitome,* 24. For Thallus, of whose life and writings little is known, see F. Jacoby, *Fragm. der griech. Historiker;* for the fragments, see Pt. II B, pp. 1156-1158; for the critical discussion, vol. 2 (1929) pp. 835 f. Cf. R. Laqueur, in Pauly Wissowa, art. *Thallos,* col. 1225. Jacoby believes it probable that Thallus was neither a Jew nor a Christian. What is best established about him is that he was a thorough-going Euhemerist.

[61] Cf. the *Chronici canones* of Eusebius in Saint Jerome's Latin version, ed. by J. K. Fotheringham, 1923, p. 13: Abraham was born in the 43d year of the reign of Minus, son of Belus; and the later remark of Orosius (*ca.* 418): almost all historians, "both Greek and Latin begin their histories with the reign of Minus, son of Belus," which was also the time of Abraham, and, according to Orosius's reckoning, 1300 years before the founding of Rome [*Historiae,* I, 1].

existed in pagan opinion. On the whole, however, when writing of this matter, Lactantius follows " the poets " so faithfully as to suggest to the reader that that happy era was universal and primeval, or all but primeval,[62] even though he also dates it as late as the sixteenth century B. C. This was not merely a supplement to *Genesis*; it was an implicit contradiction of it. Of this, however, Lactantius seems to have been oblivious; he apparently kept the two stories in separate compartments of his mind.

He accordingly gives us a second, non-biblical, version of the Fall. The Age of Saturn was for him the age before polytheism and idolatry had grown up, when men still worshipped one God, superhuman and immaterial. So long as they had a right knowledge of Deity, they also possessed all the moral virtues and their life was similar to that which Aratus, Ovid, the author of the *Octavia*, Seneca, Vergil, and Juvenal, had described, except that Lactantius avoids imputing a literal community of goods to the Golden Age. According to most pagan primitivists, private property was in that age unknown; according to Lactantius, the visible signs of it—fences and boundary stones—were indeed lacking, but this was merely symbolic of the owners' abundant charity. The result, nevertheless, was approximate economic equality. The beginning of the end of this blessed state came when Jupiter, having supplanted his father, determined to establish a cult in honor of himself. The original sin was apparently the pride and *hybris* of a monarch.[63] To this enforced apotheosis of a mere man—and a peculiarly depraved one—during his lifetime, was soon added the deification of deceased rulers or heroes; and at the same time this increasing polytheism passed over into the worship of inanimate figures, which was at least indirectly due to Prometheus, who here appears in a new rôle: as the inventor of earthenware images, he initiated the " detestable and foolish art " of the statuary, which has led to idolatry.[64] These departures from true religion resulted in an ever increasing moral corruption, for the depiction of which Lactantius again borrows copiously from the classical poets.

On the relation between monotheism and the sense of human brotherhood and the consequent loss of the latter with the disappearance of the former, Lactantius amplifies in another and a striking passage.

> The first duty of justice is to acknowledge God as a parent, to fear Him as a master, to love Him as a father . . . the second is to acknowledge man as a brother. For if the same God made us, and if He generated all men in an equal status with respect to justice and eternal life, we are surely linked together in a bond of brotherhood; and he who does not acknowledge this is unjust. But the

[62] See the opening of *Epitome*, 25.

[63] That a similar Euhemeristic version of the cause of man's decline was earlier current among Jewish Alexandrian writers is apparent from *Oracula Sibyllina*, III, 110 ff. and 543 ff. Cf. Lactantius, *De div. inst.*, I, 148.

[64] *Epit.*, 25.

origin of this evil by which the mutual society of men, by which the tie of relationship, has been dissolved, arises from ignorance of the true God. For he who knows not that fountain of benignity can by no means be good himself. Hence it is that from the time when many gods began to be held sacred by men and to be worshiped, justice, as the poets tell, took flight, every covenant was broken, society based upon human law was destroyed.[65]

Lactantius then relates more circumstantially the progress of man's depravity, again drawing largely upon classical poets for his details. When the loss of monotheistic religious belief and piety had destroyed among men the spirit of fraternity and the sense of membership in a common body, cupidity was born, source of all the evils which were to follow.[66] Thus Lactantius, after insisting upon the primacy of religious error in the process of man's degeneration, now resumes what may be called the socialistic strain of classical primitivism.

Yet this Fall of Man—so different in its nature from the biblical and from the Augustinian—was destined with the aid of supernatural grace to be eventually followed by a restoration. " God," says Lactantius, " as a most indulgent parent, when the last days drew near, sent His messenger to bring back that ancient age and the justice which had been put to flight." In other words, the Christian dispensation is, in some sense, a renewal of the Golden Age and a return of Astraea, except that justice and the social order based upon it, are now not universal but limited to a few.[67]

3. In both the foregoing accounts of man's original condition, it is represented in idyllic terms. Before the temptation our first parents were innocent and therefore happy, and there is no suggestion that such happy innocence is not the ideal state. Highly characteristic of Lactantius, however, was an idea which conflicted with this assumption—the radical distinction between innocence and " virtue " and the conviction that the latter is superior to the former. This idea had already been expressed by Stoic writers, notably by Seneca;[68] it may have been derived from them by Lactantius, but it evidently was especially congenial to his temperament, and it also appealed to him because it seemed to offer a solution of certain difficulties both in the biblical story and in the facts of moral experience. The temptation could, after all, not be supposed to have occurred without the permission of the Creator; it must, in short, have been willed by Him, and, if so, must have been in itself a good rather than an evil. Similarly the

---

[65] *Epit.*, 59. Cf. *PIA*, pp. 32, 35, 37. The justice of which he says the poets speak is, of course, the Goddess Astraea.

[66] *De div. inst.*, V, 6: *Omnium malorum fons erat cupiditas.*

[67] The words, *appropinquante ultimo tempore*, would seem to be evidence in an orthodox theologian of the fourth century of the expectation of an early end of the age.

[68] Cf. *PIA*, pp. 268, 274. A similar distinction had been made by Plato, *Id.*, p. 164.

4

trials and tribulations to which, even after the coming of Christ, the faithful were subject—and subject in even greater degree than unbelievers—must
be assumed to be in accord with the beneficent purpose of God. And both
of these seemingly paradoxical conclusions became intelligible, if it were
recognized that the attainment of "virtue" by man was the end for which
he was created, and that virtue presupposes tension, the overcoming of
obstacles, and genuine struggle against real and powerful temptations.
Lactantius accordingly develops more fully and with more reiteration than
any other patristic writer the thesis of the moral indispensability of the
existence of both suffering and moral evil, as a foil for good and at once a
touchstone and prerequisite for virtue.

> Virtue can neither be discerned unless it has vices opposed to it, nor
> can it be perfect unless it is exercised by opposition. For God desired
> that good and evil things should be discriminated in this way, that
> we should know the quality of goodness through evil, and of evil
> through goodness. Nor can the meaning [*ratio*] of the one be under-
> stood if the other be taken away. God, therefore, in order that the
> meaning of virtue might stand forth, did not exclude evil. For how
> could endurance [*patientia*] have its force and its name if there were
> nothing to endured [*pati*]? How could devoted faith in one's God
> merit praise, if there were no one who wished to turn us away from
> God? On this account, then, God permitted the unrighteous to be
> more powerful, that they might be able to force us to do evil, and
> more numerous, that virtue might be precious because rare . . .[69]
> For if it is virtue to fight bravely against evils and vices, it is
> clear that without evil and vice there is no virtue; and God, that
> He might make virtue complete and perfect, retained that which
> was its opposite, so that it might have something to fight with. For
> it is through being disturbed and shaken by evils that virtue acquires
> stability; and the more frequently it is assailed, the more firmly it
> is strengthened. This is why doubtless, though justice has been sent
> back to men, it cannot be said that the Golden Age exists; for God has
> not eliminated evil, in order to retain the diversity which alone
> contains the attestation of a divine religion.[70]

Lactantius returns to the theme not only in later chapters of the *Divine
Institutes* but also in the *De ira Dei*. Epicurus, whom Lactantius quotes
had put the problem of evil with the utmost sharpness and conciseness:

> God either wishes to do away with evils but is unable; or He is able
> but unwilling; or He is neither able nor willing.[71]

In short, He is either morally indifferent or of unlimited power. Lactantius
boldly declares in substance that God, whose power is infinite, was unwilling

---

[69] A passage to the same effect from one of the lost *Declamations* of Quintilian
is here cited.
[70] *De div. inst.*, V, 7 [*MPL*, VI, pp. 570 f.]. Cf. *De ira Dei*, 15.
[71] *De ira Dei*, 13.

to exclude evil, because the power of " wisdom," which implies choice between real alternatives, would have been impossible without its existence.[72]

From all this it followed that the idyllic life of man before the Fall had far less of potential moral value than his life since. And from this conclusion two further consequences with respect to the divine purpose concerning man could be drawn. (a) The primeval state of innocence, from this point of view, could be regarded as a brief infantile prelude to man's real history, never meant to be permanent. This is expressed in a passage of the *Divine Institutes* [73] which, though probably not written by Lactantius himself, is very much in his vein: since " wisdom cannot exist apart from evil . . . the first of the human race, so long as he experienced only good, lived as an infant, ignorant alike of good and evil." (b) From the very beginning of the creation, the Creator must have refrained from making life easy for man, have subjected him to difficulties and trials, arising both from his own inner constitution and from external circumstances, and have made his attainment of real good conditional upon his own successful struggle against these obstacles. When this thought is uppermost in Lactantius's mind, he virtually contradicts the more conventional view elsewhere accepted by him, that, but for the Fall, man would have lived free from all labor and would, but for the envy of the Tempter, have " remained immortal." Immortality, like virtue, Lactantius now declares, has never been natural to man; it is a

[72] Professor A. O. Lovejoy has written the following note on this point. " The most important historical effect of the enunciation of this general thesis by Lactantius appears nearly a millenium and a half later in Milton. This influence of Lactantius on Milton is not merely conjectural. In his *Commonplace Book* under the heading of *Malum morale*, Milton, troubled by the problem which was to be the philosophic theme of his epic, wrote, *Cur permittit deus malum? ut ratio virtuti constare possit. Virtus enim malo arguitur, illustratur, exercetur, quemadmodum disserit Lactantius*, l. 5, c. 7, *ut haberet ratio et prudentia in quo se exerceret, eligendo bona, fugiendo mala. Lactan., de ira dei* c. 13, *quamvis et haec non satisfaciunt. [Op. cit.*, 1876, p. 4]. Though the thesis seemed to Milton, at his first meeting with it, not altogether satisfying, it came to be one of his favorite and most frequently reiterated ideas. E. g., *De doctrina Christiana*, I, ch. 10, on *Genesis*, ii: ' It was called the knowledge of good and evil from the event; for since Adam tested it, we not only know evil, but we know good only by means of evil. For it is by evil that virtue is chiefly exercised and shines with greater brightness.' *Ib.*, I, 9: There are ' good temptations . . . whereby God tempts even the righteous for the purpose of proving them . . . This kind of temptation is therefore happy and to be desired.' *Paradise Lost*, IX, 335: ' What is faith, love, virtue unassay'd?' Above all, the passages cited in the text from Lactantius were the inspiration of the boldest and most striking argument for the freedom of the press in *Areopagitica*: ' I cannot praise a fugitive and cloistered virtue, unexercised and unbreathed,' etc. ' The knowledge of good and evil, as two twins cleaving together, leap'd forth into the world.' ' Perhaps this is that doom which Adam fell into of knowing good by evil.' ' How much we expel of sin, so much we expel of virtue.' The whole subject has been well treated by K. E. Hartwell, *Lactantius and Milton*, 1929, esp. pp. 23 ff."

[73] The concluding part of VII, 5, not found in most MSS., and rejected by most modern editors.

prize to be won through arduous endeavor. Why, an objector is supposed
to ask,[74] did God, Who created the world for man's sake and Who loves him
as a son—"why did He make him a frail and mortal being, why did He
expose him to all evils, when it was befitting that man should be both happy,
as akin and closest to God and everlasting, as is He for the worship and
contemplation of Whom he was made?" The answer, says Lactantius, is
that the Creator could, if He had wished, "have produced innumerable
souls, like the angels, who possess immortality without any danger and fear
of evils"; but in fact, when He came to the production of His favorite
creature, He proceeded quite otherwise.

> He devised an indescribable work, in such wise that He created an
> infinite number of souls which, being at first bound together with
> frail and feeble bodies, He placed midway between good and evil,
> so that—as they were thus composed of two natures—He might set
> virtue before them; and so that they might not attain immortality by
> delicate and easy ways, but might arrive at the ineffable reward of
> eternal life with the utmost difficulty and through great labors.
> Therefore, in order to provide them with heavy and vulnerable
> limbs—for they could not subsist in the empty space between the
> worlds, because of the downward pressure of the weight and gravity
> of the body—He determined that an abode and place of habitation
> should first be constructed for them . . . When all things were
> completed that had to do with the condition of the world, He
> fashioned man himself from the very same earth which He had first
> prepared for his dwelling-place; that is, He clothed and enveloped
> man's spirit with a terrestrial body, so that, composed of two different
> and mutually repugnant things, he might be capable of both good and
> evil . . . Why then, did He fashion him mortal and frail when He
> had built a world for his sake? First, that an infinite number of
> living beings might be produced and fill the whole earth with their
> multitudes;[75] second, that He might set virtue before man, that is,
> the endurance of evils and labors, through which he might be able
> to gain the reward of immortality. For . . . two lives have been
> assigned to man: one temporal, which is associated with the body,
> the other spiritual, which is attached to the soul. The former we
> receive through birth, the latter we acquire through labor—so that, as
> we said before, immortality might not be possessed by man without
> any difficulty. The one life is earthly, as the body is; therefore it has
> a limit. The other is heavenly, as the soul is; and therefore has no
> end. The first we received unconsciously, the second knowingly. For
> it was God's purpose that we should obtain for ourselves a life in
> a life.[76]

[74] This part of the chapter, at least, is Lactantius's own.

[75] There is an echo here of *Timaeus*, 30, 39 E, 42 E, and an expression of the
"principle of plenitude"; one reason why God created men imperfect was that, if
He had not, one kind of possible being would have been lacking in the creation.
See A. O. Lovejoy, *The Great Chain of Being*, pp. 50-52 and *passim*.

[76] *De div. inst.*, VII, 5 [*MPL*, VI, p. 750]. The point of the last clause is the
attainment of eternal life through temporal life.

Thus the reason why the soul has a body is that man may thereby have implanted in his very constitution an impediment or enemy to the good— but a necessary enemy, having, therefore, its own value as an instrumental good. So, in the conception of virtue, as contrasted with innocence, Lactantius sees the rational explanation of that otherwise mysterious duality of man's nature upon which both Saint Paul and Plato had dwelt; the reason why, in this life, sense is ever at war with soul is that the soul can exercise its powers and realize its latent potentialities only through such warfare. From the same premises it followed, with respect to the story of *Genesis*, ii, that Paradise would not have been Paradise without the serpent. This last implication of his premises Lactantius does not fail to make explicit; in one passage of the *Divine Institutes* [III, 29], he virtually declares the Devil to be a necessary and useful part of the divine economy of the universe. Satan "was not at once thrust down to punishment by God at his first transgression, in order that by his malice he might exercise man to virtue. For unless virtue is in constant motion, unless it is strengthened by continual harassment, it cannot be perfect, since virtue is dauntless and unconquered endurance of evils that must be borne. From which it follows that there is no virtue if the Adversary be wanting." [77] The argument might, indeed, have been carried one step further; since a temptation to which no man was ever likely to yield could hardly furnish the real struggle without which virtue was not to be attained, it might appear that the Fall itself—or at least a fall—was also a part of the same divine purpose. An Adversary so feeble that he could never win even a skirmish would seem scarcely adequate for that purpose. From this it would follow that Paradise was "well lost." There are adumbrations of this conclusion in some of the passages cited above, but on the whole Lactantius was apparently reluctant to press his argument to this extreme. It is evident, however, that this general strain in Lactantius's thought was adverse to any simple primitivistic reading of the story of Eden; in so far as the first pair at their creation were merely innocent and wholly happy, they fell short of the full stature of man, and under such paradisaical conditions the goal of human history could not have been attained. It may be added that by virtue of his special insistence upon these conceptions, Lactantius may be called not inappropriately the most "Romantic" of the Fathers. In giving an intrinsic value to the struggle of the will against a resistant force—which therefore exists as a necessary means to the realization of that value—he distinctly foreshadowed Fichte's thesis that the first act of the Ego, since it is essentially a moral Ego, in affirming itself is to set up an *Anstoss*, an obstacle to be overcome.

[77] Or "an adversary." But Lactantius in several other passages clearly uses *adversarius*, as other Christian writers did and would use it, in the sense of "the Devil": *De opificio Dei*, I; *De martyr. persecut.*, I; *De div. inst.*, VI, 6, 23.

Saint Ambrose

Like most of his predecessors, the great Bishop of Milan wavered between a simple primitivistic fashion of appraising the earliest condition of human life and certain other conceptions with which such a view could not easily be reconciled. In his *Hexaemeron* he gives us a description of the world and of man as they came from the hands of their Creator, before their nature had been changed by sin. This description combines themes from *Genesis* and pictures of the Golden Age from classical poetry. Its general tone is that of soft primitivism.

> Spontaneously earth bore all fruits; though it could not be plowed in the absence of a plowman—for no farmer yet existed—nevertheless it abounded in the richest harvests, and, I do not doubt, with an even larger yield, since the slothfulness of the husbandman could not rob the soil of its richness. For now the fertility of a piece of land is in proportion to the labor expended upon it, and neglect, or the injury caused by heavy rains or by the aridity of the land or by hailstones or by some other cause, is punished by the barrenness of the soil. In those days, however, the earth of itself everywhere brought forth its fruits, since He so commanded Who is the fullness of all things. For the word of God fructified upon the earth, nor had the soil as yet been laid under any curse. For the time of the birth of the world is more ancient than our sins, and the guilt because of which we have been condemned to eat our bread in the sweat of our brow, to know no food without sweat, is more recent.
>
> Yet, in truth, today also the fruitful earth produces its former abundance by spontaneous fertility. For how many even now are the things which it brings forth of itself! And even in those products which are sought by means of manual labor, the divine beneficence to humanity remains in great part, so that the grain grows while we are at rest. This is, for example, taught by the text before us in which the Lord says, "So is the kingdom of God, as if a man should cast seed into the ground: and should sleep, and rise night and day, and the seed should spring and grow up, he knoweth not how" [*Mark*, iv, 26, 27]. For the earth brings forth of herself, first the blade, then the ear, then the full corn in the ear. But when the fruit is put forth, "immediately he putteth forth the sickle, because the harvest is come" [*Mark*, iv, 29]. Thus, O Man, while you are asleep and unconscious, the earth still produces its fruits; you sleep and then you rise and marvel to see how the grain has grown through the night.[78]

Adam, while he remained in the state in and for which he had been created, possessed both natural and supernatural excellences and felicities, though "natural" and "supernatural" can in strictness be said to have acquired contrasting meaning only since the Fall. He not only had, as his

---

[78] *Hexaemeron*, III, x [Ed. Schenkl, *CSEL*, XXXII, pp. 87-90]. The date of composition is doubtful, but Dudden, in his *St. Ambrose*, 1935, p. 678, places it after 386 and perhaps in 387. For a similar passage, cf. *De paradiso*, i.

nudity showed, "the sincerity and simplicity of a sound and uncorrupted nature"[79] but was "supremely blessed," "breathed ethereal air," was "ignorant of any of the cares and weariness [*taedia*] of life,"[80] was "clad in the robe of the virtues,"[81] and "refulgent with celestial grace."[82] In short, his existence was that of an angel. The anti-naturalistic strain, not infrequent in classical primitivism, is echoed by Saint Ambrose when he speaks of Adam as having been designed "to have all the world for his country." "For if the wise man today, wherever he may travel, is everywhere a citizen, everywhere finds himself at home, . . . so much the more was the first of the human race a citizen of the whole world and, as the Greeks say, a cosmopolitan."[83] When dilating upon the advantages of solitude, Saint Ambrose pushed his primitivism to the point of declaring that the best state was that in which Adam lived before the creation of Eve, apparently overlooking for the moment *Genesis*, ii, 18, and intimates that the first man, if he had been left to himself, would not have fallen.[84] This, however, is merely a passing remark which should not perhaps be taken too seriously, since Saint Ambrose did not hold that the multiplication of the human race was not intended by God. Finally, if Adam had remained in the state of nature, he would have been immortal, for death was not at the outset a part of the natural order, but was introduced into it as a correction for the evils of existence since the Fall.[85]

With respect to the psychological cause of the Fall, Saint Ambrose, like so many other theological moralists, has at least two opinions. Sometimes he conceives Adam's disobedience to have been due to a kind of excessive pride [*superbia* or *insolentia*], to a desire to make himself the equal of God,[86] sometimes he lays the responsibility for the first misstep to the desire for pleasure.[87] The latter theory of the Fall was closely akin to one of the principal premises of technological primitivism, for frequently the development of the arts has been attributed to man's expansive desire for material goods. The former theory, in the sense in which Saint Ambrose construed it, did not have this implication, for he interpreted the "knowledge of good and evil" as referring to moral and religious understanding exclusively.

But just for this reason, Saint Ambrose, like so many others, is troubled by a double difficulty in the story of *Genesis* ii. If the first pair did not

[79] *De paradiso*, 14 [*MPL*, XIV, p. 309].
[80] *In Ps. 118, enarratio*, 4, 2 [*MPL*, XV, p. 124].
[81] *De Elia*, 4 [*MPL*, XIV, p. 701].
[82] *In Ps. 43, enarratio* [*MPL*, XIV, p. 1125].
[83] *Epist.*, I, 45 [*MPL*, XVI, p. 1144].
[84] *Epist.*, I, 49 [*MPL*, XVI, p. 1154]. "Adam was alone and did not sin, because his mind clung to God. But when woman was added to him, he could not remain faithful [*inhaerere*] to the commands of Heaven."
[85] *De excessu Satyri*, II, 47 [*MPL*, XVI, p. 1327].
[86] *Epist.* 73, 5; *Expos. Ps. 118*, 7, 9.
[87] *Epist.* 63, 14.

possess this understanding before they ate of the tree of knowledge, how could they be held responsible for yielding to the Tempter? " One who does not know good and evil differs in no way from a little child. But a just judge does not attribute wrong-doing to little children. And the just Artificer of the world would never have charged a little child with guilt because he had not known good and evil, for a child is exempt from the charge of transgression and wrong-doing." [88] Saint Ambrose tries to avoid the difficulty by distinguishing between superficial and more profound moral knowledge. Adam knew at least that eating of the tree was forbidden, even though he did not know why, and thus was not a mere child, for he knew enough to be guilty of disobedience. In the second place, Saint Ambrose feels that God must have had some intelligible reason for His prohibition; he expresses none of that delight in inexplicable submission to authority which some Christian writers of his time seem to exhibit. The desire for the knowledge of moral good and evil was in itself no sin, but a virtue.[89] The " wish to be as God," far from being reprehensible, was for Christianity, as for Platonism, the best and deepest craving of man's nature. Saint Ambrose meets this difficulty by adopting the view of Theophilus, Lactantius, and others, that Adam was in a state of relative intellectual and moral immaturity, and was not yet ready for a complete understanding of those truths for which he had already a hunger. But if that is so, then man's primeval condition was not the best that God intended him to attain, and he could reach that condition only by a gradual process of education. When Saint Ambrose is in this mood, he uses this analogy not only to explain the difficulty involved in the story of the Fall, but also, following Saint Paul [Galatians, iii, 24 f.], to explain why the Jewish Law has been superseded. The Law is the teacher of the immature; " to the Jews, then, as to children, were given not complete but partial instructions." [90] This anti-primitivistic strain is obviously somewhat out of tune with the primitivism implicit in the biblical story which he is nominally following, and also with those passages of his own in which he dwells upon the blessed state of man before the Fall.

Saint Ambrose, moreover, like Tertullian and Lactantius, had moments in which he thought of man's condition before the Fall as morally inferior. He expresses the idea, which we have seen in Lactantius, of the superiority of " virtue " to innocence, of the indispensability of evil to goodness, and the inference that the Devil has a useful, if involuntary, function in the scheme of things.

> For the completion of God's work, I shall assert, even that tree which grew in Paradise was permitted by God that we might know the superior excellence of goodness. For how, if there were not a knowledge of both good and evil, could we learn to make any distinction

[88] De paradiso, I, 6, 31 [MPL, XIV, p. 288].
[89] De paradiso, 7.   [90] Epist. 74, 4.

between good and evil? For unless there were a knowledge of the good, we should not judge that which is evil to be evil; but also, the knowledge of the good could not exist unless good also existed; and conversely we should not know what is good to be good, unless there existed a knowledge of evil.[91]

If sin did not exist, he maintains elsewhere,[92] not only would vice not exist but also virtue. The Devil therefore entered Paradise with the consent of God and in spite of his desire to do nothing but evil, is by the very nature of things a contributory cause of our salvation. So Job suffered his tribulations which made his virtue more evident; so Joseph was tempted by Potiphar's wife, to test his invincible chastity. Thus virtue is not lightly given one but is the crown of victory over vice. We should consequently not find fault with the presence of the Devil in Eden.[93] But perhaps the climax of this paradoxical dialectic is found in the theory that the Fall was the cause of the Incarnation and the Redemption and was thus in no sense of the word regrettable. Adam's sin has therefore brought us more advantage than harm.[94]

Saint Augustine

The influence of Saint Ambrose upon his pupil, Augustine, needs no comment here. Into Saint Augustine flowed currents from all parts of patristic and much of pagan literature, to be merged and flow out again as a single stream. And though he owed not only his conversion, but perhaps many of his doctrines to his teacher, he was also in debt to scores of other thinkers. What is even more important in the history of thought than his debt to others is the extent of other writers' debts to him. His doctrines of history, of the Trinity, of the will, of predestination, to name only a few examples, had a prestige which was to be duplicated only in the case of Saint Thomas Aquinas. He is thus one of those great figures from whom new movements start, figures the voluminousness of whose works makes it impossible to sum them up in a few paragraphs. We shall therefore merely attempt an admittedly superficial account of Saint Augustine's position in the set of ideas we are here examining and leave it to others to round it out.

In the first place it must not be forgotten that for Saint Augustine any historical event may be interpreted in two ways: it was both something which took place in space and time and something which occurred in a

[91] De paradiso, 2[MPL, XIV, p. 277].

[92] Id., 8.

[93] De paradiso, I, 1 [MPL, XIV, p. 278]. A sermon of Bernard of Clairvaux will illustrate the persistence of this theme in the middle ages. See Sermones in cantica, 64 [MPL, CLXXXIII, p. 1084].

[94] De institutione virginis, 104 [MPL, XVI, p. 331]. A. O. Lovejoy, to whom this section is heavily indebted, not only for its substance, but in many places for its very phraseology, has developed this theme in his "Milton and the Paradox of the Fortunate Fall," ELH, vol. IV (Sept. 1937), pp. 161 ff., esp. p. 169.

symbolical universe which had what he called " spiritual " meaning.   Thus he gives us a double interpretation of the story of the Garden of Eden.

Let us now look at that happiness of man which is meant by the word, "Paradise." Since men are accustomed to find delightful repose in groves, and light arises before our corporeal senses from the East, and the sky stretches over us, a body superior to our body and more excellent, therefore, with these words the spiritual delights which are the possessions of a happy life are to be figuratively explained, together with the fact that Paradise is planted in the East. Let us understand that our spiritual joys mean every tree that is beautiful to the gaze of understanding and good for the imperishable food upon which happy souls are fed. For the Lord says, "Labor not for the meat which perisheth " [*John*, vi, 27], that is, we must seek the reason in its entirety which is the food of the soul. In the East means the light of wisdom in Eden, that is, in immortal and intelligible delights. For it [*Eden*] may mean either delights or pleasure or feasts, if it is translated from Hebrew into Latin. It is put thus, however, without translation, to appear to mean some place, or rather to serve as a metaphor. We take all the trees which were produced from the earth to signify every spiritual joy ; that is, to tower over the earth and not to be entangled and covered over with the snares of earthly desires. The tree of life, however, is planted in the center of Paradise, which means that wisdom, by which the soul ought to know that it is placed in the center of things, so to speak, so that although it have all corporeal nature subjected to it, yet may know that above it is God's nature, and it should neither bend to the right, arrogating to itself what is not, nor to the left, negligently disdaining what is. And this is the tree of life, planted in the center of Paradise.

The tree, however, of the knowledge of good and evil likewise symbolizes that centrality of the soul and its ordered integrity. For this tree too was planted in the center of Paradise, and for this reason is called the tree of the knowledge of good and evil, because if the soul, which ought to reach forth for those things which are before, that is, God, and to forget those things which are behind [*Philipp.*, iii, 13], that is, corporeal pleasures, if the soul, I say, has turned towards itself, having abandoned God, and wishes to enjoy its own power as if without God, it swells up with pride, which is the beginning of all sin. And when its punishment follows upon the commission of the sin, by experience the soul learns what difference there is between the good which it has abandoned and the evil into which it has fallen. And this is what it will be for it to have eaten of the fruit of the tree of the knowledge of good and evil. Therefore Adam was warned that he might eat of every tree which was in Paradise but that of the tree of the knowledge of good and evil he might not eat; that is, he might not enjoy it so that he would violate and corrupt the ordained integrity of his nature itself, as if by gluttony.[95]

---

[95] *De Genesi contra Manichaeos*, Bk. ii, ch. 9 [*MPL*, XXXIV, pp. 202 f.].

From this account it would appear that Adam was originally without a conscious appreciation of either his moral innocence or of his superiority to the rest of creation. He was in fact very much like the Infant-Adam. This impression is borne out by a passage from the treatise on free-will, in which Saint Augustine concludes that Adam began by being neither wise nor stupid but had the capacity of being either.

> If the first man was made wise, why was he led astray? If, on the other hand, he was made stupid, why is not God the author of vice, since stupidity is the greatest vice? As if human nature might receive no affection midway between stupidity and wisdom, which could be called neither stupidity nor wisdom. For in that case man begins by being either stupid or wise, so that he must necessarily be called one of these, although he was already capable of having wisdom unless he disdained it, in which case his will was guilty of vicious stupidity. For no one is so foolish as to call a child stupid, although it would be more absurd to call him wise. Therefore a child may be said to be neither stupid nor wise, though he is already human. From which it appears that human nature may have a middle trait which you would rightly call neither stupidity nor wisdom. So if anyone were characterized by such an affection as those have who lack wisdom through negligence, no one would rightly call him stupid whom he saw to be such not by vice but by nature. For stupidity is not a sort of seeking and avoiding of things, but a vicious ignorance. Wherefore we do not call an irrational animal stupid, because he has not the power of becoming wise.[96]

One must not, Saint Augustine warns us, fall into the error of thinking that our first parents lived a purely spiritual life. The allegorical interpretation of *Genesis* is proper and useful, but it is only one way of reading it.[97] Adam and Eve lived an animal as well as a spiritual life, for their bodies were not as yet spiritual. They lived, moreover, in the rigid discipline of strict obedience. Before the Fall, they lived in a state of innocence, after the Fall they lived in sin and penitence, and after the Judgment their descendants will live in retribution for the Fall. Though the third phase of what became human history is in large measure a return to the first, it is in one particular an improvement over that period, for men and women then will have no fleshly bodies.

> It may be not unfairly asked whether the first man, or the first men—for there was a marriage of two—had such affections in the animal body before the Fall as we shall not have in the spiritual body when all sin has been purged from us and ended. If they did have them, how were they happy in that memorable place of happiness, Paradise? Who in short can be called absolutely happy, who is affected by fear or pain? But what could those men fear or be pained by in such affluence of such great goods, when neither death was feared nor

[96] *De libero arbitrio,* ch. xxiv [*MPL*, XXXII, pp. 1305 f.].
[97] *Civ. Dei,* bk. xiii, ch. 20, 21.

any bodily ill-health, nor was anything absent which good-will might desire nor anything present which might harm the flesh or spirit of a man living happily?

Their love for God was undisturbed, and for each other was that of those living in the faithful and unspoiled society of marriage, and from this love great joy, since it did not cease in the enjoyment of what was loved.   There was a tranquil avoidance of sin, in the duration of which no evil whatsoever could assail them to bring them sorrow.   Did they desire to touch the tree which they were forbidden to eat, but feared to die, and thus did both desire and fear already disturb them even in that place?

Far be it from us to think that such might have been the case when there was no sin whatever.   For it is not sinlessness to desire what the law of God prohibits, and to abstain from it from fear of punishment, not from love of justice.   Far be it from us, I say, to think that before all sin there was already existing such a sin as to commit with reference to a tree what the Lord says of woman, " Whosoever looketh on a woman to lust after her hath committed adultery with her already in his heart " [*Matth.*, v, 28].

Therefore the whole society of men might have been as happy as those two were and agitated by no disturbance of mind nor aggrieved by discomforts of body, if they had not done that evil which they passed on also to their descendants, and if none of their stock had committed the iniquity which brought on damnation.   And they would have been blessed with that enduring felicity, until through that blessing in which it was said, " Increase and multiply," the number of predestined saints had been completed, another blessing would be given, such as has been given to the most blessed angels, in which there was a sure certainty that none would sin and none would die, and such would have been the life of the saints, had there been no experience of labor, pain, and death, as will be true after experiencing all these, when the dead are resurrected with the incorruption of the body restored.[98]

This picture of primal felicity is repeated in a passage in which Adam and Eve appear even more like Stoics.   Their freedom from want and their self-control reach a point which would have seemed perfect to Seneca and which had already been attributed to Adam, if not to Eve, by Saints Gregory of Nyssa and Basil.

Man lived in Paradise as he wished, so long as he wished what God had commanded.[99]   He lived in the enjoyment of God, from Whose

---

[98] *De civitate Dei*, XIV, 10 [Ed. Welldon, II, pp. 101 f.].

[99] This would make little sense, if the subject of the verb were anything other than " God." But to Saint Augustine, God could not have commanded anything which Adam would not have wished, had Adam stopped to think. On the other hand, if Adam was an infant morally, then he could not stop to think, and his sin was blind—and hence pardonable?—disobedience. If he was not an infant morally, but could foresee the consequences of his disobedience, then his primal state was not such as he wished. Neither Saint Augustine, nor his successors, ever solved that dilemma.

goodness he was good. He lived in need of nothing, having it in his power always so to live. He had food lest he be hungry, drink lest he thirst, the tree of life lest old age wear him away. No corruption was in his body nor did he feel arising from his body any threats to the acuity of any of his senses. No inner disease was to be feared, no blow from without. The soundest health was in his flesh, in his spirit complete tranquility.

Just as in Paradise there was no excessive heat nor cold,[100] so in its inhabitant no mishap befell his good-will from cupidity or fear.

There was nothing sad, nothing vacantly joyful. True gladness unceasingly flowed from God, in Whom was glowing " charity out of a pure heart, and of a good conscience, and of faith unfeigned " [I *Tim.*, i, 5]. And between them the faithful society of spouses linked in honest love, an harmonious watch over mind and body and the keeping of the commandment without toil. Fatigue did not weary their leisure, sleep did not come upon them involuntarily.

Let us be far from suspecting that with things so easily acquired and with man so happy, offspring could not have been begotten without the disturbance of lust. On the contrary, those parts were moved by that act of will which moves the other members, and without the ensnaring stimulus of hot desire, in tranquillity of soul and no loss of corporeal integrity did the husband pour out his seed into the womb of his wife. Nor, because this cannot be tested by experiment, must it therefore not be believed, since violent heat did not stimulate those parts of the body, but a spontaneous power, as it was needed, appeared, so at that time it was possible for the man's seed to enter into his wife's womb with the integrity of the female organ unbroken, just as now it is possible, with that same integrity preserved, for the menstrual flux to proceed from the womb of a virgin.

In fact, just as the one could be injected, so can the other be ejected. For as there were no groans of pain in childbirth, but an impulse at maturity relaxed the female organs, so for gestation and conception there was no lustful appetite, but voluntary exercise united both natures. We are speaking of things which are now shameful and therefore, although we think of them so far as possible as they could have been before they were matters to be ashamed of, yet it is necessary that our discussion be checked by that reverence which restrains us, rather than encouraged by the eloquence with which we are too scantily supplied.

For since that of which I am speaking was not known to them who might have experienced it—since by hasty sinning they won exile from Paradise, before they united in the work of procreation with tranquil will—what now, when those things are spoken of, would rise before the human senses except the experience of violent lust not submitted to calm volition?

Therefore I am ashamed to continue speaking, although my reason supports my thoughts on the matter.[101]

[100] This becomes a commonplace in descriptions of the Earthly Paradise. Cf. Eve's lament in Kuno Meyer's *Selections from Ancient Irish Poetry*, 2d imp., London, 1911, p. 34, and below, the essay on Earthly Paradises.

[101] *Id.*, XIV, 26 [Ed. Welldon, II, p. 125].

The absence of toil does not imply that man lived a life of idleness before the Fall. In the second version of God's creation [*Genesis*, ii, 15], Adam is put into the Garden of Eden " to dress it and to keep it." Consequently he must have done some work. But Saint Augustine has plenty of classical texts in praise of agriculture to justify his opinion that it is an agreeable occupation and, since the climate of Eden was perfect, agriculture must have been always rewarding. Therefore Adam could be said not to have labored in the sense of " painful labor," but to have co-operated with his Maker in preparing a scene upon which divine creativity would play its rôle. Thus the primitive gardener " conversed with nature " and learned from her that the real source of growth and fruition is God. Such an exercise could not be fairly called " labor."

> Did the Lord wish the first man to engage in agriculture? Would it be credible that before his sin He had condemned him to labor? So we should think, unless we saw some do agricultural work with such great pleasure that it would be a great punishment for them to be called away to another kind of work. Therefore whatever delights agriculture has were much fuller when nothing adverse ever befell either from earth or heaven. For it was not the affliction of labor, but the gladdening of the will, when those things which God had created grew up gladly and fruitfully with the help of human work; wherefore the Creator Himself should be praised more copiously, Who gave to the soul established in an animal body a reason and a faculty for working, as much as was sufficient for the willing soul, not so much as the need of the body forced upon one reluctantly.
>
> For what greater or more wonderful spectacle is there, or where, one might say, can reason speak more [intimately] with Nature than when setting out seeds, planting slips, transplanting saplings, planting mallet-shoots, as if each force of root and seed were asked what it could do or what it could not do; whence it could produce, whence it could not; what was the strength in it of the invisible and internal power of numbers; [102] what diligence contributed from without; and to perceive, while considering all these things, that neither he who plants anything, nor he who waters, but that he who gives increase is God [*I Cor.* iii, 7]; that that part of the work which is brought in from without is done through him whom nevertheless God created and whom God invisibly rules and commands? [103]

Since the primeval life was the best life and contained no trace of evil, all evil, no matter what its apparent source, must be attributable to the Fall. Saint Augustine does not hesitate to draw this conclusion and lists crimes, both civil and religious, moral and intellectual, crimes of the body and of the soul, as the inevitable result of Adam's original transgression. Nor can man avoid committing them, for, as is well known, according to this Father

---

[102] The seminal reasons?
[103] *De Genesi ad litteram VIII*, viii, ix [*MPL*, XXXIV, pp. 379 f.].

all men are damned from birth.[104]   But in addition to human criminality, there are certain evils rooted in external nature itself, catastrophes such as floods and earthquakes; there are evils over which man has no more control than he has over catastrophes but which exist on a more limited scale, such as poisons, hostile animals, accidents of travel, disease, famine, nightmares, all of which would not have existed if Adam had not sinned.   His pen runs on like that of the author of the *Axiochus* and indeed no Cynic ever surpassed him in this diatribe on human misery.[105]   The only escape from this terrestrial hell is God's grace.

Saint Augustine would appear to be the first Christian author to give what might be called a metaphysical explanation of the corruption of the human race.   The Pagans were ready with psychological accounts of the increase of evil, for they knew of the pleasurableness of most immoral practices and had no religious reasons for going behind psychological hedonism.   But to them evil was a natural result of some human desires. It was not a punishment supernaturally visited upon men.   A Christian could not accept so simple an account of the matter and was consequently faced with the problem of a just God's punishment of individuals for a crime which they did not seem to have committed.   But that we all sinned in Adam seemed clear enough from *Romans*, v, 12-19.   Now it was clarified by Saint Augustine in the following manner.

> God, the author of the original natures of things, but not of their vitiated forms, created man upright.   But of his own will he was depraved and justly damned and he generated depraved and damned children.   For all of us were in that one man, since all of us were that one man, who fell into sin through that woman who was made from him before his sin.   For not yet were our individual forms created and distributed to us one by one, those forms in which we were to live as individuals; but there did exist at that time the seminal nature from which we were to be procreated and when this was vitiated by sin and bound in the chains of death and justly damned, man could not be born from man in a different condition.
>
> And so by this, through the evil use of our free-will, the continuation of this mischief was begun, which by a linkage of miseries leads the human race from its depraved source as from an injured root to the gates of a second death which has no end, from which they alone are exempt who are freed by the grace of God.[106]

[104] See esp. *De civitate Dei*, Bk. XXII, ch. 22.

[105] The *topos* of human misery became a favorite in the Renaissance.   For a selection of examples which contrast human infelicity with animal felicity, see G. Boas, *The Happy Beast*, ch. III.   It would be sheer ostentation to multiply citations from Saint Augustine as evidence of his belief in man's original perfection and subsequent corruption, but it may prove interesting to a reader to look into *De nuptiis et concupiscentia*, II, iiii, 9 and *Contra duas epistolas Pelagianorum*, IV, iv, 6, for these give his own comparison of his views with those of the Manichees and some other heretics.

[106] *De civitate Dei*, Bk. XIII, ch. 14 [Ed. Welldon, II, p. 56].   Cf. Orosius, *Apologeticus*, 26.

No law of either amelioration or degeneration describes the course of human affairs between the universal corruption of the Fall and the Judgment. Whatever decency appears in history is attributable to the inexplicable desire of individuals to be decent and thus to rehabilitate themselves in the eyes of their Maker. At times their good intentions seem to be repaid, but the bestowal of grace is unpredictable and incomprehensible. Yet at the same time there remain in Saint Augustine traces of legends which fit in with a theory of progressive degeneration. He is, for instance, a firm believer in the decrease in human stature and longevity.

> No one who shrewdly weighs the evidence would doubt that Cain could have founded not only some sort of city but even a great one, since human life used to be so long, unless perhaps some infidel would question us because of that very length of life which our authorities ascribe to men of that time and should deny its credibility. For they do not believe that even the size of bodies was much greater then than it is now. In reference to this, their own renowned poet, Vergil, says in reference to the huge stone which was set up as a boundary mark of the fields and which a strong man of that time snatched up while fighting and ran along and swung it and threw it,
>
> > " Scarcely twelve men whose frames are such as earth now produces could have carried it on their shoulder,"
>
> meaning that earth was then accustomed to producing bigger bodies. How much the more was this true before that renowned and widely known Deluge, than in relatively recent times! But the incredulous are frequently convinced of the size of those bodies by tombs stripped open by the wear and tear of time or by the force of rivers and by various accidents. Therein have appeared or from them have rolled out bones of unbelievable magnitude. I myself, not alone but in company with several others, have seen on the coast of Utica a human molar so huge that if it had been cut into pieces to the measure of our teeth, it seemed to us that it could have made a hundred of them. But that, I should imagine, belonged to some giant. For though the bodies of all men were then larger than ours, the giants overtopped the others by far. But just as in other times, so in ours there have never been wholly lacking men whose height was much greater than that of other men, though indeed they are rare.
>
> Pliny, a most learned man, maintains that as the course of time goes on, nature makes smaller bodies.[107] This he says even Homer often lamented in his poem, nor does Pliny laugh at this as poetic fiction, but assumes it to be historically correct in his capacity as a writer about natural wonders. But, as I have said, the many bones which have been found prove the size of ancient bodies even to much later ages [than that of Homer], since these bones are lasting.
>
> The length of each man's life, however, as it was in those days, cannot be brought to the test by any such evidence. Yet faith in

---

[107] See *PIA*, pp. 101, 349, n. 113.

sacred history must not be withheld on that account. It would be the more shameless not to believe its account of the past, since we see its prophecies the more certainly fulfilled. The same Pliny even says that there is still a people which lives for two hundred years. If then places unknown to us are believed to have a span of life today of which we have no experience, why should not times also be believed to have had such things? Or is it credible that elsewhere exists what does not exist here and incredible that at other times there existed what does not exist now? [108]

[108] *De civitate Dei*, Bk. XV, 9 [Ed. Welldon, II, pp. 143 ff.]. The quotation from Vergil is from *Aeneid*, XII, 899-900.

5

ORIGINAL CONDITION OF MAN: MEDIEVAL PERIOD

Saint Jerome

Saint Augustine's contemporary, Saint Jerome, is more noted for his translations and commentaries than for any contribution to Christian doctrine. His opinions on matters which interest us are to be found, not in treatises devoted to them but in *obiter dicta*. Thus speaking of the future life, he mentions Adam's original perfection as if it were unquestioned. "We are to be resurrected as a perfect man and in the measure of the stature of the fulness of Christ [*Ephesians,* iv, 13], in which the Jews believe Adam to have been created and in which we read that our Lord, the Savior, was resurrected." [1] Precisely what human perfection consisted in is a matter for further discussion and is not expatiated upon by Saint Jerome in this passage. For he was there interested merely in the age of resurrected souls and whether it would have any relation to that of their former bodies at the time of their death.

In his commentary on *Ecclesiastes,*[2] there is another passing reference to Adam's condition before the Fall. In this passage he justifies the existence of evil on the theory that man was created *insensibilis et stolidus,* but gifted with intelligence, so that his free-will would be guided by reason and discrimination; the doctrine of Adam as an intellectual infant is here clearly discarded. Again,[3] later in the same work man is said to have been created in order to worship God "in fear and respect and the keeping of His commandments." Adam and Eve before the Fall are described as "immaculate virgins" elsewhere,[4] an opinion in harmony with the earlier doctrine that the Fall was sexual in nature. But such hints are only hints and should not be used as proof of anything more than Saint Jerome's acceptance of certain earlier views or possibly of the lack of interest which he had for the subject.

Saint Prosper of Aquitania

The Augustinian tradition is continued by one of Saint Augustine's disciples, who is almost forgotten by all except specialists in medieval thought, Saint Prosper of Aquitania, a fifth century writer, who repeats the doctrine of our inclusion in Adam, our lapse into misery and sin through his Fall, and the impossibility of salvation without grace. Saint Prosper, as became the custom, simply lists all the evils which are of interest to him, attributes them all to the Fall, and thus implies that humanity, in its embodiment in the first man, lived in a state of complete moral purity. Questions of

---

[1] *Epistles,* cviii, 25 [Ed. I. Hilberg, *CSEL,* vol. 54 (1912), s. I, p. ii, 343-44].
[2] *MPL,* XXIII, p. 1120.
[3] *Op. cit.,* p. 1172.   [4] *Adv. Jovianum,* I, 4.

the material conditions of primeval life do not arise, so that earlier discussions about Adam's food and his technological knowledge seem to have had no effect upon his imagination.

> All of us men were born in the first man without vice, and all of us lost the innocence of our nature by the sin of the same man. Thence our inherited mortality, thence, the manifold corruption of body and mind, thence ignorance and distress, useless cares, illicit lusts, sacrilegious errors, empty fear, harmful love, unwarranted joys, punishable counsels, and a number of miseries no smaller than that of our crimes. Then when this and other evils rushed into human nature, when faith was lost, hope abandoned, intelligence blinded, the will taken captive, none discovered in himself a means of rehabilitation. Because, even if there was someone who by his natural intellect strove to shake of his vices, yet he gave profitless adornment to this mortal life only, nor did he attain to the true virtues and eternal bliss. For without the worship of the true God, even when there seems to be virtue, there is sin, nor can anyone be pleasing to God without God. He who is not pleasing to the true God, to whom, unless to himself and the Devil, is he pleasing? [5]

John Cassian

John Cassian, who died about 435 A. D., and was thus contemporary with Saint Prosper, was anti-Augustinian in matters concerning the will and was actively opposed by him. Believing that the first steps to salvation could be taken by the individual without the help of divine grace, he was believed to be dangerously close to Pelagianism. His conception of primitive man is of interest because it retained a measure of Greek intellectualism, modified by a conception of innate knowledge not unlike that of some of the English Platonists. Man was not created in a state of infancy. He came into this world with a complete "knowledge of the law" enrooted in his nature. The Fall was thus not an attempt to acquire that wisdom which is the special prerogative of God, but on the contrary the loss of that wisdom. It is clear from the context that the law of which John Cassian is speaking is a moral law and the question arises whether he did not believe, to use modern, if not scientific, language, that primitive man knew the difference between right and wrong "instinctively," "wrong" being simply disobedience, a kind of "unnatural" behavior. To assert that John Cassian was aware of the complexities of his word "*naturaliter*" would be unjustified. But his total conception is one whose apparent implications, as is demonstrated by the attacks made upon him, were not ignored by even his contemporaries.

> When God created man, He instilled in him by nature a complete knowledge of the law, which, if it had been preserved by man according to God's design, as at the beginning, would have made it unneces-

---

[5] *De vocatione omnium gentium*, I, vii [*MPL*, LI, pp. 653 f.].

sary that a second law be given which He later promulgated in writing. For it was superfluous to bring in from without a remedy which up to that time had been in action within. But because this inner law, as we have said, had been corrupted already in consequence of man's possession and exercise of the freedom to sin, there was added to this law, to complete and defend it, and, to speak in the very words of Scripture, to strengthen it, the stern severity of the Mosaic law, so that by the very fear of present penalty the good of natural knowledge might not be completely extinguished, according to the word of the prophet who says, "He gave the law as a support" [*Isaiah*, viii, 20].[8] And according to the Apostle [*Gal.*, iii, 24], the law is said to have been given as a schoolmaster to children, that is, as a teacher and guardian, lest in forgetfulness they stray from that knowledge which was rooted in their nature. For that man's knowledge of the law was instilled in him at the time of his creation in its entirety, is evident from the fact that we know all the saints to have observed its commands without reading it, before it was written down, even before the Deluge.[7]

Pseudo-Eucherius

Eucherius, bishop of Lyons, was a writer of the first half of the fifth century. A friend of John Cassian and apparently influenced by him, he wrote mainly books of edification for members of monastic orders. His fame is fully evidenced in the list of printed editions of his various writings which are available.[8] To him are attributed a number of exegetical works which most editors are agreed are either definitely spurious or doubtful. Among the latter is a *Commentary on Genesis*, which would appear to be of the fifth century, but of the Augustinian school, rather than of John Cassian's. For in it is a long passage, to be indicated below, which is quoted *verbatim* from the *City of God*, a distinction typically Augustinian and, of course, Pauline, between *spirituale* and *animale*, Philonic allegorizing, and certain linguistic arguments. The main points of this document are the following: the pre-existence of man in his "material cause," the immortality of the body when formed, the interpretation of Adam as reason and of Eve as bodily sense, which derives from Philo.

And the Lord formed man of the dust of the ground.

In respect to the causal reason he was made among the works of the six days; in respect to his temporal origin he was also formed at this time. For when it is said that man was made, God had made the cause itself from which man was to be made in his time. The cause, however, from which he was to be formed, that is, the earth, this had existed previously. Some have understood that when it is said later,

---

[6] The Latin here, *legem dedit in adjutorium*, follows, as the commentary by Alardus Gazaeus, cited by Migne, points out, the Septuagint.

[7] *Collationes*, VIII, ch. xxiii [Ed. Michael Betschenig, *CSEL*, vol. 13, pp. 241 f.].

[8] The list was compiled by Schoenemann. See *MPL*, XL, p. 687 f.

"The Lord formed man of the dust of the ground," the words, " in
His own image," were not added because the subject is the formation
of [Adam's] body.   But the inner man, however, is meant when it is
said, " in His own image, after His likeness."   The question, however,
is raised whether man was formed as an adult, or whether he grew
through time and whether God made him a servant of His will.   But
if this was the cause of future men, from which they were implanted
and pre-established on the day when heaven and earth were made
and God created all things at once, we must understand that Adam
was made from the dust in a perfect state, for it is not credible that
he was made as weak as our infants are.   He was already established
in those causes when God made man among the works of the six days.
And God made man from the dust of the ground.   As the body would
seem to have been created for the first man before his sin, it was not
already mortal, if this body in which we now are is such as it either
was or will be, because the first man's body had a sort of natural
ability not to die, but if it sinned, it could be sundered by death.
The body, on the contrary, whose corruption has been brought about
by sin and whose mortality leads to death, after it fell into the necessity of dying, was so altered by the creation of the first man's body
that it could not pass into immortality except through death.   But
that body which we believe will exist after the resurrection will be
made immortal once and for all, and will not be able to die thereafter.
For when the body of an immortal soul has been made, just as the
quality of dying can never be recovered by the immortal soul,
so it can never be recovered by its body.   If the vital body of
the first man lost the quality of not dying, it became mortal by
the very necessity of dying which it underwent.   Because it will
be absolutely immortal in the future, now it cannot entirely die.   And
there is another reason, namely, that the body has the faculty of not
dying from nature.   This body has the condition of dying as a
penalty; that immortal body has the felicity of never dying in the
world of glory.

   The phrase follows: *And breathed into his nostrils the breath of
life; and man became a living soul.*   By the breath of life we understand that the soul was joined to the body.   If man, when he was
made from the dust, was both body and soul, his soul was added
from the souls belonging to God [?] [9] in the act of breathing, when
man became a living soul.   When it is said, *He breathed into him
the breath of life, and man became a living soul,* one should not
believe that, so to speak, a part of God's nature was turned into
man's soul, so that we should be forced to say that God's nature is
mutable, as the soul is, which now grows strong, now weak, now
wise, now foolish.   Therefore, the soul which is mutable must not
be believed to be of the nature of or a part of God, as the Prophet
testified who says," And he that keepeth thy soul, doth not he know
it?" [10]   And the spirit itself is the soul of man, as the Evangelist

---

   [9] The passage is very obscure and is not, of course, classical Latin.   Our translation is purely conjectural.

   [10] *Proverbs*, xxiv, 12.   This is not an exact translation of the Latin, which is not
attributed by its author to any specific chapter and verse of the Bible.   It is close

testifies about the soul which Christ receives in the flesh, when the Lord said, " I · have the power to lay down my life [*animam*] " [*John*, x, 18]. Then He laid it down when He bowed His head and gave up the ghost [*spiritum*] [*John*, xix, 30]. Wherefore it can in no way be doubted that the spirit is the soul, which God made neither from Himself, nor from some underlying elemental matter, but from nothing. For if He had made it from Himself, never could it have been hurt or changeable or sick. If it had been made from visible elements, it would have the solidity of earth or the dampness of water or the lightness of air or the heat of fire. . . . He created it not from any breath of His own nor from Himself, but He either created it from nothing in the act of breathing or He breathed it into the body in the act of creating it. Not that the breath was turned into a living being, but that it vivified the soul. Yet we should understand that man was not yet spiritual because he became a living being, but was so far only animal. For he was made spiritual when he was established in Paradise and received the precept of perfection. And so, after he had sinned and was sent out of Paradise, he remained in the condition of an animal. And therefore we all bear the animal man, who have been born after his sin, until we follow the spiritual Adam, that is, Christ. For thus speaks the Apostle, " That was not first which is spiritual but that which is natural [animal] [I *Cor.*, xv, 46]. *And God formed man from the dust of the ground*; that is, Christ was made, for the Apostle says, " From the seed of David according to the flesh " [*Rom.*, i, 3], as if from the dust of the ground. *And he breathed into his nostrils the breath of life*: that is, the infusion of the Holy Spirit, who made the man Christ. *And he became a living soul*, that is, He Who was a perfect God, would be believed to be a perfect man.

[There follows a passage interpreting the planting of the Garden of Eden and the trees.]

For the tree of life was in the midst of the garden. Some wish this to be understood merely allegorically, as signifying " wisdom," which is the tree of life. But just as the rock which when struck gave forth water, although it symbolized Christ, was yet a historical rock, so also the tree of life, although it symbolized Christ, was yet corporeally and sensibly a tree. It was called the tree of life because if the men of that time ate of it, they would never suffer disease nor old age. In one sense it was food, in another a sacrament. *The tree of the knowledge of good and evil*. Not that the tree was rational in its nature or had knowledge of good and evil. But it was called the tree of the knowledge of good and evil because men learned through experience from it what is the good of obedience and the evil of disobedience. *And they were both naked, the man and his wife, and were not ashamed*. Not that their nakedness was unknown to them, but the nakedness of shame was not yet known, because lust did not yet move those members involuntarily. For they had as yet felt no law in their

---

to a translation of a Latin translation of the Septuagint. There may, to be sure, be in it a reminiscence of *Zach.*, xii, 1.

members repugnant to the law of their own mind. So they thought that nothing should be veiled, for they felt that nothing should be restrained. But from the penalty of his sin it happened to man that his flesh be rebellious to him, since he himself had been rebellious to his Creator in his deeds, and therefore he afterwards was ashamed of his body. *And the eyes of them both were opened.* They were not born blind, as the ignorant crowd believes, since he saw the animals to which he gave names; and of the woman it is said, "the women saw that the tree was good." Their eyes were not closed, but they were not open in this sense, that is, not attentive to the knowledge of what would prove a vestment of grace for them when their members were unable to resist their will. When this grace was removed, in order that their disobedience might be involved in a common penalty, there arose in the body's behavior a certain new shamelessness, because of which nakedness was indecent, and it drew their attention and made them ashamed.

The phrase follows, *They knew that they were naked,* that is, stripped of grace, by which it was brought about that the nudity of the body which had sinned against the law, made their minds ashamed by its repugnance. But why it is that the trap was sprung by the woman, not by the man? Because our reason cannot be seduced into sinning without previous delight in the feeling of carnal weakness, which ought on the contrary to be controlled by the reason, as if by the commanding man. For this occurs in each man in a certain secret and hidden wedlock. In fact, we interpret the serpent as suggestion, the woman as the animal bodily sense, the man, however, as the reason. . . . *The woman saw that the tree was good for food . . . and she took of the fruit thereof and did eat.* The woman, not the man, ate first because the carnal are more easily persuaded to sin and the spiritual are not so quickly ensnared. *And gave also unto her husband with her; and he did eat.* And this because after the delectation of our carnal concupiscence, our reason is subjected to sinning. The verse follows, *And they sewed fig leaves together and made themselves aprons.* These we now call *campestria.* Afterwards they knew that they had been miserably stripped of grace, by which it was brought about that their bodily nakedness did not trouble their minds with repugnance because of any law against sin; as soon as they knew this, of which they would have been in blissful ignorance if, obeying God and believing in Him, they had not committed what [the serpent] urged them to try; but then, troubled by the disobedience of their flesh, as if by a witness, because of the penalty of their disobedience "they sewed fig leaves together and made themselves aprons" or *campestria,* which we also call by another name, *succinctoria.* The word *campestria* is derived from the custom of the youths who used to exercise naked in the athletic field [*in campo*] of covering their genitals. Wherefore those who were thus girdled were popularly called *campestrati.*[11] *When they knew that they were naked, they sewed fig leaves together,* with which they might cover themselves. They who embrace the rough ways of secular life, who

---

[11] This is taken over word for word from Saint Augustine's *City of God,* XIV, 17.

crowd together for the religion of carnal pleasure, and who are ensnared by heretical depravity and stripped of the grace of God, bind together a covering of lies, as if of fig leaves, and make themselves girdles of vanity when they lie about the Lord or the Church.[12]

Julian Pomerius

Among the obscurer figures of the late fifth century is Julian Pomerius, author of a treatise on the contemplative life. In this work occurs a passage which describes man's original condition in terms clearly within the tradition of soft primitivism.

> If the first man had been willing to watch over himself in the blessedness of Paradise, to refrain from eating the fruit of one forbidden tree, he would not have lost his so great happiness, nor would the deliberate transgression of the saving precept have sentenced him to the necessity of corruption and mortality, so that corrupted by sin he must corrupt or lose the great gifts of his God, which he had received by the very nature of his condition. For who could properly enumerate of what and of how great goods his contempt for that abstinence deprived him? Endowed with a noble intellect, he was made in the image of his Creator; subject to God alone, he beheld all visible things subject to himself; for his sustenance he could use all the trees which were in Paradise [Gen., II, 9]; their divine fruitfulness was at his orders. The tree of life, as a duty to its Creator, served him its mystic food, not that he might live upon it, but that he might not end his bodily life. As long as he perceived this food, so long did it keep him who was perceiving it in one condition, by the figurative meaning of a certain hidden sacrament, so that he was not permitted to be corrupted by any infirmity, nor to change in age, nor to grow old, nor to be dissolved in death. No worrisome care disturbed his rest, no troubled labor fatigued him in his leisure. Sleep did not weary him reluctant to receive it, nor did the fear of losing his life vex him, secure in his immortality. He had easily acquired food, a body in all ways healthy, tranquil emotions, a sound heart. He knew nothing of penal evil, he dwelt in Paradise, he was free from sin, full of God.
>
> What then could be more happy than he, to whom the world was subject, who had no enemy, whose mind was free, who saw God face to face?[13]

The restoration of this condition, its calm serenity, its truthfulness, its universal goodness, are projected into the future life. There was little in the Bible itself to suggest that heavenly felicity was a restoration of life in the Golden Age, but there was an abundance of pagan material to do so. Julian thinks of Heaven as a city of Platonic philosophers contemplating the Idea of the Good.

[12] Commentary on Genesis, I and III [MPL, L, pp. 905-912, with omissions as indicated].

[13] De vita contemplativa, II, xviii [MPL, LIX, p. 463].

What now shall I say of the quality of the future life itself, which we ought to believe in rather than talk about? But the fact that I cannot speak as I would ought not to prevent me from speaking as well as I can. Because we believe God to be ineffable ought not to prevent our talking of Him to the best of our ability. So that life should be believed to be more than we can say. For only that much may be expressed in speech as may be comprehended by the mind. And the human mind's comprehension, however profound, conceives less when the magnitude of the things which it is trying to comprehend is very great. Therefore, the future life is believed to be everlasting and everlastingly blessed. There is a certain security in it and secure tranquillity, tranquil joyousness, joyful eternity, eternal happiness. There, there is perfect love, no fear, eternal day, eager affection, and the spirit of all united in their contemplation of their God and secure in their dwelling with Him. There the city itself, which is the blessed congregation of the holy angels and men,[14] shines like a star with radiant goodness, and eternal well-being abounds, and truth reigns. There no one deceives nor is deceived. Thence no blessed man is cast out and into it no wicked man is admitted.[15]

Saint Maximus of Turin

The strain of soft primitivism is again sounded in Saint Maximus of Turin in his account of Adam's life before the Fall. The commandment not to eat of the Tree of Knowledge is interpreted as an order to remain in a condition of rustic simplicity of mind, the anti-intellectualism which so often accompanies soft primitivism.

It has often been suggested to you not only by the Divine Scriptures, but also by our preaching, that the original sinful transgression in Adam was the allurement of the intellect and that the cause of his fall consisted in the desire for food. For since amid so many rich feasts of Paradise he would not abstain from one food alone, he lost the pleasure of all the delights and let slip what was permitted since he lusted after what was forbidden. And so, if he had been able to bear abstinence from one food, deprivation of so great good would not have occurred. Wherefore, we, brothers, knowing the cause of our author's transgression, should cut off from ourselves the cause of the offence. And desire, which he extended beyond the limits of the law, we should hold within the bounds of commanded duty, nor should we suffer, because of the appointed fast of very brief duration, the loss of a whole life's sweetness. If Adam sinned in tasting, why should I not be virtuous in fasting? If his eating led to death, why should not my abstinence lead to salvation? The fool clearly is he who is not instructed by precept, who does not learn by example. See, therefore, if such a precept is not given to us when we are reborn as was set forth to Adam when he was created. For we are told, although we have been placed in a garden of delights and repose pleasantly beside

---

[14] We follow the text as given in Migne. One MS reads, *angelorum sanctorumque omnium*—" of all the angels and saints "—which may be preferable.

[15] *De vita contemplativa*, I, ii [*MPL*, LIX, p. 419 f.].

the fountains of the Lord, that we may eat of the fruits of all the virtues, but solely the little tree of the knowledge of good and evil may we not taste. Who would not be satisfied with such a law, to abstain from one delight for the sake of many? From the tree, I say, of the knowledge of good and evil we are ordered to abstain. We ought to know what this tree is. Since the saints feast upon the fruits of discipline, what is the justly forbidden tree but secular lack of discipline? Each man who has tasted of secular wantonness after receiving grace has learned the difference between good and evil. For he begins to know what he has lost of sanctity and what he has gained of perdition. Not because the taste of the tree in itself informed man of this, but because his conscience was innocent. When it later became corrupted, it bewailed the good it had lost and groaned over the evil it had gained. Life and knowledge are not retained, however, unspotted; for holy or honest life always thinks that alone to be in man which is pure. But wantonness makes a man ill endowed for the most part through the experience of sinning. It is therefore good for a Christian to hold rusticity sacred, but fame wicked. Tree of the knowledge of good and evil, I do not wish thy knowledge. For what does it profit to know what it does not profit to know, what one should be sorry to know? For the Lord has decreed such a law for man in the tabernacle of the Church as He commanded in the possession of Paradise. Paradise is in fact the Church of the different virtues, protected by beautiful trees, from whose center flows like a crystal fountain Christ, and, as in Paradise, four rivers take their rise in the four streams of the Gospels. For the blessed apostles and evangelists are to be compared to streams, because the face of the whole earth [lit., people] is watered by the spirit of their teachings. There is indeed no Christian soul who does not drink at the holy fountain of the Gospels.[16]

Late fifth and early sixth century poetry

In that curious group of Christian poets which includes Prudentius, Sidonius, Ennodius, and Corippus, one finds a mixture of pagan and Christian themes, a borrowing of classical phrases, a use of literary allusions, which would appear to be characteristic of the time. One finds whole verses of Vergil and Horace incorporated in their poems, and the pagan pantheon and mythology are called upon to furnish eulogistic parallels to men and events which recall the same practice in the Italian Renaissance.

Apollinaris Sidonius

Thus Apollinaris Sidonius, wishing to celebrate the advent of a new emperor, continues a tradition which goes back to Calpurnius, himself an imitator of Vergil,[17] and hails the new reign as a return of the Golden Age. The earth began to bare spontaneously again, the seasons were defied, and the world took on some of the aspects of the Land of Cockaigne.

---

[16] Sermon XIV [*MPL.*, LVII, pp. 559 f.].
[17] See *PIA*, pp. 89 ff. The new Emperor is Anthemius.

The beginning of your reign was radiant with great events and the prescient earth promised a return of the Golden Age with renewed fertility. When thou wast born the rivers flowed with fresh honey, slowed in its progress by its sweetened waves, and oil ran through astonished oilpresses from the hanging olive. Meadows brought forth waving grain without seed and the vine envied the grape, born without its aid. Roses blushed in winter. Spurning the cold, lilies burst forth dotted with frost. How often has Lucina brought about such a birth! The laws of nature have given way and our faith in thy future kingdom is strengthened by the strangeness of events.[18]

Such extravagant rhetoric, to be sure, was nothing more than a literary flourish and did not indicate on Sidonius's part any fundamental belief in any of the forms of primitivism. In fact, in his *Third Epistle* he expresses clear antiprimitivistic sentiments.[19] A literary style had been set many centuries before and was faithfully followed. We find a similar use of the theme in the middle of the sixth century in Corippus's eulogy of Justin II.[20]

Corippus

When peace was restored, the glad throng throughout the city adorned its holy walls with woven garlands. The fields were despoiled of their glory, each tree was stripped of its fruit and the leaves were torn from the green olive. They decorated their doorposts and put plaited reeds upon the entrances and stretched festive awnings over whole streets. Then the youths began to play and to add praises to praises. They danced with their feet and marched with gentle step and chanted new songs in wondrous modes. They called the pious Justin and Sophia two stars. Organs, lutes, and lyres played throughout the city. A thousand kinds of pleasure, a thousand cries, dances, laughter, speeches, joys, and applause! They wished long life to their rulers with glad shouts. "After its old age," they said, " the world rejoices to grow young again, and seeks the first signs of its ancient form. The iron age departs and the golden age emerges in thy time, Justin, hope of the city and of the world, splendor of the Roman Empire, jewel added to all the princes before thy coming, whose conquering wisdom has reached the greatest heights of thy fathers' rule." They joined the name of Sophia [to thine] and spoke next of this star and added a new song with applause.[21]

---

[18] *Carmina*, II (Panegyricus) lines 94-114 [Ed. Lvetjohann, *MGH*, 1887, p. 176]. The plural pronoun in the opening refers to the imperial couple; the singular which follows to the Emperor himself. It should be noted that the translation " the laws of nature " should literally be " the custom of the elements."

[19] See his Epistle III, 8.

[20] Justin II ruled from 565 to 578. Since he became insane in his later years and was unfortunate in war, the poem ought probably to be dated in the earlier part of his reign.

[21] *In laudem Justini*, III, lines 62-84 inc. Cf. Id., lines 173-186. [Ed. Partsch, *MGH*, 1879].

Boethius

Ennodius also utilized this figure when he found it convenient,[22] but the only writer of this period whose use of it had extended influence was Boethius.[23] His picture of the Golden Age, which is quite without Scriptural color, was read wherever the *Consolation* was read, and, when one thinks of the extraordinary popularity of that book, one sees that its author must be second only to Ovid as the main source of the legend for medieval readers. Boethius's picture of the Golden Age is not that of the soft primitivist. His primeval man was Juvenal's, acorn-eating, innocent of war, ignorant of luxury.

> Too happy was that earlier age, satisfied with its faithful fields and not given over to inert luxury, that age which was accustomed to slake its prolonged hunger with easily gathered acorns. Its people knew not how to mix the gifts of Bacchus with clear honey nor to dip the shining fleeces of the Seres in Tyrian poison. They slept healthily upon the grass and drank from the flowing stream. The tall pines shaded them. Not yet did they as strangers cleave the depths of the sea nor visit new shores for merchandise gathered in from far and wide. Then the cruel trumpet kept silent and blood poured out in bitter hate stained not the stubble of the fields. For how could hostile fury wish to brandish arms, before men saw savage wounds or any reward for bloodshed? Would only that our times would return to those ancient ways of living! But more cruel than the fires of Aetna, a fervent love of possession is burning. Alas, who was he who first dug up the weight of hidden gold and gems, demanding only to lie concealed, costly perils? [24]

Readers of classical Latin verse will recognize in this passage echoes of both Ovid and Vergil, and may therefore see in it no serious opinion about primeval man. When Boethius was discussing Christian doctrine, he outlined a theory of man's original condition in which three states were differentiated. There was first man's condition before the Fall, in which, though free from the possibility of death and unstained by sin, yet "the will to sin was able to be in him" [*poterat tamen in eo voluntas esse peccandi*], an awkward phrase which may very well have meant that he had the will to sin *in potentia*. The second condition is that in which "he could have changed, if he had chosen to remain steadfastly within God's commands," in which case he would have had neither the wish nor the power to wish to sin, as an additional gift from God. The third condition is that

---

[22] See *Epistle*, xi; *Lib. pro synode*, 136, line 10, p. 67; *Epistle*, cdlv., p. 316, line 30; *Epistle*, xviii, p. 22, line 30. Page references are to F. Vogel's edition, in *MGH*.

[23] We omit Avitus, since he adds nothing to the history of this idea and his poem is too long to quote. The reader, curious of what this sixth century Milton said, is referred to Peiper's edition of his poems in *MGH*, *De mundi initio*, I, 218-244; II, 35-76, 145-160, 185-203.

[24] *Consolatio philosophiae*, II, met. 5 [Ed. G. Frieflein, Leipzig, 1897].

which obtained after the Fall, in which are found death, sin, and the desire
for sin.[25] The second of these states is proposed as one of two alternatives
which would have been distinguished from man's original condition. It is
presumably a better state than the first. Man was therefore not created
perfect, according to this passage, but created potentially perfect, a poten-
tiality which was not to be realized. Had it been realized, man would have
attained the rank of the angels.[26] The doctrine, thus, by making the possibility of sin plausible, attributable to man's original imperfection, achieved
something which none of the earlier writers had achieved. It is a doctrine
which seems to have had little if any influence. One of the major difficulties
which it presented was obviously the problem of man's resemblance to God
when originally created.

Dionysius Exiguus

The Fall of Man for Dionysius Exiguus, the friend of Cassiodorus and
introducer of time-reckoning by the Christian era, is essentially the loss of
a kind of divine knowledge which would appear to be an intuition into the
nature of things in which the absolute simplicity of each "kind" or
"nature" would appear. The reason, therefore, why God forbade man to
eat of the Tree of Knowledge was not His divine jealousy. Because that
knowledge was mixed and logically impure, it was corrupting. God presumably knows no evil; man, had he retained his resemblance to God, would
have known none. But the serpent, by disguising evil with an appearance
of good, was able to deceive the first couple and to vitiate their cognitive
processes.[27]

> What then is that which contains the knowledge of good and evil
> and at the same time seems to be most gratifying in sensual pleasure?
> Do you think that in my zeal for interpretation I am deviating not
> far from the truth, taking advantage of my understanding of knowl-
> edge to obtain this insight? I believe that this knowledge cannot
> at present be felt to be the acquired learning of those who have
> trained senses, but I find it to be the custom of the Holy Scriptures
> to distinguish between knowledge [scientia] and discernment [dis-
> cretio]. For to distinguish good from evil as a consequent of acquired
> learning is said by the Apostle to be the more perfect state of those
> who have trained senses. Therefore he has taught us to put all
> things to the test, and has said that it is the peculiarity of the
> spiritual man to be able to judge and to distinguish between all
> things. But knowledge does not always introduce everywhere ac-

[25] There may be here an echo of Saint Augustine's distinction of Adam's *posse non
peccandi* and his *non posse non peccandi*.

[26] See *Contra Eutychen*, VII, 40-50; *De fide catholica*, 72-58.

[27] Such, at any rate, would appear to be the meaning of the passage which follows
in the text above. But one would be very self-confident to say that this interpretation
is unquestionable. The difficulties of the Latin—to say nothing of the vagueness of
the thought, when it can be divined—make translation largely conjecture.

quired learning as well as thought if one argues from the meaning
of the term, but very frequently it is said to be a consequence of
grace, as in the phrase, " The Lord knoweth them that are His "
[II *Tim.* ii, 19].   And God says to Moses, " I have known thee
before all others." And of those things which are censured as evils,
He who knows all asserts and says, " I never knew you " [*Matth.*,
vii, 23].   Therefore that tree which brings to fruition a knowledge
which is mixed and jumbled is of those things which are forbidden
to us by the Lord.   For that fruit seems to be compounded of contrary qualities and is proved to have the serpent as its advocate.   It
is perhaps for this reason that evil is not offered to us naked and
unveiled, lest it be suspected of being what it is in itself, as a consequence of its own nature.   On the contrary, wickedness itself has
remained ineffectual when colored by no semblance of the good,
through which he who is deceived may be allured into the desire for
it.   As a matter of fact, the nature of evil is somehow complete, containing disaster in its depths to be sure, as if laying open snares for
us.   But in this concealed seduction it shields itself with a certain
image of the good, for the good appears to the avaricious and the
greedy to be of matter, that is, to be golden in color, but the love
of money is the root of all evil.   And who would rush into the mire
of filthy and loathsome lust, unless he thought sensual pleasure to be
a commonly accepted good, since he is allured to the disease of passion
by a kind of bait?   So, too, the other sins have an absolutely mixed
differentia and they are thought at first sight to be very acceptable
and, because of their seductive dye, are sought by thoughtless and
imprudent people in place of [real] goods.   Because, therefore, many
people think the good to be that which is gratifying to the senses,
and because of a certain kinship either with the truly good or with
that which is thought to be good and is not, the concupiscence which
attracts us to evil as if it were good is called by the Holy Scriptures
the knowledge of good and evil; whereas knowledge would declare
that a state of mind, not absolutely bad, since it has the superficial
hue of goodness, nor utterly good, since the outlet to evil lies hidden
in it, but mixed, that is, compounded of both, is stated to be the
fruit of the forbidden tree whose taste, it has said, draws those
touching it to death.   Proclaiming this, one might say, with clear
teaching and phrase, that what is truly good is simple and unique,
foreign to the nature of all [other] things.   But evil is various and
dyed that it may be thought to be one thing, whereas experience shows
it to be another, the knowledge of which, that is, the effect of action,
is the cause of death and the beginning of corruption.   Therefore
the serpent when he pointed out the evil fruit of sin, did not exhibit
it as having an evil nature in itself—for man would never have been
led astray by obvious evil—but adorning it with a showy appearance
and recommending it by the sensual pleasure it would bring and
urging a taste of it, he persuaded the woman to sin, as Scripture says,
" And when the woman saw that the tree was good for food, and that
it was pleasant to the eyes, and a tree to be desired to make one wise,
she took of the fruit thereof, and did eat."   By that food she was
made the mother of human death.   Nor was the result vague.   For
the account clearly reveals the reason why that tree should be called

the knowledge of good and evil. Just as poison smeared with honey is believed to be good because the sweetness introduced into it soothes the senses, so, since it also makes away with and destroys those eating it, it becomes more harmful than any evil. As therefore deadly poisons have prevailed against the life of man, *man*, a great thing and a great word, and the image of the divine nature, *has been made like unto vanity*, as the prophet says. Thus the image of God is fitly discerned in those things known to be best in us, but whatsoever things in our life seem worthy of pity and are downcast, they are shown to be absolutely foreign to our divine likeness.[28]

Petrus Diaconus

The *De incarnatione* of Petrus Diaconus, a sixth century work, repeats the Augustinian doctrine of Adam's fall, the original freedom of his will entailing either death or immortality, according to its use. It is cited here as simply a link in a chain of theory, for it contributes nothing novel to doctrine.

And so we believe Adam to have been made good and without any carnal weakness by God, the Creator of all, and endowed with great freedom so that he had it in his own power to do good and to commit evil if he wished. And there was death as well as immortality in his possession of free-will. For he was susceptible of both, so that if he kept the commandment, he would become immortal without the experience of death, but if he broke it, death would immediately ensue. And so, depraved by the serpent's wiles, he was by his own will made a violator of the divine law and thus, according to what he had been told, he was condemned by God's just sentence to the penalty of death, and was entirely—that is, both in body and soul— changed for the worse, his peculiar freedom lost, and delivered over to the subjection of sin.[29]

Saint Isidore of Seville

Though Saint Isidore of Seville was a compiler of legends and miscellaneous information, rather than an original thinker, his works were more influential than those of any other sixth century writer in passing on ideas to posterity. In his account of man's life before the Fall the usual themes of soft primitivism are repeated. But he adds to the tradition the notion that the degeneration of the physical world—admitted of course by many pagan as well as Christian writers—was a consequence of Adam's sin.

Since after the waters the earth was established next in the order of elements, let us speak first of Paradise, which was the home of the first men, although our discussion must be made as a reminder of a subject about which many men have handed down a variety of opinions, e. g., whether immortal life itself, with which men were

---

[28] *De creatione hominis*, ch. xxi [*MPL*, LXVII, p. 380 f.].

[29] *Liber de incarnatione*, ch. vi [*MPL*, LXII, pp. 89 f.]. This passage is found word for word also in Saint Fulgentius's *Epistle* XVI, ch. vi, 15 [*MPL*, LXV, p. 447].

endowed before the Fall, was called by the name "Paradise," or whether the whole world was called "Paradise" because it was so conveniently arranged for men living in innocence, who would possess it as long as they lived blamelessly without any sin. For life in that land was entirely happy and it was carried on without any labor, but presently when they had sinned and degenerated, the very world was changed by their vice and by the pronouncement of their sentence was darkened as well—as we have said of the sun and the moon— and it lost its beauty and fruitful power, if not entirely, at least to a very large degree, so that the things which had increased the blessed happiness of those living well augmented the punishment of those living ill.

[Saint Isidore proceeds now after an explanation of the three ways of interpreting Scripture, the literal, the figurative, and the "mystical," to expatiate on the possibility of Adam's power over all creation, his painless and labor-less life.]

But when the dweller in Paradise sinned in the place of his earthly bliss, he was thrust out to dwell in a land accursed, and straightway all those things which he had previously possessed, he lost in part and in part preserved by labor. And when he was shut out from the abode of bliss, the possibility of returning there was precluded, and it was so done as in the case of the fallen angel, who, cast out of the high serenity of Paradise with his [legions], was allotted this realm of darkness. So too man was excluded from the earthly blessedness of his Paradise into the habitation of this cursed land.[30]

In a later chapter Saint Isidore hints at a doctrine of natural goodness which has a certain likeness to that of John Cassian. According to Saint Augustine and his school, man's original goodness has been irrevocably lost: all men were depraved by Adam's fall and could be saved only by an act of grace. But Saint Isidore apparently believes in the possibility of retaining what he calls the *primae conditionis jura*. According to some of the pagans, this possibility had been realized in the life of the Noble Savage. Isidore, however, did not share this feeling.

Men, destined to inhabit this temporary world after the original sin, did not lose all the natural good which they had had at their creation, but, vitiated first by their parents' sin, they added to its corruption by depraved morals, and so it came about that just as they gather the fruits of the cursed earth with labor, so they can keep their natural good which exists within them only by laborious care.

And just as in the serpent, the woman, and the consenting man, they triply fell into original sin, similarly all their children are afflicted with a triple plague: they fail from pain, from old age, and from death, and every good which they received implanted in them naturally by their Creator, they discover by zealous toil and barely preserve by great vigilance of mind. And whatever good they discover, sought zealously as a gift from God, with the exception of evil riches they do not leave to their heirs, and all arts, which they receive

---

[30] *De ordine creaturarum*, ch. x [*MPL*, LXXXIII, pp. 938 f.].

individually in life, they also lose as this life departs, when they breathe forth their spirit.

Paupers and kings, fools and sages, are harassed by the same condition of weakness. For similarly all need sleep and must be refreshed by food and clothed in garments. With carnally vicious passions are they bowed down or corrupted. With emotions, anger and love, desire and fear, are they cramped. They are undone by pain, old age, and death. Of the past they are quickly despoiled, the present they can use in moderation, of the future all things are uncertain.

Similarly they feel and live by hearing, vision, touch, taste, and smell. With the same knot of original sin are they bound, enriched by the same gift of the Redeemer are they washed in the waters of baptism and in the Holy Spirit. But to these men, too, if they neglect the faith that redeems or the works of faith, equally with the transgressing angels and their prince, the Devil, will eternal punishment be given. But for those who guard either through the warnings of Scripture, or through natural goodness, the fortifications which are the laws of their primal condition, a future life has been prepared as a gift of the Redeemer.[30a]

Saint Boniface

In the pagan legends of the Golden Age, it was frequently mentioned that after the departure of the gods from earth, one divine being, the goddess Astraea, Justice, remained on earth. This Virgin goddess had entered into Christian poetry through Vergil's fourth eclogue. That her legend was still remembered as late as the eighth century is demonstrated by her appearance in one of the riddles of Saint Boniface. Christian interpretation of Vergil's Virgin naturally identified her with Saint Mary. In this poem of Saint Boniface no such identification is made, however, and she remains what she was for the pagans.

> Lo! fiery Jupiter is said to be my father and I, the Virgin, am said by the words of the stupid to have left the wicked earth because of hunger, but it was really because of the various crimes [of men]. My face was but rarely thereafter perceived by the earth-born, though I was the glorious daughter of heaven's king, regulating the world with such laws as my sire [proclaimed], rejoicing in my father's bosom and imprinting kisses on him. The golden race of men would have rejoiced for all time, had they obeyed the rule given them by the protecting virgin. But when I was spurned, a host of evils weighed the peoples down, while they continually trampled under foot the orders of the thundering Christ. Therefore in tears they enter the gloom of black Erebus, the fiery Tartarus of King Pluto.[31]

John Scotus Erigena

The outstanding thinker of the ninth century was unquestionably John the Scot. The historian may assume that any of his works were widely

[30a] *De ordine creaturarum*, ch. xii [*MPL*, LXXXIII, pp. 943 f.].

[31] *Aenigmata*, in *Poetae Latini Aevi Carol.* [Ed. Duemmler, Berlin, 1881, I, p. 5].

read and very influential. Consequently his views on the original condition of man are of peculiar interest.

John Scotus selects from the intimations in *Genesis* as to Adam's state before the Fall one characteristic only, his asexuality. Since the peculiar metaphysics of this author would have made Adam a universal, rather than a particular, as he was also presumably in Saint Augustine, and as his essence would have been multiplied as is that of the angels, by an instantaneous logical emanation, there was no division into male and female. It is worth noting that until this time we have found no evidence that this distinction was considered a defect, though conduct entailed in it was of course commonly considered lamentable, even if legitimatized by the sacrament of marriage.

> We believe man to have been made in the image of God in mind alone and in those virtues naturally implanted in him, for he has present within him wisdom, knowledge, the power of reasoning, and the other virtues by which the soul is adorned, expressing his inner likeness to his Creator. We also believe that all men were made together and at the same time in that one man, of whom it is written, " Let us make man in our image, after our likeness " [*Gen.*, i, 26] and " for that all have sinned " [*Rom.*, v, 12]. For at that time that one man [Adam] was all, and in him all were expelled from the happiness of Paradise. But if man had not sinned, he would not have been subject to a division of his simplicity into bisexuality. This division is entirely devoid of the image and likeness of the divine nature and would by no means have existed, if man had not sinned, just as it will by no means exist after the restoration of nature to its original condition, which will be made manifest after the universal resurrection of all men. Wherefore, if man had not sinned, none would be born of the union of both sexes, nor from any seed, but just as the angelic essence, while it is one, is at the same time multiplied into infinite thousands, without the slightest temporal intervals, so human nature, if it had been willing to obey the commandment and had obeyed it, would have blossomed all at once into a number foreknown to the Creator alone. Since God, who neither deceives nor is deceived, foresaw that man would desert his rank and dignity, He added the creation of a second manner of human multiplication, by which this world is riddled with spatio-temporal intervals, so that men may pay the common penalty of the common sin, being born from corruptible seed like the other animals.[32]

The question of whether the human race would have been multiplied by sexual union if Adam had not fallen had been discussed in earlier centuries, but there was no agreement on the matter. Gregory of Nyssa and John of Damascus had both agreed that if Adam had not sinned, there would have been no marriages and the human race would have been procreated asexually in a manner unknown.[33] Saint Cyril of Alexandria, on the other hand,

---

[32] *De divisione naturae*, IV, 12 [*MPL*, CXXII, p. 799].
[33] *De hominis opificio*, ch. 17, 18 and *De fide orthodoxa*, Bk. II, ch. 30, respectively.

maintained that sexual union was intended from the beginning, a view which later became generally accepted.[34] That some form of multiplication of the human race had to be provided was, of course, necessitated by *Genesis*, I, 28, " And God said unto them, Be fruitful and multiply." Otherwise a man of John Scotus's platonistic views might have held that unless Adam had sinned, there would have been no particularization of the universal, Mankind.

Bandinus

When we come to the twelfth century and its revival of learning, we naturally find more comment on man's primeval state. The Augustinian tradition survives in Bandinus with minor changes. Adam's original free-will lay either in the choice of mortality or immortality, rather than in the choice of sin or freedom from sin. In keeping with many of his contemporaries, he intimates that the Fall had certain corporeal consequences; in his case, it produced the feeling of hunger.

> There occurs here a threefold consideration on the condition of man: what he was like before the Fall, after the Fall, and what he will be like in the resurrection. In the first state he had the ability to die and the ability not to die. In the second, that is, after the Fall, he had ability to die and the inability not to die. In the third state he will have the ability not to die and the inability to die. . . . .
>
> Adam's flesh seems to have been immortal before his sin from its very nature, to be helped by the sustenance of foods, to be brought to perfection by eating of the tree of life. Wherefore Augustine says that the flesh of Adam before his sin was created immortal so that it might be preserved by the sustenance of the other trees of which he was ordered to eat until, brought to a state agreeable to his Creator, he should at God's own orders, eat of the tree of life by which made perfectly immortal, he would require no further food. . . . .
>
> But some men disagree at this point, thinking that our first parents did not take food before their sin, and they say, If they had not sinned, they would not have died; they would not, however, have sinned, if they did not eat, because they could live without food. To these men we reply, that they would not only have sinned by eating of the forbidden tree, but also by not using the things which they were permitted to use. For they had a double commandment: to use the one, to abstain from the other. Wherefore says Augustine, Both were contained in the commandments, to eat of the permitted and to abstain from the forbidden.
>
> Hence if they had not sinned, they would not have felt hunger, since it is the penalty of sin. Without hunger, however, they might have eaten immediately. To which we reply, Hunger is indeed the penalty of the sin, for it is an immoderate appetite for food. Man would not have been subjected to it, if he had not sinned, yet he would have had a natural and moderate appetite which he had the right to satisfy before the Fall.[35]

[34] At least according to Petavius's *Theologica dogmata*, 1700, II, p. 178. For Cyril, see *Contra Julianum*, III [*MPG*, LXXVI, p. 618 D].

[35] *Sententiae*, II, *dist.* xix [*MPL*, CXCII, p. 1046].

Ernaldus of Bonneval

Perhaps the most extravagant account of the delights of primitive life is to be found in the *Hexaemeron* of Ernaldus of Bonneval. Here is a kind of Christian Land of Cockaigne, whose corporeal delights satisfy all the senses and where only an innate moderation prevents their abuse. There was of course no Biblical authority for most of what Ernaldus writes; his account is an excellent example of the use of the literary imagination playing with a few simple texts. A trace of cultural primitivism colors the picture: Adam works, but does only agreeable work—gardening, and this not because it was necessary—the earth was spontaneously fertile as in the Golden Age—but as an act of reverence to the Creator. This cultural primitivism is not, however, as, for instance, in certain passages of Seneca,[36] combined with anti-intellectualism. Adam was both a natural scientist and a metaphysician. Presumably this knowledge was innate, not acquired.

> Man was made outside of Paradise and, lest any grace seem to be lacking, was led into it, where woman is related to have been made later from his rib. For the delightfulness of that place was suitable to a man who had been made in the image of God, and, although no harm could befall him in his innocence wherever he might be, it was nevertheless provided that a multitude of all things delightful to the outer senses be brought together in one place, lest if anything be lacking there, his appetite be fatigued by searching and seeking for what was at a distance, whereas he was to have the immediate use of all things. If he had persevered, his intellect would have had in the Creator a plenitude of rational truth and peace, and the contemplation of His goodness alone would have filled his whole mind. Similarly, the outer man would have had before his senses whatever soothing and pleasant things can delight human nature, so that God would have been the culmination of all man's spiritual joys and Paradise sufficient for all temporal comfort. For this reason that place was called Eden, that is, Pleasure, and a garden of delight, because of the fertility of its soil and its fruitful orchards. From its centre there flowed a crystal spring, thoroughly watering and refreshing every herb, yet not too copiously flowing but by underground infiltration moistening the garden's extent. Spreading leaves on the tall trees shaded the grass beneath and both the moisture below and the equable atmosphere above maintained an everlasting verdure in the turf. There was a gentle breeze arising at mid-day, which blew away and drove off the heat, if by chance there were any. The place was entirely free of snow and hail and was jocund with an unbroken and perpetual spring. There arose from the fruits and the very twigs a spicy emanation and from the trunks there exuded perfumed gums. Styrax dripped and balsam, when the bark was ruptured, copiously flowed upon the earth. There ran through the meadows streams of nard-breathing perfumes, and since aromatic gum oozed forth without the force of the press, the whole region was

---

[36] See *PIA*, pp. 275 ff.

bathed in countless sweet odors. No gloom was there, no corruption, to impede other things, for all the trees of that garden were sweet with the perfume of Him Who planted them and they proclaimed the grace of celestial glory. The trees exuded fragrant oils, the charity of the saints was later to give forth purity, and in that soothing odor was suggested not only the integrity of prophecy but also the fullness of eternal happiness. That fragrance was like a kind of ecstacy, symbolizing the bodily senses, yet not lulling man to sleep nor calling him away from his duties, but sharpening the mind's subtlety and cleansing it for zealous work. Stacte and myrrh, amonum and nard and medicinal herbs, freely sown, enriched the fertile glebe, and, though nature had no need of them, she took pleasure in the superabundant grace. There was no fever but already its cure existed; there was as yet no weakness of constitution, but already the remedy for lassitude was being produced. Man was busy not building something new with toilsome labor but with the delight of caring for what he had; he was either bringing something into the light or shading it, or preparing some barrier or guard against the beasts, lest wandering here and there, they tread with heedless step upon those places for which their outward beauty demanded reverence. These and other such things man, the cultivator, could lovingly do without tedium, without vexation. For these things in combination with his great happiness rendered the pleasant work seductive. He kept guard within the garden, not because he feared that anything would be stolen from him, but that he would allow something to enter for which he would deserve to be expelled from the garden, keeping safe the things that had been entrusted to him and put under his rule by God, rejoicing in the obedience of all and providing for future generations, as well as for himself. Would that he had guarded as well the gardens of his soul and the herbs of the virtues and guarded them with proper diligence, doing useful things and keeping watch, learning from the obedience of the lower animals how great subjection he owed to his Creator. If he had persevered under His rule and kept His commandments, he would quickly have assured what was hanging until that time in suspense, and would have been borne from this agreeable corporeal garden of delight into that spiritual tranquillity whose peace passes all understanding.

Having discussed the pleasures and virtues peculiar to the sense of smell, Ernaldus now proceeds to discuss those of taste and vision, being careful to point out that none of the pleasures was *aliqua passione desiderii inflammata*. The description of the beauty of flower and tree and fruit becomes as rhapsodical as a page of Bernardin de Saint-Pierre. Passing on to the sense of hearing, he says that the birds of Eden sang canticles in the trees, turtle-doves prophesied in their songs the state of the future church.

Such were the flute players who stood about the table of the First-Made; such were the harpists of earliest antiquity; and yet this was corporeal consolation, not the felicity that was foreordained. In Paradise there was no mime nor actor. All things simply acted their own rôle. No simulation of masks rendered comic scenes with de-

ceptive illusion. No drunken sensuality weakened dissolute souls
into lasciviousness, nor did excessive itching of the carnal feelings
transcend their legitimate bounds. But the flesh restrained itself
within the law. And the form of all things, determined by the
Creator according to fixed rules, was kept within its assigned bounds
by voluntary action and the will was not restless, but, satisfied with
reasonable sufficiency, did not grow feeble, burning in endless intemperance. For every intemperate use of things is foul, and shameful abuse and whatever enjoyment of things is not satiated make a
man wretched and he does not use fixed weights and measures and
numbers and the experience of things. And therefore the appetite
for pleasures and its indulgence press an unbridled and dissolute
mind into torment, for the vehemence and gluttony of intemperance
are not quieted by throwing straws upon the fire but are stimulated.
Man did not use his corporeal pleasures before the Fall so that as a
wanderer he might sink into the dregs of debasement, but deliberat-
ing on all things with decent and modest approach, he honored the
excellence of his station as rational overseer and dominated his
emotions with discreet moderation, not with tyrannical oppression.
In those matters upon which we have touched slightly in some
measure, sight, hearing, smell, taste, and touch, persevering in
keeping their virginity intact, they kept their lamps lighted without
any smirch of curiosity, and in pure obedience the wakeful troop
met the Bridegroom as He came with the lights of all the senses
burning.

As for the trees which God planted in the garden, besides those
of which we have spoken, many remain to be explained spiritually
. . . Of all the trees in Paradise, two are spoken of in the Book of
Genesis, the tree of life and the tree of the knowledge of good and
evil, although that there were many others in that dense woods cannot
be doubted, because we read also of the tree of wisdom and we cannot
doubt that the names of the virtues were given to other trees according to their powers. Nor do we take it upon ourselves to uproot the
material plant from the corporeal Paradise, but we harvest spiritual
fruit in the visible orchard and from olives we gather both fruit and
oil. And even in gems, which are rolled about in the gravel of a
stream's head-waters, and, carried on by the flow of the rivers, reach
us, we have found very great virtue to exist,[37] so also in trees which
surpass the odors and savors to which our senses are accustomed, who
would doubt that there is a singular power or remedies for various
things? So the tree of life would prevent the decay of senility and
the tree of temperance would extinguish the heat of gluttony and
the tree of chastity was also there, no doubt, whose power would so
temper man's nature that the genital organs would no more be moved
to copulation than the other members. These each without any
stimulation do what they are ordained to do in orderly sequence. For
even now in this sort of weakness, camphor acts efficiently with an
enfeebling or drying effect and when smelled often or drunk dessi-

---

[37] For the powers of gems, see any medieval lapidary. An excellent synoptic table
of them will be found in Studer and Evans, *Anglo-Norman Lapidaries*, Paris, 1924,
p. 12 f.

cates the receptacles of the sperm and shrivels up the hardened instrument of that function. Many seeds and roots now nearly extinct have this effect. How much the more when the world was young and in Paradise, when all things were in ferment because of the newness and purity of their freshly made humors, would there not be found somewhere not one herb, but seed or fruit to fill the cup of salvation and incorruptibility as a pledge to their Lord and Care-taker, in obedience to man for whose sake they were made, some for this purpose, others for some other. But if Solomon " spake of trees, from the cedar tree that is in Lebanon even unto the hyssop that springeth out of the wall " [I Kings, iv, 33] and so many natural scientists through conjecture or experience could reach an under-standing of so profound a thing, could Adam, who belonged to God, ever be ignorant of this, Adam who possessed this power because he was made in the image and likeness of God, so that he understood the laws [rationem] of every creative subordinated to him? The First-born knew the seasonal changes of all corporeal things; he knew the causes and motions and essences and effects of all things which the elemental source produced sensibly and visibly, and which the mate-rial essence nourished . . .[38]

Saint Hildegard of Bingen [39]

The importance of this mystical writer for our purposes is her introduc-tion of a new element into the story of the Fall. Adam—or man in a state of nature—was sanguine, that is, in perfect health; after the Fall, the humors became unbalanced and disease arose. In Adam's case, the melancholy temperament predominated. As melancholy was responsible, according to the medical theories of the time, for most art, science, and philosophy, it is perhaps not an unfair inference that there was concealed in Saint Hilde-gard's account of the Fall a kind of anti-intellectualism typical of cultural primitivists. Along with the coagulation of Adam's black bile, he lost his musical voice; its place was taken by loud laughter and boorish jeering.[40]

---

[38] *Hexaemeron* (*MPL*, CLXXXIX, pp. 1535-1540). The whole passage should be read in connection with the emphasis which the Franciscan school was to put upon natural beauty as evidence of God's goodness. One can appreciate the popularity of this theme in the later Middle Ages, when one remembers that apparently it became the subject of rhetorical exercises. An unpublished MS, advertised by A. Rosenthal, Ltd., in Catalogue I, no. 9, p. 4, *Secular Thought in the Middle Ages and Renaissance*, 1939, entitled *De commendatione naturae in creaturis* is presumably an example of such a school-boy exercise.

[39] For Saint Hildegard's position in the history of science, see Charles Singer's " The Scientific Views and Visions of Saint Hildegard," in *Studies in the History and Method of Science*, Vol. I, 1917, p. 43.

[40] How popular these theories became and how influential is shown by Dürer's *Melancholy I*, the iconography of which has been exhaustively studied by I. Panofsky and F. Saxl in their *Melancholia*, a reprint of their " Melencolia I, ein quellen- und typengeschichtliche Untersuchung," Berlin and Leipzig, 1923 [*Stud. d. Bibl. War-burg*]. See also Panofsky's *Studies in Iconology*, N. Y., 1939, pp. 209 ff.

When God created man, mud was compounded with water and from the mixture man was fashioned. And He put into that form the breath of life, igneous and aerial. And since the form of man came from mud and water, the mud was turned into flesh from the fire of the same breath of life and from its air the water with which the mud was compounded was made into blood. When God was creating Adam, the splendor of divinity shone about the mass of mud from which he was created, and so the mud, when the form was put in, appeared outwardly in the lineaments of the limbs and inwardly there was a void. Then God created internally in the same form from the same mass of mud the heart and the liver and lungs and stomach and viscera and brain, as well as the eyes, tongue, and other internal organs. And when God put the breath of life into it, its matter, which is the bones and marrow and veins, was strengthened by this breath; and the breath separated itself in this mass as a worm twists itself into its home and as greenness is in a tree. And these things were strengthened as silver becomes changed when the silversmith puts it into the fire. And so the breath of life was established in man's heart. Then in this mass were made flesh and blood from the fire of the soul [41] . . . There are some men [who are called sanguine] in whose blood melancholy often arises. It makes the blood black and dries up the matter which is in it, so that men waking as well as sleeping are often heavily fatigued from this cause.

When Adam sought the good and did the evil in eating the apple, melancholy arose in him as a consequence of that change, which without the suggestion of the Devil is not in man either in waking or sleeping, because gloom and despair come from melancholy and these Adam had in his transgression. For when Adam violated the divine command, in that very moment melancholy was coagulated in his blood, as radiance withdraws when a light is blown out and as the wick, glowing and smoking, remains to stink. Thus it happened to Adam, because when the radiance was extinguished in him, melancholy was coagulated in his blood from which gloom and despair arose in him, for the Devil in the fall of Adam stirred up melancholy in him, which made man finally doubtful and unbelieving. But since man's form is bound, so that it cannot raise itself up without limitation, he fears God and is sad, and so frequently he despairs in that sadness, worrying lest God observe him. And since man was made in the image of God, he cannot omit to fear God and therefore it is difficult for the Devil to converse with a man who resists him, because man still fears God more than the Devil. Thus man has hope in God, but the Devil has none for himself. But the suggestions of the Devil frequently worm their way into the melancholy and make man gloomy and desperate, so that many men of this type in desperation are strangled and worn out, but many so resist this evil that they are like martyrs in the battle [42] . . . Before Adam transgressed

---

[41] *Causae et curae*, II [Ed. Kaiser, Leipzig, 1903, p. 42].

[42] *Ib.* [Ed. Kaiser, p. 143]. For an account of the humors and temperament contemporary with Saint Hildegard, see Honoré d'Autun, *De philosophia mundi*, IV, xx [*MPL*, CLXXII, pp. 93 f.]. Honoré bases his account on the *Isagoge* of Johannitius [Honein ben Is'hak], an Arab medical writer of the ninth century. See Lynn Thorn-

against the divine law, what is now the gall in man shone in him like crystal and had the taste of good works. And what is now melancholy in man shone in him as the dawn and contained the knowledge and perfection of good works in it. When, however, Adam sinned, the splendor of innocence was darkened in him and his eyes, which previously saw celestial things, were extinguished and his gall was changed to bitterness, and melancholy into the blackness of impiety, and he as a whole was changed into another type of being. And so his soul contracted gloom and sought a release at once in anger. For anger arises from gloom, and for this reason men have contracted from their first parent gloom and anger and all harmful things [43] . . . Adam also before his sin knew the song of the angels and every kind of music and had a voice which sounded like a monochord. In sinning, however, there crept into his marrow and thigh from the serpent's wiliness a sort of wind which is even now in every man. And from that wind man's spleen grows fat and improper gaiety and laughter and jeering are emitted by men.

Now just as in Adam's sin the holy and chaste nature of begetting children was changed into a mode of carnal delight, so too the voice of higher joys which Adam also enjoyed was turned into the contrary mode—laughter and jeering. For improper gaiety and laughter have a kind of affinity with carnal pleasure and therefore that wind which excites laughter as it arises from man's marrow shakes his thighs and his inner organs. And then after too great shaking laughter brings the water from the venous blood to the eyes in the same way as the foam of man's semen is expelled from the venous blood in the ardor of pleasure.[44]

Honoré d'Autun

We have already seen suggestions that the two famous trees in Eden, that of Life and that of Knowledge, were not the only marvelous plants in the garden. Honoré d'Autun, a contemporary of Saint Hildegard, in the following passage specifies what some of these were. Other details of interest are his emphasis upon man's original free-will, his power to procreate without lust or pleasure, and painless child-birth. Honoré also believes that Adam's children—if he had not sinned—would have walked and spoken at birth, an opinion which Hildebert was to combat. The selection from Honoré given below is in the form of a dialogue between Master and Pupil.

Pupil. Where was Adam created? *Master.* In Hebron, where he later died and was buried, and he was established in Paradise.

dike's *History of Magic and Experimental Science*, Vol. II, esp. pp. 756 ff. The new interest in the physical state of primitive man which we have mentioned in the text may have been due indeed to the introduction of Arabian medicine into Western Europe.

[43] *Ib.* [Ed. Kaiser, p. 145].

[44] *Ib.* [Ed. Kaiser, p. 148]. Readers whose appetite for Saint Hildegard's writings is as yet unsatisfied will find another, but similar, account of the Fall in her *Scivias*, I, ii [*MPL*, CXCVII, p. 391].

P. What is Paradise and where? *M.* A very lovely place in the East, where divers trees were planted, useful against various failings. For instance, if a man should eat of one at the proper time, never more would he thirst; of another, never would he grow weary. Finally, if he ate of the tree of life, he would never grow old, nor weaken, nor ever die.

P. Where was woman created? *M.* In Paradise, from the side of man while he was sleeping.

P. Why from man? *M.* That just as in flesh she was one, so through love she might be one in mind with him.

P. Why were not all the elect created at once, as the angels were? *M.* Because God wished Adam to be like Him in this respect, that just as all things are born of Him, so all men should be born of Adam, wherefore even Eve was born of him.

P. Why did not God create them such that they could not sin? *M.* To be more deserving. For if they had not consented when tempted, they would have immediately become so strengthened that neither they nor their descendants could ever have sinned. Therefore God wished them to choose the good freely and to receive this [immunity from sin] as their reward.

P. How would they have been born if they had remained in Paradise? *M.* As hand is joined to hand, so would they have been joined without concupiscence, and as the eye is raised to see, so without pleasure that sensitive member would have fulfilled its function.

P. How would woman have brought forth children? *M.* Without uncleanness and without pain.

P. Would an infant be weak as now, and unable to speak? *M.* As soon as born, he would have walked and spoken perfectly. For each of his defects he would have used the tree planted there and at a time pre-ordained by God he would have eaten of the tree of life and thus remained in one state thereafter.

P. How long were they to have remained in Paradise? *M.* Until the number of fallen angels had been made up and that number of the elect which was to be made up if the angels had not fallen.[45]

P. How could Paradise have held them all? *M.* Just as now a generation passes away in death and a generation arrives in life, so then parents were assumed into a better state, whereas their children in a predetermined time—which is believed to be about thirty years—after eating of the tree of life, would have given way to their descendants and finally all would have been on an equal footing with the angels in heaven.

P. Were they naked? *M.* They were naked and no more blushed for those organs than for their eyes.

P. Why is it said, After the sin they saw that they were naked, as if they had not seen this before? *M.* After the sin they immediately burned with concupiscence for each other and in that organ there arose that disorderly union from which human propagation proceeds.

P. Why in that organ more than in the others? *M.* That they

[45] The theory that the number of human souls must be terminated some day, after which time there would be no birth or death, was stated as early as the fourth century by Gregory of Nyssa. See his *De anima et resurrectione, MPG*, XLVI, p. 148.

might know that all their posterity would be held guilty of the same crime . . .

P. Why did the Devil lead them astray? *M.* Out of envy; for he envied them because they had attained to that honor from which he in his pride had fallen.

P. What approach to temptation did he find? *M.* Pride. For man wished to retain power over himself, since he said, "And in my prosperity I said, I shall never be moved." [*Psalm* xxx, 6].

P. Why did God permit man to be tempted when He knew that he would be overcome? *M.* Because He foresaw how great goods he would make from his sin . . .

P. Was there knowledge of good and evil in the apple? *M.* Not in the apple, but in the transgression. Before the sin, man knew good and evil: good through experience, evil by knowledge. After the sin, however, he knew evil by experience, good only through knowledge.[46]

The distinction between Adam's knowledge of good and evil through experience and knowledge [*scientia*] seems to have been original with Honoré. Presumably he is maintaining that even before Adam ate of the tree of the knowledge of good and evil, he possessed knowledge, if not the experience, of evil. This may be in keeping with the doctrine of Dionysius Exiguus cited above, that man before the Fall had an intuitive knowledge of all the essences. On the other hand, it is questionable whether Evil was an essence, there being good reasons for believing that many Christian thinkers, following Saint Augustine, held it to be what Aristotle called a "privation." Honoré may not have been one who agreed with Saint Augustine on this point. It is nevertheless difficult to make clear how a person could have had an intuitive knowledge of the nature of evil and yet have been willing to commit an evil act, especially since he had not as yet been accustomed to wrong-doing.

It will be noticed that Honoré says nothing of labor's being one of the effects of the Fall. His contemporary, Abelard, however, makes this clear in a brief passage in his commentary on the creation.

Abelard

There was not a man.[47] This does not simply say man was not, since earlier he was understood and shown to have been made between the generations of heaven and earth; but he did not exist for working the land, because there was no need as yet for him to engage in laborious agriculture, which he later received as a penance for his sin and which he now practices everywhere on earth.[48]

[46] *Elucidarium*, Bk. I, 13 and 14, with omissions as indicated [*MPL*, CLXXII, pp. 1117 ff.]. Cf. Hildebert, below.

[47] Abelard comments on the first part of the last phrase of *Gen.* ii, 5, which in the Vulgate reads, *Et homo non erat qui operaretur terram.* Though his readers would presumably have supplied the conclusion of the clause from memory, Abelard treats it as a whole sentence, with the consequences shown in the passage cited.

[48] *Expositio in Hexaemeron* [*MPL*, CLXXVIII, p. 774].

Hildebert

A more extended account of the life of Adam before the Fall is given in Hildebert. Here there is an emphasis upon what is called "the natural life," into which are woven strains from Saint Augustine, frequently echoed in the Middle Ages: the primeval possibility of either mortality or immortality, of either sinning or not sinning, the notion of procreation without lust—which Hildebert believes is the manner of animals, of child-bearing without pain. A relatively new note is struck in this passage in the introduction of "nature as norm." Adam and Eve are said to have had "natural" appetites and by "natural" is meant "moderate," which in turn is defined as "that which is necessary for one's nature." The knowledge, moreover, of what is necessary and what superfluous is a *praeceptio naturalis*, a term derived originally from Cicero, the best modern equivalent of which would probably be "instinct." Primitive man thus becomes instinctively temperate and potentially immortal and righteous.

"God took the man and put him into the garden of pleasure" [*Gen.*, ii, 15]. With these words Moses clearly shows that man was created outside of Paradise and afterwards was put into Paradise. This is said to have been done because he was not to remain there, or in order that he might not attribute the benefactions of God to nature instead of to grace. Paradise is said by the sacred writers to be the highest place in the East, so that not even the waters of the Deluge could reach it, and in it were trees of various kinds: the tree of life, the tree of the knowledge of good and evil, and several others. The tree of life was so-called because its fruit prevented death and the threat of any weakness. The tree of knowledge was different, because it did not receive its name from its nature—to confer knowledge—but from God's prohibition, so that he who would eat of its fruit would quickly know by his experience of evil what a difference there was between the good which he had lost and the evil which he had found. For he had knowledge of good and evil previously, of good by experience and not by knowledge, of evil by knowledge only and not by experience. Here must be seen what was man's condition before the Fall.

Thus says the Apostle, "The first man, Adam, was made a living soul" [I *Cor.*, xv, 45], that is, a sensitive body, which to this extent was animal, in that he needed the nutriment of foods; he had a mortal body in that he could either die or not die; he could either sin or not sin. But when a certain number of years had elapsed, he would change to that condition in which he could neither die nor sin. Therefore before the Fall he was immortal in the sense that he had the power not to die, but not immortal in the sense that he was unable to die. But if Adam and Eve had not sinned, as Augustine says, there would have been a spotless wedding-bed in Paradise, conception without lust, child-bearing without pain.

But how their children would have been born if they had not sinned, whether soon [after conception?] and able to walk and to speak and do other things, we have no certain authority to tell us.

Yet Augustine seems to think that, however quickly they might have been born, they could have done these things. For he says, If the first men had not sinned, would they have had children such that they would have used either tongue or hands? Because of the nature of the uterus, it would perhaps necessarily follow that their children be born as babies, although, in spite of the rib's being a very small part of the body, God did not on this account make a tiny wife for the man. Wherefore the Omnipotent Creator could also have made their children tall, as soon as brought into the world. But aside from this, it was surely possible, since He did this for many animals, such as poultry which, although very small at birth, nevertheless, as soon as they are born run and follow their mother. But the feet of man, when he is born, are not suitable for walking, nor are his hands even able to grasp things, and though the breasts lie near them, they are more likely to cry when hungry than to reach up to them. In a similar way this weakness of the baby agrees with its weakness of mind. But since Augustine says nothing about this question, it does not seem absurd to some that even then the proper age was awaited for these functions and the like, not because of any vice— since they had not sinned—but because of their natural constitution. Similarly they were not able to abstain entirely from eating, yet not because of any vice, but from their natural condition.

To this one can reply, If they had not sinned, they would never have died. Therefore, even if they did not eat, they would never have died, unless they had sinned. Consequently, they could live without food.

To which we say, not only would they have sinned, if they had eaten of the forbidden tree, but even if they had not used what they were permitted to use so long as their appetites were natural. For in so doing, they would be acting contrary to the natural reason which was given for this end, that they might use the proper things.

It is again objected, Since hunger comes from sinning, they would not have suffered hunger unless they had sinned. But to eat without hunger seems unnecessary.

To which we reply, Although they had not sinned, they would have had a desire to eat, by which act they would use foods to prevent hunger, and that appetite is natural and moderate. But hunger is an immoderate desire for food.

From this condition, which we have been describing, man had to be carried upwards with all his offspring to that highest good which had been prepared for him, without the pain of death. For just as there are two natures in man, the corporal and the spiritual, so two sorts of goods have been prepared for him, the temporal and the eternal. And because the animal is prior to the spiritual, the temporal good was bestowed upon him first. The other, that is, the eternal, was not given then, but was postponed. For the preservation of that which He had given, God laid down a natural law. The natural law was *discrimination*, by which man was inspired with a knowledge of what was needful for his nature and what was harmful. As for the reward which He had postponed, He gave a commandment of obedience, saying, " But of the tree of the knowledge of good and evil, thou shalt not eat . . ." [*Gen.*, ii, 17]. Then the Devil, seeing that man through obedience was going to ascend to that place from which he himself had fallen through pride, was envious of him, and he who had previously been through pride the devil [*diabolus*], that is, *flowing downward* [*deorsum fluens*], through envy was made Satan, that is, the *Adversary*, wherefore he tempted the woman, in whom he knew that the reason was less vigorous than in the man. But to keep his temptation well hidden and thus to prevent her from being on guard against it, he was permitted only to tempt her in the guise of a serpent, so that by his external disguise she might possibly notice his cunning. As Augustine says on *Genesis*, Since the Devil succeeded in the temptation and could not have done so unless he were permitted to, he could succeed only through the means which had been given him.

Is it asked why the woman was not afraid of the serpent? We reply that when he was newly created, he is thought to have received the function of speech from God. The temptation was carried out in this way: first he approached her with a question in order to gather from her reply how he ought to converse with her about the rest of the matter: " Why do you not eat of the tree of the knowledge of good and evil? " To which the woman replied, " Lest perchance we die . . ." In these words, " Lest perchance we die . . ." was given the ground for tempting her. Wherefore the Devil immediately said, " Eat and ye shall be as gods, knowing good and evil." By three things did he tempt her: by gluttony, when he said, " Eat "; by vainglory, when he said, " Ye shall be as gods "; by avarice, when he said, " Knowing good and evil." Gluttony is the immoderate desire for eating; vainglory, the love of self-praise; avarice, the immoderate love of possessions." [49] Since one temptation is internal, another external, the man was tempted by external temptation. External temptation is made from without by a sign or word, so that he to whom it is made may be inclined to a participation in sin. Internal temptation is the stimulus of base delight, by which the mind is impelled to sin. It is conquered with much greater difficulty. The man who was impelled by external temptation and fell was the more severely punished since he was laid low by a less powerful impulse.[50]

Alexander Neckam

The speculations on the physiological effects of the Fall are continued by Alexander Neckam into the beginning of the thirteenth century. He adds to them the effect of this primeval sin on all creation. According to him, primitive man was in command of all the beasts and there were neither flies, gnats, fleas, nor other pests to annoy him. All things within their genera were alike; there were no degrees of normality—an observation which would seem to imply that at this early period in the history of biology, variations within a species had been observed and had seemed puzzling.

---

[49] Hildebert here uses the Vergilian phrase, *amor habendi*. For its significance in Vergil, see *PIA*, p. 58.

[50] *Tractatus theologicus*, xxvi [*MPL*, CLXXI, p. 1121].

The dietetic state of nature was common to animals and men. The very light of the stellar bodies was brighter. Finally, woman did not menstruate, and Neckam considers menstruation monstrous.

The willing pen shrinks before the task of treating once more of man. What wonder if the art of writing does not refuse to serve man, him whom the elements serve! Oh, if the noble creature would only recognize his dignity, the lovely country of his fatherland, his God! The sun does not shine for itself, but for man, to whose coming and going the four seasons are submissive. The sun with continuous motion traverses the signs of the zodiac, now illuminating the hemisphere from above, now from below. Aurora with rosy countenance announces the coming of the sun, calling man to the work of daily toil. The moon presides over the order of the stars, conferring manifold good on man. The heat of the day and the moisture of the night extend their benefactions to things, and the four-horse chariot of the sun with the two-horse chariot of the moon serve the cause of human needs. Earth does not deny that her fertility exists for human needs, since she gladly responds to the farmer's labor. The trees do not begrudge the delights of their fruits to man. The sea and the rivers put their riches at his disposal. The very herds and flocks serve him to remind him of the glory of his primitive dignity, which he had before the Fall. If man had not sinned, the lion would obey human commands as quickly as the dog. But it was only right that man, who wished to deprive his Lord of the use of the service due to God, should lose his lordship over the things subjected to him by the Lord. Nevertheless, the sweetness of divine pity yielded to man as a consolation the use of certain animals, that man might confess that God, even if angered, was well disposed to him. Yet, to lower his pride and keep him mindful of his deceit, even tiny animals bring many annoyances to man. For this reason both gnats and stinging flies confuse the sight of man's eyes, annoying him by suddenly flying into them, to remind him that he has abused the inner light given by God Himself against God. The flea, a persistent pest, disturbs the rest of sleep, and unhappily despises the tranquillity of that most agreeable contemplation wherein one enjoys supernal delights. By a luckless progeny of the body, armed with a multitude of feet against the parent who brought it forth, is man molested, so that he may reflect that his own body is the heritage of the worms. The fly at any time alights on food and drink, that man may know what an importunate pest is a host of disordered thoughts. Unseasonable thoughts disturb and annoy the mind with troublesome concerns.

It should also be known that if man had not sinned, there would be no noxious poison. Likewise every animal would be of a temperate complexion in his own genus. Nevertheless there would be some animal of a complexion more temperate than that of another. For before the sin of the primal deceit, Eve was of a temperate complexion, but Adam was of the most temperate. If then man had not sinned, there would be no [differences of] degree, for a degree is a lapse from the norm. Therefore will it not appear to one versed in physical science that complexions may be changed, although many think this to be impossible? Likewise it ought to be carefully considered why man alone is said to be an animal tamed by nature. For if man had not sinned, every animal would obey his orders. Some say this does not arise from the nature of animals, but from the pure will of God. But why? Since in no humor was there an excess of heat or moisture, of cold or dryness, whence would have arisen either the fervor of wrath or the impetus of indignation? That man therefore is said to be an animal tamed by nature should not be referred to the original state of his nature, boasting of its great worth, but to a state of his nature already damaged and disturbed. For the subtle investigation and laborious diligence of physicians do not consider the state of his first nature but that of his second. And so there would have been no disease, no disturbance of health, if man had remained in the state of his glory. The nature of men and beasts alike would have been satisfied with vegetables and fruits alone, and the hawk would not have pursued the lark, nor the lion the bull, nor the wolf the lamb. Wherefore also it is said in *Genesis,* " Behold I have given you every herb bearing seed, and every tree, in which is the fruit of a tree yielding seed; to you it shall be for meat. And to every beast of the earth, and to every fowl of the air, and to every thing that creepeth upon the earth, wherein there is life, I have given every green herb for meat " [*Gen.,* i, 29-30]. At which place the gloss says, " It is obvious that before the Fall of Man the earth brought forth nothing harmful, no poisonous herb nor barren tree. For all herbs and trees were given to men and birds and beasts of the earth for food." Wherefore it is clear that at that time animals did not live on the flesh of other animals, but in peace lived on herbs and fruits.

And behold how before the Deluge men did not live on meat nor were there any rains before the Deluge. The earth was made fertile from the dew and the overflow of springs.

Now it should be noted that if man had remained in his state of felicity, no animal would have felt pain nor trouble in the dissolution of soul and body. Man in fact would never have died, but when a certain number of years had elapsed and been completed, he would have been carried off to heaven and his body would have been clothed in eternal glory.

Nor must we pass over the fact that because of the sin of the first deception, the light, not only of the planets, but of the stars as well had been dimmed. If therefore man were willing to consider to how great a change things were subjected because of his sin and to how harmful an alteration, he would be contrite and bowed down. For he ought to recall that he was formed from the dust, and that his exaltation may be reduced. But let him know that his soul was created in the image of God, that he may strive towards Him whose image he is.

For humility is nourished in man if he considers that he is born of woman who alone is a menstural animal, whose fluxes deserve to to be counted among monstrosities. Seeds touched with them will not germinate, trees will lose their fruits, iron will be seized with rust, bronze will grow black. If dogs should eat of them, they will become mad and will bite men and drive them mad. The bitumen in Judea which produces the Asphalt Lake which cannot be thinned, will dissolve when put in that blood. Moreover, women themselves during their periods cannot look at things with harmless eyes. At their sight mirrors are so spoiled that their brightness is extinguished, stricken by the ray of their sight, and their gleam will not return the accustomed image of the countenance and the face will be clouded by a sort of mist of dull lustre. Let man consider that he has been nourished in his mother's womb by the menstrual blood. For the said blood is converted into mother's milk.[51]

Maimonides

The position of Maimonides in Scholastic philosophy is not unlike that of Philo in Patristic. Both men succeeded in presenting the Hebraic tradition in a form acceptable to minds which desired to be critical and had as yet no vocabulary for expressing their convictions in rational form. Philo's eclectic metaphysics, combined with his allegorical method of interpretation, served this purpose in the early centuries of Christianity; Maimonides was no less eclectic, but the predominant character of his metaphysics was Aristotelian and his method was more severely logical than Philo's. To us, who see in him reflections of the Greeks, there appears little that is novel in his ideas. But the medieval mind knew only fragments of the total teachings of the ancients and the Arabian and Jewish thinkers proved a stimulus to what later became the characteristic method of Catholic philosophy.

Maimonides in discussing the condition of Adam before the Fall, insists upon his intellectual ability. He is not the infant of some of the early fathers, nor the pampered darling of God of Ernaldus of Bonneval. He is a strictly rational being. In fact, his sole guide before the Fall was his reason. After the Fall desire became a stimulus to action and the ethical categories of good and bad took their place alongside of the logical categories of true and false. This loss of perfect reason and the exclusive employment of it as a guide to conduct reduced Adam to the condition of the beasts, at least in respect to the food which he now ate and " many other requirements " which Maimonides does not specify.[52]

Maimonides brings us to the thirteenth century and thus to the voluminous and complex works of the great Scholastics. To deal adequately with them would entail the composition of another volume. We propose therefore to leave the matter here, hoping that we have suggested what the background was against which those greater and more influential minds would set their ideas. It is clear enough perhaps that for most Christian fathers the condi-

---

[51] *De naturis rerum*, Bk. II, ch. 156 [Ed. Th. Wright, London, 1863]. Another picture of man before the Fall is given in Alexander's *De laudibus divinae sapientiae*, lines 315-330 [Ed. Wright, p. 493], a poem which does not bring out the gruesome consequences of the Fall.

[52] The passage may be found in the *Guide for the Perplexed*, tr. by M. Friedländer, 2d. ed., London, 1910, ch. II, pp. 14-16. The writer of this essay knows no Arabic, and it seems reasonable not to reprint so accessible a translation.

7

tion of primitive man before the Fall was whatever the writer might believe to be most noble and valuable and that as the centuries progressed, the western European writers began adding more and more calamities to the original list of those produced by the primeval sin.   However fantastic some of these effects may now seem, it is important to remember that each of them gave added impetus to chronological primitivism, if not to cultural, each of them furnished a new detail in the picture of primitive earthly felicity.   It is also clear that there was no generally accepted doctrine about the condition of primitive man which could be called orthodox.   On this, as on so many other questions, Catholics, even those in positions of authority and influence, were sharply divided.   It cannot even be said that Adam before the Fall was happier than anyone who lived later than he, for the Twelve Apostles and certainly many of the saints were believed to have been much less unhappy.

CHRISTIANITY AND CYNICISM

1. *The Appeal to Nature*

A study of Greek and Roman thought shows how the concept of something called " nature " served as a normative corrective to the variations in standards. It appeared in such contrasts as nature vs. custom, behaviour " in accordance with nature " and behaviour "' contrary to nature," the instinctive or innate vs. the acquired or learned, reality vs. appearance. When the question arose of determining what precisely was the natural and what the unnatural, recourse was had to a variety of expedients. Since it was customary to believe that the standard of standards must be single and immutable, one looked for a single and immutable something under the film of multiplicity and change, and that something might turn out to be almost anything: the " 'heart " as contrasted with the " head," the universally accepted, the life of primitive man or of savages, of even the life of animals. By attributing to such things the magic word " natural," all difficulties seemed to be removed. The assumption that animals, for instance, remained in a " natural " condition, whereas man had abandoned it, was fortified by the additional assumption that man was simply an " unnatural " animal. The Fall of Man in pagan thinkers who accepted Nature as a norm was always interpreted as a deviation, for reasons which no one could discover, from this norm. It was in fact one of the differentiae of men to be able and willing so to stray. The very multivalence of the term gave it apparently a kind of power which less ambiguous terms could not have. Why so few of the Ancients ever questioned its use is one of the more puzzling problems of the history of thought. We can but note that the appeal to this mysterious standard has continued down to our own times and that there is still as great reluctance to inquire into its meaning or to make it more precise.

" Nature " had the advantage, to be sure, not only of a supposed immutability and unity, but also of accessibility. A man in doubt about what he ought to do could easily consult Nature, if Nature was as close at hand as his heart or his dog or his infant son. When she was the life of primitive man, one had only to recall one's Hesiod, Vergil, or Ovid; when she was the life of Noble Savages, one had Homer or Vergil again, a score of edifying geographers, legends of Anacharsis. No great amount of moral casuistry was needed to justify temperance or chastity or the simple life—or even their opposites—if one could turn to this fertile source of counsel. Like an indulgent parent, Nature justified every whim and her spoiled children saw no reason to criticise her inconsistencies.

The Christian had no such moral problem. His standard of right and wrong was written down in the Decalogue and in its revised version in the

Sermon on the Mount. There might be dispute about the correct interpretation of these texts, but there could be none about their authority. No
Christian need turn to the life of savages and animals for exemplars; he
turned to the Word of God. And though there were scores of differences
in the translations of this Word—for even the earliest Christians were far
from being " all one body "—yet none turned away from it to seek authority
in some non-scriptural authority.

For one of the prime facts of any Christian metaphysics was the opposi-
tion between the Creator and His creation and the perhaps Platonic inference
that the latter was inferior to the former. Every sense of " nature," except
that which equated it with God, made it part of Creation and, if it were to
serve as a standard of values, it could do so only vicariously, as man, for
instance, being the image of God, might serve as some sort of indication,
faute de mieux, of his Original's mind. The product, that is, was bound to
show traces of its producer's genius, and hence might elicit praise from those
who found these traces in it. But if one had other and more direct access
to God, there would be no point in lingering over substitutes.

The Greek use of " natural " and " unnatural " was echoed in the New
Testament. Saint Paul, writing to the Corinthians, bases his commands
to women to cover their heads when praying not only upon the symbolical
arguments which are too well known to be cited here, but also on the
teachings of Nature. " Doth not even nature itself teach you, that, if a man
have long hair, it is a shame unto him? But if a woman have long hair, it is
a glory to her: for her hair is given her for a covering " [I *Cor.*, xi, 14, 15].[1]
The " teachings of nature " also appear in the *Epistle to the Romans* in
which some of the Gentiles are described as doing by nature the things which
are commanded by the Law. Here " by nature " means " unconsciously "
or " instinctively " and its use implies neither a necessary conflict between
nature and the law nor a necessary harmony between them.[2] His reference
to sodomy as " unnatural " is again merely the utilization of a Greek term
of speech and should not be interpreted as an appeal to Nature, rather than
to the Law, for moral guidance.

Tertullian

The early Christian fathers, if we may judge from the scanty writings
which survive, show very little interest in any of the things which were called
" nature " by the Pagans. It is therefore with something of a shock that one

[1] Saint Paul must have known that custom alone kept men's hair short. He was
perhaps thinking that a custom which sharply differentiated the appearance of men
and women was " in accordance with nature."

[2] *Romans*, ii, 14. Saint Paul himself made use of the Greek word *nomos* as anti-
thetical to *physis*, the rhetorical effect of which was greater than that of the English
" law " and " nature." But since *nomos* meant " law " as well as " custom," and
was thus understood by the translator of the Vulgate, the ambiguity of the term
should not be emphasized here.

finds Tertullian's eulogy of the Christian soldier who refused to don a wreath to honor the Emperor, resorting to the appeal to Nature in justification of his conscience. After utilizing the argument from custom—for he says that he can find none in Scripture—he ironically enough turns to that from Nature, as if Christian custom and Nature were not at odds but harmonious.

Nature lays it down, he argues,[3] that a crown does not become a head. Flowers were made to be enjoyed by vision and odor, not by the head. It is, he says, as unnatural to long for a flower with the head as to long for food with the ear or for sound with the nose.

> Everything which is against nature deserves to be branded as monstrous among all men: but with us it is to be condemned also as sacrilege against God, the Lord and Creator of Nature.[4]

Here the "teachings of Nature" have doctrinal importance, for Tertullian makes it clear that he believes that the words of Saint Paul quoted prove the law of nature, as he interprets it, to be an indication of that part of the law of God not found in Scripture. But should one know only the law of Nature, one would be ignorant of its higher source, and therefore of what is much more important for the salvation of the individual. It would seem, then, that according to Tertullian there are some rules of conduct which cannot be found in the Bible; these it is permissible to seek in Nature whose teachings can be inferred from the organic teleology of the universe.

Tertullian, therefore, does not hesitate to seek evidence for his beliefs beyond the Scriptures. In one place, arguing against the heretic Marcion, to whom he attributes gnostic views of the physical world, he maintains that Nature, in the sense of "all creation," is permeated with the spirit of God and that one looking at it could not fail to admire its Creator. It is perhaps unnecessary to point out the similarity between this attitude and that of a Stoic like Seneca.

> Though you may laugh at the smaller animals, which the Most Great Creator has purposely made great with inborn powers, thus showing that greatness can be tested in lowliness, just as according to the Apostle virtue may be tested in weakness, imitate, if you can, the hive of the bee, the hill of the ant, the web of the spider, the thread of the silkworm. Resist, if you can, those beasts of house and bed, the poison of the cantharis, the sting of the fly, and the proboscis and lance of the gnat. What of the larger animals, since you so enjoy or suffer from those little ones that you do not despise the Creator in His small creatures? Finally survey yourself; consider man both within and without. Will this work of Our God please you, which your Lord, that better God, loved, because of which He worked to descend into these poor elements from the third Heaven, for the sake

---

[3] *De corona,* 5. Since A. O. Lovejoy has made a special study of "Nature as Norm in Tertullian," we treat the question here in the most summary manner. See his *Essays in the History of Ideas,* 1948.

[4] *Ib.*

of which He was even crucified in this shrine of the Creator? But
he up to now has not disdained the water of the Creator, with which
he washes his people, nor His oil, with which he anoints them, nor
the mixture of milk and honey on which he suckles them, nor the
bread, in which He represents His body, demanding even in His own
sacraments the poor simplicity of the Creator. But you, a pupil
superior to his Master, a servant superior to his Lord, your knowledge
is more sublime than His, for you destroy what He loved. I should
like to examine, if you are acting by any chance in good faith,
whether you do not seek for what you destroy. You turn against
Heaven and hold Heaven's freedom captive in your houses; you look
down on earth—clearly the womb of your enemy the flesh—and you
squeeze out its marrow for your food; you condemn also the sea, but
not its bounty which you consider sacred food. If I should hold out
to you a rose, you would not disdain its Creator. Hypocrite, even
were you to prove yourself a Marcionite by voluntary starvation, that
is by a repudiation of your Creator—for that is what should be your
practice if you really despised the world—you would be resolved into
some sort of matter, you would possess the substance of the Creator.
How obstinate is your pig-headedness! You make light of the very
things by which you live and die.[5]

The argument in this passage has perhaps a special turn in view of its
purpose. If one is opposing people who maintain that the physical world has
a kind of secondary reality, that the flesh is entirely bad, and that man should
turn completely away from both, it is perhaps inevitable that one emphasize
the skill of the Creator, as manifested in that world, to a degree which is
somewhat unusual. But in another passage, where Tertullian is arguing for
the resurrection of the flesh, he also turns to the cosmic scene for evidence,
pleading that natural rhythms and cycles supplement the evidence of
Scripture.

Look now upon these examples also of divine power. Day dies into
night and is buried everywhere in shadows. The beauty of the world
is darkened and all substances turned black. All things grow dim,
silent, and benumbed. All occupations cease. Thus the departure
of the light is mourned. And yet once more with its beauty and riches,
with its sun, the same and whole and entire it is born again throughout the world, slaying its own death, the night, opening its own grave,
the shadows, arising as its own successor and heir, until night shall
come to life again, on its own eminence. And the rays of the stars
are kindled once again, which the morning's glow extinguished. And
the absent constellations, which had been concealed for a time, return.
And the mirror of the moon, which had been tarnished for a month,
is polished once more. Winters and summers come and go, springs
and autumns with their powers and laws and fruits. For even earth
receives its orders from heaven, to clothe the trees, after their de-
foliation, to color the flowers anew, to spread out the grass once more,
to bring forth the very seeds which were consumed and not to bring

---

[5] *Adversus Marcionem*, I, 14 [Ed. Kroymann, in *CSEL*, vol. XLVII, p. 308 f.].

them forth until they have been consumed.   What a marvelous
rational order! From the defrauder, the preserver; to take away in
order to return; to lose in order to keep; to injure in order to make
whole; to lessen in order to increase! In fact, the restitution has
been richer and more beautiful than the destruction, in truth a
profitable destruction, a useful injury, a gainful loss. I might even
say, the law of the universe is recurrence. Whatsoever you may
come upon, that has already been. Whatsoever you lose, will exist
once more. Nothing is that will not be again. All things return to
the state from which they departed. All things begin again, when
they have ended. Thus they are terminated that they may be made.
Nothing perishes save for its salvation. Therefore the whole revolv-
ing order of things is witness to the resurrection of the dead. God
inscribed this in His deeds before He put it in the Scriptures,
preached it in His power before He preached it with His voice. He
has sent forth Nature to you as a teacher, and He will send you
prophecy also, so that as a pupil of Nature you may the more easily
believe in prophecy, that you may immediately admit when you hear
what you now see all about you, nor doubt that God is also the
reviver of the flesh, since you know Him to be the restorer of all
things. And so, if all things rise again for man, for whom they
were prepared, and not merely for man but also for his flesh, why
should that perish entirely for which and because of which nothing
perishes? [6]

Lactantius

In attacking "philosophy" Lactantius employs as one of his weapons a
type of epistemological primitivism employed by Cicero. "Philosophy"
has, by the admission of Cicero, Lucretius, and Seneca, only recently come
into the world.[7] Seneca has said, "It is not yet a thousand years since the
beginnings of wisdom were undertaken." "But there is great force in that
argument . . . which is used by [Cicero's] Hortensius: that philosophy is
not wisdom because its beginning and origin are apparent." True wisdom,
in other words, must be innate in the human race and anything which has
the appearance of true wisdom and is not innate but acquired must on that
account alone to suspect. For if genuine wisdom were so recent an acquisition, it would follow that mankind had existed for years *sine ratione*, which
to Lactantius is a manifest absurdity. Consequently before the appearance
of philosophy among men, there must have been another kind of knowledge
which was inborn in human nature and which was "higher" than philosophy.

That knowledge which did not appear on earth with the appearance of
the human race is suspect, would, one might imagine, have been applied as
an argument against the truth of so recent a revelation as Christianity. Of
this consideration Lactantius here appears oblivious. There were, of course,
various possible rejoinders to it. One might reply that revelation, being
supernatural, is not subject to the same tests as philosophy, or that—as was

---

[6] *De carnis resurrectione*, 12 [Ed. Kroymann, in *CSEL*, vol. XLVII, p. 40].
[7] See *PIA*, pp. 252 ff., 235 ff., 263 ff.

to be said by many other Fathers—Christianity was new only in the form in which it was revealed, its substance being identical with that of the truths of the Old Testament, or that the new revelation was but a new step in a long religious education which had begun in the Garden of Eden, an actualization of certain potentialities which had always been dormant in the human race.

The influence of the normative use of " nature " in another of its senses may be seen in Lactantius's struggles with the Pauline dualism and the Platonistic otherworldliness and distrust of the senses. Under these influences Lactantius, though admitting marriage to be permissible for the procreation of children, continues in an intensely anti-hedonistic vein: " Let no one think," he says,[8] " that he must abstain solely from that pleasure which arises in sexual intercourse, but [he should abstain also] from the other sensory pleasures, because they also are in themselves vicious, and it is the part of virtue to condemn them . . . Virtue ought to fight stoutly against them, lest, ensnared by their lure, the mind be turned from heavenly to earthly things, from things eternal to things temporal." But Lactantius is far from being consistent on this point, for writing on what he believes to be the three basic passions—anger, avarice, and lust—he actually attacks the Stoics and Peripatetics for having gone too far in repressing them. Neither of these schools of philosophy, he maintains, " judges rightly [in this matter]; for these passions can neither be wholly eliminated— since they are implanted by nature and have a certain and great reason for being— nor yet diminished, since if they are evils, we ought to dispense with them altogether, even when restrained and moderate in degree, and if they are good, we ought to use them to the full. But we say that they ought neither to be eliminated nor diminished. For they are not evil in themselves, God having implanted them in man for a reason; but while they are assuredly good by nature, since they are granted us for the protection of life, they become evil through evil use." [9] Here, again, whatever is the natural equipment of man, must be a standard of goodness, it being inconceivable to Lactantius that God could have created man in anything other than a perfect condition.

The Carpocratians

Two of the early heretical sects, the Carpocratians and the Marcionites, also made curious use of nature as norm. The former, according to Clement of Alexandria, preached an extreme form of equalitarianism which they based upon this use. Their doctrine included a kind of erotic primitivism according to which the marital state of nature was the ideal for humanity.[10]

---

[8] *Epitome*, 62.   [9] *Ib.*, 61.

[10] The heresy recurred in the thirteenth century in the *Roman de la Rose*. For the conception of erotic primitivism in pagan writers, see *PIA*, Index, under " marital state of nature."

He says then in his book "On Justice," that the justice of God is a kind of community with equality. Heaven, at any rate, is spread out equally in all directions and encompasses the whole earth in a circle. And night exhibits all the stars equally. And the cause of day and the father of light, the sun, has been caused by God to shine forth from on high equally upon all the inhabitants of the earth capable of seeing; and they all see in common, since He does not distinguish between rich and poor, the ruler or the people, the foolish or the wise, women, men, free, or slaves. Nor is there even any different method of treating the irrational animals, but pouring Himself forth from on high upon all the animals equally, good and bad, He firmly establishes His justice, since no one can have more nor rob his neighbor, to have twice his share of God's light. The sun causes food to grow in common for animals since He has given an equal and common justice to all. And among them there are as many bulls as cows, as many boars as sows, as many rams as ewes, and so on for all the rest. For justice among them appears to be community. Since according to the communal principle, all things are similarly distributed within groups, and a common food is eaten by them who feed on the earth, by all the cattle and by all equally, controlled by no law, justice is given to all harmoniously and in abundance at the Donor's orders. Nor is procreation controlled by any written law, for it would have been altered. But they sow and beget in equality, having an inborn sense of communal justice. To all in common and equally has the Creator and Father of all given an eye for seeing by the decrees of His justice, not distinguishing male from female, rational from irrational, and, in short, nothing from anything else. But in equality and community He has divided seeing and has bestowed it upon all similarly in one command. But the laws, he says, of man, unable to punish ignorance, have taught lawbreaking. For it is the peculiarity of the laws to chop and nibble at the community of the divine law, not understanding the words of the Apostle, saying, "I had not known sin, but the law." [Rom., vii, 7].[11] And the mine and the thine, he says, have crept in by stealth through the laws. No longer is there common enjoyment— for these things are common—of earth or possessions or even of marriage. For He made the vines for all in common. They are denied neither to the sparrow nor to the thief. And so too the grain and the other fruits of the earth. But the violation of community and equality by the law has produced the thefts of flocks and fruits. Since then God made all things for men in common, and joined the female to the male in common, and welded together similarly all the animals, He pronounced justice, community with equality. But those thus born denied the community which had brought about their birth. And he says, if anyone has married one woman, let him keep her, although they are unable to share in all, just as the other animals beget children. Saying such things in these words, he again says, "For He has put into males a powerful and vehement desire for the begetting of offspring, which neither law nor custom nor anything else is able to destroy. For it is a law of God." [12]

[11] Cf. Rom., iii, 20.
[12] Stromata, III, ii, 6-8 [Ed. Stahlin, II, pp. 197-199.].

The Marcionites

In the Marcionites that " Nature " which had been a norm of goodness to the Carpocratians became a norm of evil. For to them Nature, as the physical world, including the animals, was—at least as their doctrine developed—the work of an evil deity, and instead of making a contrast between " nature " and " law," they made a contrast between " nature " and God. Nature was thus God's enemy and anything which might be presumed to be dictated by its laws, was to be abjured. Consequently to them the moral law demanded absolute sexual continence, lest they be guilty of perpetuating the material world. Again, the animals, which were moral exemplars to the Carpocratians, were objects of contempt to the Marcionites, and for precisely the same reason which made them admirable to their opponents, namely, that they were more " natural " then man.[13]

Saint Ambrose [14]

Equalitarian notions, based ultimately on pagan concepts of the " natural " appear in Saint Ambrose, but he confines his inferences largely to the economic domain. He reverts to the pagan commonplace that in the Golden Age no boundary-stone separated field from field; all things were held in common. This, he maintains, was God's original intention. He meant the earth and all its fruits to be owned and enjoyed by all, but avarice—again a pagan theme—broke down communal ownership.[15] Private property is thus " unnatural " and has to be controlled by law for that reason alone.[16] *Natura . . . jus commune generavit, usurpatio jus fecit privatum.*

The argument that " nature has poured forth all things for all in common," and that God has ordained that " the earth be common property for all," is obviously not based upon Hebraic tradition. There was no warrant in the Old Testament for attributing communism to life as it would have been if Adam had not sinned. There were in the New Testament such stories as that in *Matthew* xix, and its parallels, which condemned riches, but even these did no more than advocate an extreme form of charity. Saint Ambrose seems to be recasting a pagan doctrine in Christian form. He apparently treats Adam as a symbol for the whole human race, as Origen had in certain passages, and God's gift to Adam of the earth and its fruits is interpreted as a gift to all mankind without distinction of persons.

---

[13] The views of the Marcionites and Carpocratians are contrasted in Clement's *Stromata*, III, iii.

[14] A fuller treatment of the communism of Saint Ambrose by Professor Lovejoy in his " The Communism of Saint Ambrose," *Journal of the History of Ideas*, III (1942), pp. 458-468, makes it unnecessary to do more here than to indicate briefly his argument.

[15] *Expositio in Psalmum cxviii*, 22 [*MPL*, XV, p. 1372]. It is worth noting that Lactantius, a believer in the reality of the Golden Age, omitted communism from his account of it.

[16] *De officiis ministrorum*, I, xxviii, 132 [*MPL*, XVI, p. 67].

That mankind for him forms a corporate unity, whose cement is the *lex naturae*, appears clearly from the following passage.

> How serious it is to take something from one with whom we ought to sympathize and to be deceitful and injurious to him to whom we owe a sharing of labor. This is the law of nature which so binds us to all humanity that we act towards one another as if we were parts of one body.[17]

Because of this corporate unity, charity to all is the prime duty of a Christian.

> Consider, O Man [*homo*], whence you have taken your name. From the soil [*humo*] which has deprived no one of anything, but has given all things bounteously to all, and has poured out her various fruits for the use of all living beings. Therefore the special and personal virtue of man is called " humanity," which helps one's fellow-man.[18]

It is clear that in such passages as these Saint Ambrose makes no distinction between the law of nature and the law of God. He may be using pagan language because it is the language to which he is accustomed, as a modern philosopher might try to express his doctrine in the terms of " common-sense." But in his letters he utilizes what we may loosely call the " Pauline conception " of the Law of Nature, according to which " nature " is that which is innate in man rather than acquired. Saint Paul, however, does not appear to imply that it is on that account higher or more valid than the written law. He simply states without criticism that Gentiles do " by nature " " the things contained in the law." Saint Ambrose, however, ranks the law of nature definitely above the written law and seems to identify it with instinct. If this instinct had been preserved, there would have been no need of written law; all would have been good instinctively, and, he seems to suggest, the instinctive doing of good is better than the conscious or rational doing of good.

But what is even more striking and in some ways more important for the history of primitivism, is his finding a model for the kind of behavior he is thinking of in children. The child, who is innocent, follows the *lex naturae*; he is a living example of what Adam was like before the Fall, he thus takes the place occupied by the Noble Savage in the writings of cultural primitivists.

> If man had been able to keep the natural law which God, the Creator, instilled into the breasts of each, there would have been no need for that law which, written on tablets of stone, bound and tied together the weakness of mankind more than it freed and loosed it. That there is, however, a natural law in our hearts, the Apostle teaches when he writes that " the Gentiles do by nature the things contained

---

[17] *De officiis ministrorum*, III, iii, 19 [*MPL*, XVI, pp. 158 f.].
[18] *Ib.*, III, iii, 16 [*MPL*, XVI, p. 158].

in the law, and though they have not read the law, yet have the work of the law written in their hearts" [*Rom.*, ii, 14].[19] Hence this law is not written, but is innate. It is not perceived by any reading, but is expressed in each of us by the overflowing of nature's fountain, so to speak, and is drunk by human nature [*ingeniis*] . . .

Finally, let us investigate infancy; let us see whether any sins are discoverable in it, whether it is avaricious, ambitious, guileful, cruel, insolent. It knows nothing as its own, it assumes no honors, it is unacquainted with self-advancement, it wishes for no revenge, nor can it. What insolence is, a pure and simple mind cannot understand.

This law was broken by Adam, who wished to take for himself what he had not been given, so that he might be like his Creator and Author, and receive divine honor. And so through disobedience, he committed sin and became guilty through insolence. If he had not broken the commandment, and had remained obedient to the heavenly orders, he would have preserved the privileges of nature and innate innocence for his heirs. And so, since through disobedience the privileges of natural law were corrupted and annulled, on that account it was thought necessary that law be written down, so that he who lost the whole might retain at least a part, and that he who had destroyed the heritage of his birth, might regain it to a certain degree and preserve it through education.[20]

The anti-intellectualism of such a passage is reinforced by what Saint Ambrose has to say of the Tree of Knowledge. Knowledge in his mind is the source of cunning [*astutia*] and the reason why God forbade man to eat of the tree whose fruit was knowledge was to avoid the rise of cunning and its attendant vices in the Garden. This tree was not alone in producing certain *affectus* in those who ate of their fruit, but the other such trees—which were not trees of knowledge—produced the virtues.[21] Thus virtues were not rooted in the intellect, but, it is perhaps not unfair to argue, in instinct. The good Christian, then, is a man in a state of nature, childlike because unreasoning, and somehow better for what intellectualists would call a defect.

He established a nursery-garden of the knowledge of good and evil; for man alone of the living things on earth has the knowledge of good and evil. There were also other different plants there, whose fruits are the virtues.

But since man's disposition, which is capable of knowledge, is known to God to incline him more speedily to cunning than to the heights of prudence—for the quality of His work could not lie hidden from the Judge Who had established fixed limits in our soul—He wished to eliminate cunning from Paradise, in His rôle of provident author of our salvation, and to enroot more deeply the devotion to

[19] These words in the Latin are not an exact translation of the Greek Testament, but do appear to preserve its meaning. We have followed Saint Ambrose.

[20] *Epistolarum classis*, II, lxxiii, 2-3, 4-5 [*MPL*, XVI, pp. 1305 f.]

[21] For the continuation of this tradition, see Index under *Garden of Eden, Trees.*

life and the discipline of piety; and so He told man that any tree which grew in Paradise might be tasted but that the tree of the knowledge of good and evil might not be tasted.[22]

Saint Augustine

The danger to Christian orthodoxy in the appeal to Nature was the possible disregarding of God. It must therefore be proved either that the Law of Nature was the Law of God or that the appeal to Nature was illegitimate.

In Saint Paul there had been a pronounced dualism between the flesh and the spirit and when the flesh was identified with matter and matter with the physical world in general, it was easy to lapse into Manicheeism and see throughout the cosmos the same dualism that Saint Paul had seen within the human individual. If that were done, then Nature, in the sense of the physical world and its presumed implicates, was the pronounced enemy of God and he who lived " in accordance with Nature " was by that very fact living contrary to God's commands.[23]

Although the Manichean heresy gave a metaphysical explanation of some ethical difficulties, it had the great disadvantage in the minds of men sick of pluralities of decreasing the power of God and of removing Him from that part of the world in which human beings had the misfortune to spend the major part of their waking life. At the same time, it seemed to solve what has always been a problem to most types of theists—those who believe that their God is good—namely, the problem of evil. For if God was all-good and the sole creator of things, how could one explain His creating evil? Accordingly, a person who wished to avoid heresy had to incorporate evil into an all-good universe and, if he wished to retain the appeal to Nature, to interpret that multivalent concept as fulfilling some perfect design of God.

This task was undertaken by Saint Augustine. For him the very definition of evil proved it non-existent. Evil is defined as that which is " contrary to nature." But " nature " is used here in the sense of the generic character of a thing,[24] and it is assumed by Saint Augustine, as by most of the Ancients, that a thing could be what it essentially is not.[25] Since the verb " to be " in Latin, as in English, served as logical copula, as a symbol of identity, and as an expression of existence, it was possible by a familiar kind of philosophical pun to prove the non-existence of evil. God, therefore, could not be its author, since He is not the creator of the nonexistent.

> Often, in fact almost always, Manichees, you ask of those whom you strive to convert to your heresy, whence is evil. Imagine now that

[22] *Epistolarum classis*, I, xlv, 8, 9 [*MPL*, XVI, p. 1192].

[23] Cf. Saint Jerome, *Epistle 133*, par. 9 [*MPL*, XXII, pp. 1157 f.].

[24] See *PIA, appendix*, nos. 3, 24, 25.

[25] In Aristotelian language, a thing is what it essentially is not, when one of its accidents becomes its final cause. Thus the ethical problem for Aristotle was to bring about the identification of man's formal and final causes.

I have fallen among you for the first time. I shall ask something of you, if you do not mind: That you set aside for a moment the doctrine by which you think to know these matters and try to straighten out with me so great a matter, even if roughly. Ask me whence is evil and I in turn shall ask you what is evil. Whose question is the more just? Theirs who ask whence it is without knowing what it is, or his who thinks that one should first ask what it is to avoid seeking the origin of an unknown thing—which is most absurd. Very true, you say. For who is so blind in mind that he does not see that evil for each kind of thing is what is contrary to its nature? But when this is settled, your heresy is avoided; for no nature is evil. You tell us, however, that evil is a certain nature and substance. For [evil] occurs because something is contrary to nature, and is even inimical to nature, and strives to annihilate it. Thus it attacks that which is, to bring about that it cease to be. For nature itself is nothing other than that which is believed to be something *in suo genere*. And so, as we now call its being by a new name, "essence," from the fact that it is, which we also call commonly "substance," so the Ancients, who did not have these words, used "nature" in place of "essence" and "substance." [26] Therefore evil itself, if you will consider the matter very carefully, is a relinquishment of the essence and an attempt to prevent its existence.

Wherefore, when in the Church it is said that God is the author of all natures and substances, it is at the same time understood by those capable of understanding this, that God is not the author of evil. For how can He, Who is the cause of the existence of all things which are, be again the cause of their non-existence, that is, of their relinquishment of their essence and their tendency towards non-being? For this is what the truest reason declares is evil in general. But that type of evil of yours which you wish to be the greatest evil, how would it be against nature, that is, against substance, since you say it is nature and substance? If it acts against itself, it deprives itself of its being, but if it succeeds, then only shall it reach the highest evil. But it will not succeed, because you not only wish it to be but to be eternal. Therefore it cannot be the highest evil, because it is said to be a substance. [27]

The Manichean heresy was a constant preoccupation of Saint Augustine, since he himself had been an adherent to it in his youth. [28] After having proved that evil, as Plotinus had also maintained, was non-being, he might have rested satisfied. Yet he no doubt realized that even this shadow of existence, like a bad dream, could and did have real effects upon man's behaviour. The non-being of evil must consequently be interpreted in some way which would leave it its causal efficacy, if not its reality. Accordingly,

---

[26] *Essentia* was not so novel a word as Saint Augustine thought. Seneca, *Ep.* lviii, 6, holds that Cicero invented it.

[27] *De moribus Manichaeorum*, Bk. II, ch. i [*MPL*, XXXII, pp. 1345 f.].

[28] He gives his definition of this heresy in *De haeresibus*, I, 46. Cf. also *Contra Julianum*, I, lxvi; III, clxxxvi.

man's " unnaturalness " is emphasized, as in the Cynics, but his unnaturalness consists not in his departure from the life of the beasts or that of the
savages, but in his falling short of the Platonic idea of humanity. This
short-coming was of course attributable to Adam's fall. It is, however, a
defect which is curable and which in principle—if not in fact—has been
cured by Christ's atonement.

> All of us who believe in the living and true God, Whose utterly good
> and immutable nature neither does nor suffers any evil, from Whom
> all is good which can be diminished and Who in the good which is
> Himself cannot in any way be diminished, when we hear the Apostle
> saying, " Walk in the Spirit, and ye shall not fulfil the lust of the
> flesh. For the flesh lusteth against the Spirit, and the Spirit against
> the flesh: and these are contrary the one to the other; so that ye
> cannot do the things that ye would," [*Galat.*, v, 16, 17], far be it
> from us to believe what the insanity of the Manichees believes, that
> two natures are indicated here, made up of contrary principles con-
> flicting among themselves, one of good, the other of evil. Absolutely
> both of them are good, both the Spirit is good and the flesh is good,
> and man, who consists of both, the one commanding, the other
> obeying, is likewise good, but changeably good, which he could not
> become except by the agency of an unchangeable good by which all
> good is created, whether little or great; but however little, yet it
> was made by a great, and, however great, yet it is not to be in any
> way compared to the greatness of its maker. In truth, in this nature
> of man, good and well established and ordained by the good, there
> is now war, since there is not yet health. When his sickness is cured,
> there is peace. But his guilt rightly brought on that sickness; it has
> not been rooted in his nature. That guilt clearly has been washed
> away from the faithful by the waters of regeneration through the
> grace of God, but hitherto under the hands of the same physician his
> nature has been struggling with his sickness. But in such a struggle,
> health will be a complete victory, not temporary but everlasting
> health, when not only will this sickness be ended, but no other will
> ever again arise. Wherefore the just man addresses his soul saying,
> " Bless the Lord, O my soul, and forget not all His benefits; Who
> forgiveth all thine iniquities; Who healeth all thy diseases " [*Ps.*,
> ciii, 2, 3].[29]

Saint Augustine also appeals to Nature in the sense of " the whole of
things." But here too he had to indulge in metaphysical apologies in order
to preserve its all-goodness. Such apologies are of two sorts: first, the Stoic
type in which Nature is a " whole " which is beautiful and ordered, whose
beauty and order require the presence of apparent ugliness and disorder;
second, the type of natural teleology which was a commonplace of pagan
thought, according to which anything which Nature gives, however evil in
appearance,—poisons and hostile beasts, for instance—has a purpose useful
to man.

[29] *De continentia*, Bk. I, vii, 17, 18 [*MPL*, XL, pp. 359 f.].

This cause, that is, God's goodness in creating good things, this cause, I say, so just and worthy, which when diligently considered and piously thought of terminates all the controversies of those seeking the origin of the world, certain heretics have not seen. For many things offend the poor and fragile mortality of this flesh, the result of a just punishment, (although these heretics do not agree), such as fire and cold and wild beasts or something of that kind. Nor do they consider either how those things flourish in their proper places and according to their natures, and are organized in a beautiful order, and how much beauty they confer upon the whole of things in accordance with their portion as in a common state, or how much use they bestow upon us ourselves, if we utilize them fittingly and intelligently. So the very poisons, which are dangerous if improperly employed, when properly taken became wholesome medicines. And how, contrariwise, these things in which they delight, like food and drink and light itself, are experienced as noxious if immoderately and inopportunely used. When Divine Providence warns us not to blame things foolishly but diligently to seek their utility, and when our wit or weakness is at fault, to believe it hidden, just as were certain things which we were barely able to find: for that concealment of utility itself is either for an exercise of our humility or a wearing down of our pride. For in no wise is anything in nature bad and this name is that of nought but a lack of goodness. But from heaven to earth, from the visible to the invisible, some things are good, others better than others. In this they are unequal, so that all kinds of things might be.[30] God, however, is so great a creator in great things that He is not less great in small. These small things are not to be measured by their greatness—for they have none—but by the wisdom of their Maker. Just so in the appearance of a man, if one eyebrow is shaved off, practically nothing has been removed from his body, but how much from his beauty, since that does not consist in size but in the equality and measure of parts.[31]

There is still another use of the appeal to nature as norm in the underlying idea of the *City of God*. If man in a state of sin could do things which were in manifest contradiction with what he would have done in a state of grace, there were—at least from the phenomenal point of view—two orders of existence. These two orders in the Platonistic tradition were called the sensible and the intelligible worlds, but in Saint Augustine they became the City of Man and the City of God, the latter of which was the immutable pattern of the former.[32] The former was temporal and changing, the latter eternal and immutable. Accordingly, the former was to be judged by its approximation to the latter, which was, in Saint Augustine's terminology, its " nature." This distinction, which appears frequently in his writings, as

[30] Note the introduction of the " principle of plenitude." Cf. Lovejoy's *The Great Chain of Being*.

[31] *Civ. Dei*, Bk. XI, ch. xxii [Ed. Welldon, pp. 490 f.].

[32] It is probably obvious that the two terms derived from the City of Cecrops and the City of Zeus.

the distinction between the Law of God and " custom " or " temporal law," is analogous to the Roman juridical distinction between *jus naturale* and *jus gentium*. A passage in the *Confessions* clarifies the distinction in a manner recalling some of the discussions of the Cynics.

> I did not know true inner justice, which judges not from custom but from the most righteous law of God, the All-powerful, by which were formed the customs of places and times in accordance with their needs, though it is everywhere and at all times itself, not one thing here, another there, according to which Abraham was just, and Isaac and Jacob and Moses and David and all those praised by the mouth of God, but judged unrighteous by the ignorant, who judge according to the time of man and measure all human acts by their own ways of living. They are like a man who is ignorant of armor, who does not know what is proper for each member of the body and wishes to cover his head with leggings and to shoe himself with a helmet, and complains that they do not fit. Or as if on a day when business is forbidden in the afternoon, someone were angry at not being allowed to set forth his wares since he could have done so in the morning. Or as if he should see in a house a servant handle something which the cup-bearer is not allowed to touch, or something permitted after dinner which is forbidden before meals, and would be angry that though there is one dwelling and one household, the same things are not allotted on every occasion to all. Such are they who are indignant when they hear that something was permitted in the past to the just which is not now permitted to the just, and because to those men God commanded one thing, to these another, in accordance with the needs of the times, though both obey the same law. Yet in one man on one day and in one house, they see one thing fit one limb, another another, and one thing permitted at one time, at another forbidden, something permitted or ordered in that corner which in this is justly punished and forbidden. Is justice therefore various and mutable? No, but the times over which it has the command are not all alike, for they are times. Men, however, whose life upon earth is brief, since they can make no sensible connection between the causes of prior ages and of other races of which they have no experience and those of which they have experience, yet in one body or day or house can easily see what is fitting for each limb or amount or part or person, are shocked by the former and submissive to the latter.[33]

This distinction was made even clearer in Saint Augustine's treatise on free-will.

> A. Let us carefully investigate, if you will, to what extent evil deeds are avenged by that law which restrains people in this life; then we shall undertake the remaining question, namely, what is punished more inevitably and secretly by the Divine Providence.
> E. I should be very happy to, if only one could reach the end of so great a question. For I think it is endless.

[33] *Confessions*, III, vii, 13 [*MPL*, XXXII, pp. 688 f.].

A. Nay, pay strict attention and trusting in piety proceed upon the way of reason. For there is no road so arduous and difficult that with God's help it may not become level and easy to travel. And so dependent upon Him and beseeching His aid, let us ask the questions we have decided upon. First, tell me whether that law which is written is of help to men living this life.

E. Obviously. For both peoples and states are made up of such men.

A. What? Are men and peoples of the same kind of being as cannot pass away or be changed and are utterly eternal? Or rather are they changeable and subject to time?

E. That this kind of being is clearly changeable and subject to time, who would doubt?

A. Then, if a people be temperate and serious and a diligent guardian of the common good, upon which depend each man's private affairs as well as the public, would not a law be rightly passed by which this people would be permitted to create its government by which its affairs—that is, its public business—would be administered?

E. Of course.

A. If then the same people, becoming corrupted bit by bit were to put private before public interest, and should offer its votes for sale, and debased by them who love honors, should entrust its government against its own welfare to wicked and vicious men, would it not likewise be right, if any good man should then exist, who had very great capabilities, for him to deprive the people of the power of giving honors and to put it at the disposal of a few good men or even of one?

E. Yes, and rightly too.

A. Then, since those two laws seem to be in such conflict that one of them gives the power of bestowing honors to the people and the other revokes it, and since the second has been so framed that both can in no way exist at the same time in a single state, should we say that one of them is unjust and ought never to have been passed?

E. Not at all.

A. Then let us call that law, if you will, temporal, because, although it is just, it can justly be changed as times change.

E. Let us call it so.

A. What now? Can that law which is called the highest reason, to which obedience is always due, and in accordance with which in fine that which we have said should be called temporal is rightly framed and rightly changed, can it not appear to any intelligent man immutable and eternal? Or can it sometimes be unjust that evil men be wretched, whereas the good are blessed, or that a temperate and serious people create its own government, whereas a dissolute and worthless people lack that power?

E. I see that this law is eternal and immutable.

A. For I believe that you see at the same time that there is nothing just or legitimate in that temporal law which men have not taken from the eternal. For if that people at one time gave honors justly and again at another time unjustly, this temporal occurrence, in order to be just, depended upon that eternal law by which it is always just for a serious people to give honors and for a thoughtless people not to give them. Or does it seem otherwise to you?

E. No, I agree with you.

A. That I may give you briefly as concise as possible a verbal expression of the eternal law of which we have gained an impression, it is that it is just that all things be in the highest degree of order. If you think otherwise, tell me,

E. No, I agree with you.

A. Since, then, this is one law of which all those temporal laws for human government are variations, can it itself ever vary?

E. I do not think so. For no force, no accident, no stroke of misfortune has ever made it true that it is not just that all things be in the highest degree of order.[34]

In the *157th Epistle*, Saint Augustine identifies the law of God with the law of nature, which obtained before the Fall when man " was able to use his reason." The importance of this concept, as developed by Saint Augustine, is that natural law was instinctively known to primitive man and was inherited by all his descendants regardless of race. Thus we have a reversion not only to Origen's theory of natural law, but also to that of the Cynics, who likewise believed that no learning was required in order to know the teachings of nature. Moreover, the violation of this law could be committed by anyone, whether he had been lucky enough to receive the fruits of Revelation or not. For man, whether Barbarian, Hellene, or Jew, was man and equally a descendant of Adam. He might not be censured for breaking the laws of a nation which was not his, but he was justly punished for breaking the law which was a part of his nature as man, incorporated into his being by his Creator. In such places the appeal to Nature was an appeal to God. And inasmuch as the only uncorrupted and natural man was Adam before the Fall, the appeal to Nature is chronological primitivism. But in so far as Nature is known not by learning but by instinct, it is also, to a measure not realized by Saint Augustine himself, cultural primitivism.

> But what [Paul] adds to those words which we were discussing when he says, " Moreover the law entered, that the offence might abound," [*Rom.*, v, 20], does not now pertain to that sin which is inherited from Adam, of which he said earlier, " Death reigneth by one " [*Rom.*, v, 17]. For by " law " we understand either the natural law, which appeared in the time of those who were still able to use the reason, or the written law which was given through Moses, since it could not vivify in itself and liberate from the law of sin and death which was inherited from Adam, but added rather an increase of transgression. " For where no law is," says the same apostle, " there is no transgression " [*Rom.*, iv, 15]. In the same way, since the law is likewise in the reason of a man who actually uses his free will, being written by nature in his heart, by which it is commanded that he do nothing to another which he himself would not be willing to have done unto him, according to this law all are transgressors, even those who did not receive the law given through Moses, of whom it

[34] *De libero arbitrio*, I, vi [*MPL*, XXXII, pp. 1227-1229].

is said in the psalm, " All the sinners of the earth are weighed as transgressors " [35] [*Ps.*, cxix, 119]. For all the sinners of the earth did not violate the law given through Moses; but nevertheless if they had not violated some law, they would not have been called transgressors, " For where there is no law, there is no transgression." Therefore when the law which was given in Paradise was broken, man was born of Adam with the law of sin and death, of which it is said, " I see another law in my members, warring against the law of my mind, and bringing me into captivity to the law of sin which is in my members " [*Rom.*, vii, 23]. Yet if this were not fortified afterwards by evil habits, it would be more easily conquered, but not without the grace of God. But when the other law is broken, that which is in the use of the reason of a rational soul at the age when man uses his reason, all the sinners of the earth become transgressors. But when that law which was given through Moses has been broken, the offence is more fully abundant. " If there had been a law given which could have given life, verily righteousness should have been by the law. But the Scripture hath concluded all under sin, that the promise by faith of Jesus Christ might be given to them that believe " [*Galat.*, iii, 21, 22]. These words, if you know them, are apostolic. Of this law it is said once more, " It was added because of transgressions, till the seed should come to whom the promise was made; and it was ordained by angels in the hand of a mediator " [*Galat.*, iii, 19]. It commends us to Christ for Whose sake all are saved, both children from the law of sin and death with which we are born, or their elders, who, using badly their free will, break the natural law of their reason, or they who have received the law which was given through Moses and breaking it are cut down by its letter. But since by the teachings of the Gospel man transgresses, as a man four days dead stinks, yet one must not despair even of him, because of the grace of Him who said not slowly but " cried out with a loud voice, Lazarus, come forth " [*John*, xi, 43].[36]

2. *The simple life*

By the first century B. C. the ideal of self-sufficiency common to Stoic, Epicurean, and Cynic gave rise in all three schools to closely similar conceptions of the good life. Cicero spoke of the Stoics as " virtually Cynics "; Epictetus called his own ideal " 'Cynic " and frequently cited Diogenes; Juvenal sarcastically remarked that the Stoics differed from the Cynics " only by a tunic "—referring to the peculiar cloak which the school of Diogenes wore.[37] The Epicurean likewise practised a simplicity of living which, though it does not seem to have reached the extremes of self-denial

[35] The traditional English rendering does not follow the Latin closely enough to be quoted. We have therefore translated directly from Saint Augustine.

[36] *Epistle* 157, ch. iii, 15 [*MPL*, XXXIII, p. 681].

[37] See *PIA*, pp. 117 f. for a fuller discussion of this point and textual references. Cf. Farrand Sayre, *Diogenes of Sinope*, Baltimore, 1939, for a detailed analysis of the sources of Cynicism.

imputed to Diogenes, was nevertheless inspired by the same motives. These men differed less in their ways of living than in their metaphysics; there was little similarity between Lucretius's world of swerving atoms and Cleanthes's "ordered universe circling round the earth," but a consistent Epicurean and a consistent Stoic would have lived lives almost impossible to distinguish outwardly.

Similar remarks could be made about many of the early Christians and the Pagan moralists. Thus Justin Martyr, in spite of his debates with the Cynic, Crescentius, continued to wear the philosopher's cloak after his conversion.[38] And in appearance a monk in his soiled garments, with wallet and staff, was outwardly the double of any Cynic.[39] Julian the Apostate, for one, saw this and compared the two in his *Oration to Heraclius* [VII, 224 C]. And even Saint Basil, when he compares his love of poverty with that of Zeno and Diogenes, appears to be no more aware of the differences between the pagan ethical schools and Christianity, than he is of the different motivations of Stoicism and Cynicism.[40] He turns to pagan exemplars as naturally as he might be expected to turn to Biblical. He mentions the (probably) Epicurean notion of the "life in oblivion" as among the "primary values." [41]

By this time the philosopher's cloak had already been adopted by the Eastern monks and apparently many of its wearers thought it sufficient proof of saintliness, for the Synodal Letter of Gangra, written to the Bishops of Armenia in 340 A.D., condemns its use when it alone is held to confer righteousness.[42] But the Christians not only used the external marks of Philosophy, they also utilized the writings of Pagans to support their cause. So Eusebius inserted Oenomaus's book against the oracles in his *Praeparatio evangelica* [V, 19; VI, 7 ff.] and Renan cites the use of Epictetus's *Manual* by the Christian monks.[43] The former work was of course a case of Paganism testifying against itself; the latter, however, was used for the moral edification it might provide.

The recognized similarity between pagan and Christian ideals is most impressively shown in the legend of the friendship of Seneca and Saint Paul. Tertullian had already called Seneca *saepe noster*[44] and Lactantius had said that he would have been a worshipper of the true God, if anyone had taught him to be.[45] Since Saint Paul was preaching in Rome during Seneca's lifetime, it was easy enough to imagine that they had met and exchanged ideas. Yet this was apparently not thought of until the fourth

---

[38] See Eusebius, *Hist. eccl.*, IV, xi, 8. [40] See *Letter IV* [Deferrari].

[39] See Lucian's *Peregrinus*, 15. [41] *Letter* IX [Deferrari].

[42] See E. F. Morison, *St. Basil and his Rule*, Oxford, 1912, p. 147. The whole letter is interesting as a condemnation of extreme asceticism.

[43] See *L'Eglise Chrétienne*, 1879, p. 311, n. 4.

[44] *De anima*, 20.

[45] *Inst. div.*, iv, 24. It is curious that Lactantius did not mention the possibility that Saint Paul might have taught him.

century. As Boissier points out,[46] the primitive Church never thought of
seeking prestige by allying its doctrines with those of the learned world.
The accusations of Celsus, that only the dregs of society were Christian,[47]
were by no means denied by early Christians, but were admitted, and that
not in a spirit of self-depreciation, but of pride. The " dregs of society "
were after all the poor in spirit, the mourners, the meek, they who hunger
after righteousness, the persecuted, the reviled, in fact, most of those whom
Christ had blessed in the Sermon on the Mount. Tertullian, for his part,
preferred such simple souls who had not been spoiled by Academies.[48] But
this was not the attitude of fourth century Christians. Just as Constantine
turned to Vergil for a prophecy of Christ's birth,[49] so his contemporaries
turned to the great name of Seneca, and the Seneca-Paul letters would appear
to date from this period.[50] Even Saint Jerome, so hostile to the use of the
Fourth Eclogue as prophecy,[51] listed Seneca *in catalogo sanctorum*.[52] This
was in part the effect of Seneca's stoicism, so similar to Christianity in its
belief in the fatherhood of God and in the compelling force of duty, in part
the effect of his terminology.[53] But perhaps the best evidence that Christians
found the similarity between their own and pagan ideas striking, is the fact
that as late as Eusebius it was believed to be necessary to explain it away
by the device of making the Pagans plagiarists or pupils of Moses.[54]

The confusion was warranted by certain outstanding doctrines which

[46] *La religion romaine*, 1878, II, pp. 49 ff.

[47] Origen, *Contra Celsum*, III, 44.

[48] See *De testimonia animae*, I.

[49] Though earlier Christians may have used the *Fourth Eclogue* as prophecy,
Constantine's is the first name to be associated with this practice.

[50] We have seen that Lactantius does not appear to have been aware of these
letters, or even of the supposed friendship between the two men. We accept the
dates of Boissier, *Op. cit.*, II, 49 ff. The correspondence, trivial as it must seem in
content, had great fortunes in the following centuries. As late as 1853, Amedée
Fleury published a two volume work, *Saint Paul et Sénèque*, to prove that Seneca
was a Christian.

[51] See his attack on " garrulous old women " and " raving old men " who try to
teach the truths of Christianity by quoting such people as Vergil and Homer. *Quasi
non legerimus, Homerocentonas, et Virgiliocentonas: ac non sic etiam Maronem sine
Christo possumus dicere Christi anum. qui scripserit.Jam redit. etc.* See *Epist.*
LIII, 7 [*MPL*, XXII, p. 544]. Yet Saint Augustine in the fifth century utilized the
Fourth Eclogue in the *City of God* (X, 27), in *Epist.* cxxxvii, ch. 12 and *Epist.*
cclviii, ch. 5, and as late as Innocent III medieval writers continued to quote it.
See e. g., Innocent's *Sermon II* in *MPL*. CCXVII, p. 457. It was even used to convert
Marcellianus, *qui et ipse sapientissimus erat et Christianorum persecutor*, to Christi-
anity [*Acta Sanctorum*, II, pp. 407]. Jerome himself cites Cynics as moral exemplars
for Christians in *Adv. Jovinianum*, II, 12, 13, 14 [*MPL*, XXIII, pp. 315 ff.].

[52] *De viris illustr.*, 12.

[53] That Saint Paul was influenced by pagan rhetorical style, particularly that of
the Stoic-Cynic diatribe, has been pointed out by C. Toussaint in his *L'Hellénisme et
l'Apôtre Paul*, 1921, pp. 346 f.

[54] See *Praep. evan.*, VIII, xii, 4; IX, vi; XIII, xi, 1; XIII, xii, 13.

appeared to be common to both Christianity and Paganism. Saint Paul's battle between the flesh and the spirit was justification for Cynic asceticism; one who had read *Galatians* v, 16-24, might easily believe that the Pagan "who had not the law," yet instinctively knew it, had discovered an important ethical truth. *Colossians*, iii, 5, drew up a list of vices which almost any Stoic, Epicurean, or Cynic would also have condemned. The Cynic doctrine of poverty was paralleled by *Matthew*, xix, 24; *James*, iv, 13-14; v, 1-3; *I Timothy,* vi, 10. Indeed, the last of these references—the love of money is the root of all evil—is paralleled by a passage in the 50th letter of Pseudo-Diogenes, and Diogenes Laertius quotes the father of Cynicism as expressing the same sentiment as the Apostle, changing simply the word "root" to "mother-city."[55] This doctrine in Cynicism was accompanied by the practice of improvidence, and in the Sermon on the Mount, Christ Himself bids men to lay up treasures not on earth but in Heaven, to take no thought for the morrow, "for the morrow shall take thought for the things of itself." Paul, too, extols his freedom in a manner which, if it had been coarser, would recall Diogenes. "All things are lawful for me, but I will not be brought under the power of any" [*I Cor.*, vi, 12]; "Art thou called being a servant? care not for it: but if thou mayest be made free, use it rather" [*Ib.*, vii, 12]; "Though I be free from all men, yet have I made myself servant unto all, that I might gain the more" [*Ib.*, ix, 19]; "Stand fast therefore in the liberty wherewith Christ hath made us free, and be not entangled again with the yoke of bondage" [*Gal.*, v, 1]. Saint Paul, who of all the Apostles is the most learned in pagan thought, expresses a contempt for learning which is typical of some of the Cynics. In the first chapter of the first epistle to the Corinthians is the famous passage against the "wise," which, though in intention no more than a diatribe against them whose knowledge has not helped them to accept Christ, could easily be interpreted as a speech in praise of ignorance. Again, the "fools for Christ's sake" [*I Cor.*, iv, 10] might easily be mistaken for the Cynic Sage who turned away from reading lest he be corrupted by the ideas of others.[56]

Such texts give us a verbal picture of the Christian who is ascetic, poor in worldly goods, free even when enslaved by a terrestrial master, careless of the future, wise without learning. It is not to be wondered that such a person was confused with the pagan Sage of the "ethical period" nor that the monastic life was described as "the life of philosophy."[57]

Not only the theory of the Christian life, but the practice of monasticism was in its outer character primitivistic. When a hermit, the monk reminded one of Diogenes in his wine-jar; when a member of a community, he reminded one of the men of the Golden Age. Both reduced their wants to a minimum, thus attaining a kind of self-sufficiency, though the Christian, as

---

[55] *Vit. philos.*, VI, 50.
[56] Cf. *PIA*, pp. 132 f. and St. Bernard, pp. 124 f., below.
[57] See the two brief *Ascetic Discourses* attributed to Saint Basil.

distinguished from the Pagan, substituted " dependence upon God alone,"
for " dependence upon the self." Such resemblances are not proofs that the
Christian borrowed his ideas from the pagans, or that there was even more
than superficial similarities between the two sets of ideals. Saint Basil for
instance, describing the beauties of his retreat by the river Iris, and Tertullian showing the greatness of God in His works, both write like Seneca.
But Tertullian's admiration of the cosmic order was in reality a refutation of
the Gnostics, who believed that the physical world was the creation of an
inferior Deity. Saint Basil's appreciation of his retreat is based upon its
quietness, for only in complete quietness could he meditate. There is thus
in reality nothing of any importance which can be identified as paganism
in such passages. And yet the result of these and similar writings was to
inculcate a way of life which was almost identical with that of some of the
pagan cultural primitivists. We shall pass on now to some illustrations.

Pseudo-Clementina

The reduction of wants, common to both Cynicism and early Christianity,
was based upon different assumptions in each case. The Cynic reduced his
wants for the sake of self-assertion or independence; the Christian for the
sake of self-humiliation. The following passage from the Clementine
Homilies illustrates the outward similarity between the two views.

> Peter, hearing this, said with a laugh, " What are you thinking of,
> Clement? That by necessity itself I shall not reduce you to the
> position of a slave? For who will guard my fair and numerous
> garments with rings and foot-gear to match? And who will prepare
> the sweet and varied sauces which, being complicated, require many
> expert cooks, and all those things which are prepared for the appetite
> of effeminate men as for a great beast, provided out of superabun-
> dance? But if such a choice confronts you, perhaps you do not know
> and understand my life, that I eat only bread and olives and rarely
> vegetables—and that my wrap and cloak [58] are this very thing which
> is thrown about one nor have I any other, nor need I any others.
> For in these I have more than enough. For my mind, looking upon
> all the eternal goods over yonder, sees none of the things here below.
> But I am satisfied with your good choice and I praise you, wondering
> how a man born in luxury can so easily change his life for the bare
> necessities." [59]

Salvianus

It is in a similar spirit that Salvianus wrote of the truly Christian life.
Were it not for the Biblical texts, the following passage might well have been
written by a late Roman Stoic. It will be observed that the author, who

[58] The author here uses the word which had become symbolic of the Cynic
philosophers.

[59] *Homiliae*, XII, vi. Cf. *Recognitiones*, VII, 6. " Over yonder " and " here below "
became commonplace in Neo-platonism.

was known for pointing out the moral superiority of barbarians to Romans, does not hesitate to hold up the pagan Sage as a model to his fellow Christians. The primitivistic tone is especially clear in such a passage, though it should not be overlooked that the simple life is not praised for its own sake, but as a prelude to the rewards of an after-life.[60]

There is no reason whatsoever to grieve for these men, because they are not rich and happy and much less for the saints, because although they seem to the ignorant to be unhappy, they cannot be other than happy. It is unnecessary that anyone think them unhappy because of their weakness or poverty or other things of this sort, by which they themselves confess themselves to be fortunate; for no one is unhappy in the feelings of others, but only in his own. And therefore they who are really happy in their own consciousness cannot be unhappy because of the false judgment of anyone else. For none, I think, are happier than they who act in accordance with their own opinion and will. The religious are lowly; they will this. They are poor; they delight in poverty. They are without ambition; they spit ambition out. They are without honors; they flee from honors. They lament; they exult in lamentation. They are weak; they rejoice in their weakness. " For when I am weak," says the Apostle [*II Cor.*, xii, 10], " then I am strong." Not improperly does he so think to whom God Himself has said, " My grace is sufficient for thee: for my strength is made perfect in weakness " [*Ib.*, 9]. Therefore this affliction of weaknesses should not be cause for pitying us, this affliction which we believe to be the mother of the virtues. And so, whatsoever may be the case, they who are truly religious should be called happy, because amid whatsoever difficulties, whatsoever rough places, none are more happy than they who are what they wish to be. Although there are always some who are pursuers of shame and obscenity, even if they are happy in their own opinion, since they attain their will, yet in the thing itself they are not happy, because they will what they ought not to have willed. The religious, however, are on this account more happy than all, because they both have what they will and they could in no way have better things than those they have. And so toil and fasting and poverty and humility and weakness are not a burden to all who bear them, but only to those unwilling to bear them. For the mind of him who bears them makes them heavy or light. For just as nothing is so light that it is not heavy to him who does it unwillingly, so nothing is so heavy that it does not seem light to him who does it willingly. Unless perhaps we believe it to have been burdensome to those ancient men of pristine virtue, the Fabii, and Fabricii, the Cincinnati, that they were poor who did not wish to be rich, since they brought together all their zeal, all their efforts to the enrichment of the community and enriched the growing forces of the republic with their personal poverty. For did they sustain that niggardly and rustic life then

---

[60] Similar remarks might be made of Christian Horatian poetry in general. A good medieval example would be the *Rus habet in silva patruus meus* by Marbod of Rennes, 12th century, in *MPL*, CLXXI, p. 1665.

with groaning and pain, when they brought cheap and countrified foods before those hearths on which they cooked, and they were not permitted to partake of them before evening? Did they bear it ill that because of their stingy but rich conscience they did not coin golden talents, even when they restrained the use of silver by law? Did they think it the penalty of allurements and cupidity that they did not have pouches bursting with gold coins, when they judged that a patrician, because he wished to have the wealth of ten pounds of silver, unworthy of the curia? They did not then look down upon poor raiment, when they put on a short and shaggy covering, when they were summoned from the plough to the *fasces* and they who were to be glorified with consular robes wiped off perchance the dust matted with sweat from those very imperial robes which they were about to don. And so then those poor magistrates possessed a wealthy state, now on the contrary rich potentates make the state poor. And what madness is it, I ask, or what blindness that in a needy or beggared state men believe that private riches may stand? Such at that time were the ancient Romans and thus they despised riches, though ignorant of God, just as the followers of the Lord now spurn them. Yet why do I speak of them who in the interest of extending the empire turned their contempt of their own opportunities to the advantage of the commonwealth, and, although they were personally poor, yet increased to overflowing the common riches, since indeed certain Greek philosophers without any feeling of public utility stripped themselves of all use of their private property, by a thirst for gaining glory, and not only this, but raised the pinnacle of their teaching to the contempt of pain and death, saying that the Sage was happy even in chains and tortures. They wished virtue to have so great force that no good man could ever be unhappy. If now those men who took no fruits of their toil beyond the present praise, are not thought by some of our wise men to-day to have been unhappy, how much more ought the religious and saintly not to be thought unhappy, who receive the delights of the presence of faith and obtain the rewards of future blessedness! [61]

Saint Basil

Asceticism, which appeared earlier than monasticism, continued to be practised, after the organization of the *coenobia* in the fourth century, by many lay men and women who preferred to remain in the world, as the ideal life of a Christian. This is particularly true in the matter of the simple life and frugality. Saint Basil's directions to the monks regarding food, clothing, and other aspects of life, may contain details specifically intended for the monastic regimen, but they rest as a whole on arguments from authority and historical precedent so general in their import that they by implication might seem valid for every good Christian.[62] Moreover, views

---

[61] *De gubernatione Dei*, I, ii [Ed. Halm, pp. 4 f.].

[62] In *De renuntiatione saeculi*, 203 B, which, according to modern scholars, cannot be attributed with certainty to Saint Basil but which at any rate " hails from a Basilian monastery of early date," and has always been accepted as in the Basilian

of similar character are contained in Saint Basil's writings addressed to others than monks, as will be seen in several of the following passages.

In the twenty-second of his *Longer Rules*, the principles on which the practice of the simple life, and especially of asceticism, are primarily based, humility, and elimination of all interests conflicting with the soul's other-worldly aspirations, are reinforced by several considerations pertinent to our subject.   (a) The dress of the Christian should comply with mandates and examples similar to those of chronological primitivism: the first couple, after the sin, were given only coats of skin by the Creator [*Gen.*, iii] for the simple purpose of covering their shame, and the " saints of old " did wander about thus dressed.   (b) The use of clothes for any superfluous purpose, such as variety, show, daintiness, is against the original use which was designed by God; it is a later intrusion made by the " useless and vain arts "; there-fore, if, as Saint Basil reluctantly admits, covering from inclement weather is needed,[63] a single cloth should suffice for both decency and protection. (c) This minimum should be strictly adhered to, so that the rule of poverty [*aktemosyne*] should not be violated.   (d) A uniform dress should be a distinguishing mark of the true Christian's character, and should, moreover, aid the weaker brethren to remain faithful to their vows.

> The preceding discourse has shown that humility and frugality are necessary, as well as plainness and cheapness in everything, in order that occasions for distractions, which come from bodily needs, be kept down.   The same purposes then must be pursued in discussing dress . . . When the Apostle said, " Mind not high things, but condescend to men of low estate " [*Rom.*, xii, 16], let each one ask himself whom Christians should imitate more becomingly, those who live in palaces and are clothed in soft raiment, or the herald and messenger of the coming of the Lord, than whom no greater man born of woman has arisen, one named John, son of Zacharias, whose garment was of camel's hair.   And besides, the saints of old also " wandered about in sheepskins and goatskins " [*Hebr.*, xi, 37].   And as for the purpose of dress, the Apostle let it be understood by saying in our phrase, " And having food and raiment let us be therewith content " [*I Tim.*, vi, 8], because we only need it as cover, without falling, however, into the forbidden vanity of variety and daintiness, which comes from it, not to say anything worse.   For those crept into life later through the useless and vain arts.   It is clear what the first use of dress was,

---

tradition, the commands of the Gospels, including those prescribing renunciation of worldly cares and goods " have been laid down for all alike, and are fraught with danger for those who transgress them."   " Christ . . . was addressing men living in the world.   When once it happened that He was asked a question and answered His disciples in private, He testified saying, ' What I say unto you I say unto all.' [*Mark*, xiii, 37]."   From Clarke, *The Ascetic Works of Saint Basil*, p. 10.

[63] Extremes in weather and other imperfections of Nature are attributed by Basil to the Fall: *Reg. fusius tractatae*, lx, 397 A-D.   The ability of Socrates, the great exemplar of the Cynics, to withstand the weather and his simplicity of dress should be recalled in this connection.

which God Himself gave to the first couple who came to need it. For it is said: for them "did the Lord God make coats of skins" [*Gen.*, iii, 21]. For, indeed, such use of garments was sufficient to cover their shame. But since another purpose is added to it, that of being warmed by coverings, dress must have been desired for the use of hiding our shameful parts and of protecting us against the harm of inclement weather. Still, as among those same clothes, some are more useful, others less so, it is proper to prefer those which will carry us through more needs, so that the principle of poverty will not suffer in any way. Let not some be intended for show, and others for home use, or again some to be donned in daytime, and others at night, but let us design the possession of one such as may suffice for all our needs, both for modest covering during the day, and for protection needed during the night. From such arrangements there is added another result, that we share also in common the same kind of dress, and that a distinguishing character be placed upon the Christian from his garment. For those things which tend to one purpose, for the most part are the same towards one another.

And besides the peculiarity of dress is useful, as it announces each one and declares him a professor of life according to God. Therefore our way of living should be asked by people to conform to this profession. For what is unbecoming and shameful does not appear in the same light whether it is done by anyone at random, or by one who has promised great things . . . So that the profession of life through uniform dress serves as a discipline for the weaker brethren, as it forces them, even unwillingly, to abstain from evil actions.[64]

The Christian ideal has for Saint Basil a counterpart in the virtues chiefly expounded and practised by the Stoics and Cynics. In spite of manifest differences in the presuppositions and motives of the pagan and Christian ideals, differences which have been indicated above, Saint Basil, formed as he was in his youth by pagan Greek literature, and throughout his life imbued with its moral teachings, discovers essential resemblances between the two.[65] Since, moreover, the reading of the pagan classics still constituted a substantial part of the education of the Christian youth of the time, the Church had the problem of adapting it, so far as possible, to the inculcation of the Christian virtues. In his *Address to young men on how they might derive profit from pagan literature*, Basil seeks to furnish a guide to Christian youth in the study of the poets and moralists of pagan Greece, and to show them how to choose those parts which make for edification and to

---

[64] *Regulae fusius tractatae*, xxii [*MPG*, XXXI, p. 977].

[65] He studied for four or five years in the pagan schools of Athens, and kept afterwards in contact with pagan scholars, particularly with the celebrated rhetorican, Libanius. For a detailed study of his knowledge of pagan literature, as it is reflected in his writings, see Leo V. Jacks, *St. Basil and Greek Literature*, 1922, where further bibliographical details are to be found. Cf. also Roy J. Defarrari and Martin R. P. McGuire, preface to the *Address to Young Men*, in Deferrari's edition of Basil's *Letters*, IV, pp. 365 ff.; P. De Labriolle, *Histoire de la littérature latine chrétienne*, 1924, pp. 15-39.

shut their eyes to the rest. Under these conditions, he assigns a propaedeutic value to the writings of the Ancients, because they contain in more easily understandable language many of the hidden truths of the Scriptures, and he uses freely the *loci classici* of hard primitivism.[66]

Although Saint Basil's primary concern is otherworldly,[67] he also insists at times upon the value of hard and austere living, not far removed from that of a practising Cynic, as a means of attaining happiness in this world.

> But remembering the words of him who admonished that one should choose the life which is excellent by itself, and hope that it would become pleasant through habit, we should undertake what is best. For it would be shameful if, casting away the present opportunity, we should at some later time recall the past when all our suffering would avail us nothing.[68]

Hesiod's praise of the life of renunciation and hardship in the *Works and Days* (lines 287-292) is paraphrased as follows.

> What thought are we to suppose that Hesiod had in mind when he wrote the poems which everyone sings, other than that of exhorting young men to virtue? He says that the road which leads to it is rough at first, and difficult to tread, and full of abundant sweat and toil, and steep.[69]

He also sets up the Cynic hero, Hercules, as an exemplar, repeating at some length Prodicus's apologue, as given by Xenophon,[70] for Prodicus " was not a man to be disregarded." And finally, in dealing with the theme that we should liberate ourselves from all demands of the body except the bare necessities, Saint Basil invokes not only the Cynics' arguments but their very expressions.

> One should not, therefore, serve the body, unless it is strictly necessary. But one should provide his soul with what is best, setting it, through philosophy, free as from a prison from its bonds with the affections of the body; at the same time bringing the body to a state where it will have the upper hand over the passions; this is to be accomplished by serving the belly only with what is needed and not with what is most delicious, as is done by those who look everywhere

[66] The importance of this work in modern times is attested by the numerous editions and translations of it; the *editio princeps* of Leonardo Bruni's translation dates already from 1470-1471 and by 1500 nineteen known editions of this translation are reported. It continued to be frequently re-edited in subsequent centuries. See Deferrari, *op. cit.*, IV, pp. 371 f.

[67] *Address to young men*, ii [Ed. Deferrari, IV, p. 383] and elsewhere.

[68] *Address to young men*, x [Ed. Deferrari, IV, p. 432]. The opening saying is ascribed by Plutarch [*De exilio*, viii, 376] to the Pythagoreans. Cf. Deferrari, *op. cit.*, IV, p. 433, n. 2. The passage as a whole should be compared with *Letter II*, to Gregory.

[69] *Address to young men*, v [Ed. Deferrari, IV, p. 292].

[70] *Memorabilia*, ii, 1, 21. See *PIA*, p. 119.

for table-dressers and cooks, and scan land and sea, paying, as it were, tribute to a harsh master, pitiable in their absorption in such things. Their sufferings are not a whit more bearable than those of men under punishment in Hades, they are actually carding wool into fire, carrying water in a sieve, pouring water into a perforated jar, and they know no end in their toil. To waste one's labor on the hair and on dress beyond what is necessary is, according to Diogenes, characteristic of men who either are unfortunate or are evil-doers. Therefore I maintain that being and being called a fine dresser ought to be considered by such people just as shameful as associating with harlots or defiling another man's bed. For what difference does it make, at least to a wise man, whether he is attired in a costly robe of fine material or whether he is wearing a cheap common-people's cloak,[71] so long as it provides sufficient protection against the severe winter and the hot summer? Likewise in other matters, one should not contrive provisions for oneself beyond what need requires, nor should one show more solicitude for the body than is good for the soul.[72]

In the matter of food, vegetarianism and abstinence from wine are prescribed, but Basil argues here partly from the life of primeval man and partly from " Nature."

In general, just as it seems right to consider bare necessity in the matter of clothing, so in the matter of food bread will fill our needs, and water will take care of thirst for the healthy person, and whatever side-dishes of vegetable food there are can preserve in the body the forces necessary for his needs.[73]

Saint Basil however, in his ascetic zeal, goes further than the Cynics and, indeed, departs from one of their principles. Whereas they consider their mode of life as favorable to health and did not turn away from the gratification of bodily needs, but even accepted pleasure when accessible without effort, Saint Basil suppresses sexual desires, rejects pleasure, and looks with suspicion even on perfect health. He cites the tradition according to which " Plato, having in mind the harm which may come from the body, chose purposely a pestilential region of Attica, the Academy, so that excessive wellbeing of the body should be trimmed out, just as excessive growth of the vine is pruned away." He adds that he has heard physicians say that extreme good health is dangerous.[74] In his rules for the monks, however,

---

[71] Cf. *PIA*, p. 136. In the *Cynicus* the *tribonion* is the Cynic's cloak and in Synesius [4th or 5th century], *Letter 147* [Herscher, *Epistolographi graeci*, p. 730], it is the monks' habit. Synesius jokingly suggests to a friend of his that a white rather than a dark one would better fit an ascetic's life and character. We may point out that in Basil it represents, as a common symbol, the meeting place of pagan cynicism and Christian asceticism. Cf. *Regulae fusius tractatae*, xxii.

[72] *Address to young men*, ix [Ed. Deferrari, IV, pp. 414 f.]. Cf. also *Letter II.* to Gregory [Ed. Deferrari, *Letters*, I, pp. 20-22].

[73] *Letter II* [Ed. Deferrari, I, p. 22]. Cf. *De jejunio*, i, 5 [*MPG*, XXXI, p. 169], *Regulae fusius tractatae*, xix, 362 [*MPG*, XXXI, p. 968].

[74] *Address to young men*, ix (182 D).

the use of medicine is allowed, provided that sickness is considered as a trial sent by God and the cure credited mainly to prayers said for recovery.[75]

The Culdees

Western monasticism, as described by the rule of Saint Benedict, does not seem to-day particularly " hard," but there were in Ireland and Scotland a group of monks, popularly known as Culdees, who apparently practised a more extreme asceticism. Much of their early history is still unknown but there is a fairly early account of the life of these monks in a manuscript reprinted by Migne presumably from Brockie's unpublished *Monasticon Scoticum* (1730-1750).[76] It is a life devoted to work and prayer; food is cut down to a minimum, speech is reduced, work horses and oxen are replaced by the monks themselves, private property is unknown, and even communal property limited to the necessary. The author, interestingly enough, believes this to have been also the life of the Egyptian hermits; it was in reality more like that of the Essenes.

> Serf, disciple of Saint Palladius, about the year 448 built the monastery of Culross, and there he assembled a great congregation of monks, whom he guarded in the fear of God and in great continence. They were called by the common people Culdeans or Colideans, but were properly called Kiledeans, so named from the cells which they lived in.[77] And they were true monks, imitating the monks of Egypt and leading a life like theirs. For in the first place, they kept a perpetual fast, eating but once a day, in the winter time when the stars appeared in the firmament, in summer, however, after sunset. This meal among them was called " supper " and they did not put upon the table dishes of various savors nor the more succulent foods, but according to the number of the company so many loaves of bread and cooked vegetables, seasoned only with salt. Never did they eat flesh or fish, nor did they permit cheese or butter, except on Sundays and feast days, when they ate two meals, breakfast and supper. For drink they had pure water, sometimes mixed with milk, for wine and beer were unknown among them. Yet the infirm or those bowed down by age, or wearied by a long journey, were given the pleasure

---

[75] *Regulae fusius tractatae*, lv. In the monasteries a dilemma arose: should failing of physical forces arising from abstinence be left to interfere with the work assigned, or should the work not be allowed to interfere with abstinence? Basil reluctantly adopts a middle position, but insists that both work and eating should be done for the glory of God. See *Regulae brevius tractatae*, 139. At any rate fasting for the sake of vainglory is condemned. Much of what has been said above concerning the similarity between Saint Basiil's view and those of the Cynics could also be said of those of Saint Gregory of Nyssa. See his *De oratione dominica*, Oratio IV [*MPG*, XLIV, p. 1169]; *Ib.*, p. 1172; and *De pauperibus amandis*, I [*MPG*, XLVI, j. 456]. The last reference particularly insists on the necessity of one's inner disposition's conforming to ascetic practices.

[76] See *MPL*, LIX, p. 562, footnote, and *Nova acta eruditorum*, 1751, pp. 620-624.

[77] This is, of course, fanciful. The Culdees were early Irish monks whose name probably meant *servus Dei*. See art. *Culdee* in Hastings.

of a blander food, though they never ate meat. At table they observed a deep silence, intent upon the divine reading and exhortations of their spiritual father, and in this way they eased their weary joints during the eating of the supper they were given, yet never to the point of satiety. For too great satiety, although only of bread, begets lust, but there in accordance with the unequal condition of their bodies or ages each could take his meal.

All slept in one place but in separate beds, and clothed and girt with a belt of skins that when aroused they might leave their beds more eagerly . . .

[After their prayers and personal toilet] all made ready to work in the monastery or the fields, so that sweating by the daily work of their hands, they might pass their lives in common toil, knowing well that carefree rest and leisure are the mother and nurse of the vices, and therefore they bent their shoulders to divine fatigue; and with great zeal they worked with foot and hand, and so with their own individual force they carried out the work of the whole congregation with joy. For girt for their works in the fields, they put the yoke upon their shoulders and dig their spades [78] and mattocks into the earth with invincible arms, and they bear the hoes and scythes for mowing in their sacred hands and perform with their own labor everything which farmers are accustomed to perform with the help of oxen and horses. For they had not a single ox or horse or other animal for cultivating their fields, or for doing any work whatever, for each was ox or horse for working. Only the litte old abbot had a pony for traveling and a few cows for milk, and similarly they kept some sheep for their wool and skins, for all other possessions they spurned, and they detested riches. When the farming lasted too long, then they sang the accustomed portions of the Psalms in the fields, having observed the due time for each canonical hour, intent upon this, that day by day they might in their devotions recite the whole Psalter. When, however, they were working, not the slightest murmur was heard, no unnecessary talk was held, but each, either praying or in right thinking, performed his allotted task . . .

[After evening tasks in the monastery] they came to table that they might refresh their tired limbs by food, though they paid more attention to the spiritual reading than to the taste of the dishes. Indeed, the whole refreshment consisted in no viands other than common bread flavored with salt, as has been already said. When they had moderately eaten, they sought the oratory with action of grace and pouring forth of prayers for a short time, at a given signal, and when the blessing of their spiritual father was given, they all went to the dormitory, old as well as young, according to the cloistral order, and no murmur of voices was heard, but they kept silent until the first crowing of the cock . . .

They especially cultivated poverty, nor did they have any possessions other than what they could make with their own hands. Hence they despised the gifts of the wicked; they detested riches. If, how-

---

[78] We are guessing that " spades " is the meaning of *sustossoria*. It would appear **to** be unknown to lexicographers.

ever, someone of the great of the earth wished to give them something as alms, they distributed it at once to the poor, to whom they gave also the offerings of the faithful. For they had in the neighborhood an asylum where they fed the poor and weak, the lame and the blind, the aged and the orphans, who were the special care of Saint Serf. He gave them all the necessaries and helped them with pious exhortations.

They were dressed in cheap clothes, particularly in skins, but white in color that they might appear to shine in both their habits and their clothing . . . Thus among those ancient monks or Kildeans shone a perfect probity of manners, a life of poverty, perpetual continence in all their deeds, as well as unfailing obedience to the commands of their spiritual father . . . These and more difficult and painful things did those ancient Kildeans perform, whose rigorous discipline, although necessary for those who would do as they did, the brevity of our account which we have proposed forbids us to expound. But they imitated the Egyptian monks in all things and led a life like theirs.[79]

Alain of Lille

When we come to the twelfth century, we find once more sentiments which might have been written by Pagans, sometimes quoted in the very words used by their ancient authors. Alain of Lille in his treatise on preaching writes a paragraph in which the familiar Biblical passages are missing and in which Nature assumes the role which she had played in the Cynics.

Consider how much Nature demands, not how much the palate desires. If you have been continent, you will arrive at the point of being content with yourself. For he who is sufficient unto himself . has been born in a state of bliss. Check concupiscence. Cast off all things which allure the mind with flattery and pleasure; stop eating before you reach satiety, drinking before you reach drunkenness, reduce your wants a little, for you ought to care only that they may cease. Yield to food, not to pleasure; let hunger excite your palate, not flavor. Let your poverty never be foul, nor your thrift sordid, nor your simplicity negligence, nor your lightness laziness. Do not bewail your own fate nor wonder at another's . . .[80]

The rest of the passage is a eulogy similar in tone upon the golden mean. The authority for it is Seneca's, not the Bible's; its purpose the life in accordance with Nature, not the life of penance. Such a shift of emphasis

---

[79] Anon; *Ordo monasticus in veteri Scotiae monasterio de Kil-Ros olim observatus*, *MPL*, LIX, pp. 563-568. Though this is dated from the 5th century by Migne, such a date is impossible. The monastery, even if founded by Saint Serf, could not have existed before the seventh century. The reference to " canonical hours " would date it from the sixth century at the earliest. But the monks described are called *antiquos*, which would certainly not be a qualification of one's contemporaries or recent forebears.

[80] *Summa de arte praedicatoria*, ch. xxv [*MPL*, CCX, p. 161].

indicates a reviving interest in pagan writers, for however much a Christian might have praised deportment which a Pagan too would have praised, he would in general have felt the need of ascribing Biblical sources to his ideas and of evaluating the acts which he discussing by a Christian standard. This paganizing tendency is seen throughout Alain's work. Thus when he is discussing poverty, he says, " If you live in accordance with Nature, you will never be poor; if in accordance with opinion, never will you be rich. Nature desires very little, opinion very much. Natural desires are limited, those born of false opinion have no stopping place." [81]   He does not say, " If you follow the commands of God, you will never be poor." Moreover, the emphasis upon the middle way is not characteristically Christian. In fact, one of the distinctions of early Christian thought was its extremism. Half-way measures were not tolerated, whence the advocacy of virginity, monastic poverty, self-abnegation of all types. But in Alain the middle way is so important that the incarnate Christ is described as midway between earth and sky:

> In terris humanus erit, divinus in astris.
> Sic homo, sicque Deus fiet, sic factus uterque
> Quod neuter, mediaque via tutissimus ibit.[82]

Alain apparently sees no more incongruity in making Christ the " mirror of nature " than in attributing to her Apollo's advice to Phaeton. It was this novel tone which may be accountable for his popularity and influence, which are to be seen in the *Roman de la Rose*, in the *Divine Comedy*, and in the *Parlement of Foules*.

Peter Cantor

The same use of pagan authorities is found in Peter Cantor, a contemporary of Alain, whose *Verbum Abbreviatum* [83] resembles the anthologies of Stobaeus. The chapter on poverty (ch. xvi, *MPL*, CCV, p. 65 f.) is a simple collection of Biblical passages such as *Luke*, vi, 20 and *Matthew*, viii, 20, supplemented by long quotations from Seneca's *Epistles* (cx, iv, and ii). One of the most interesting features of this work is this method of bringing pagan and Biblical authorities into harmony. For it is not likely that one should do this except as an apology for the study of the classics or as proof of the universality of Biblical truths or because one has become so habituated to reading the Pagans that the propriety of using them is simply not questioned. We have no reason to explain the *Verbum abbreviatum* on the first two grounds. The third is more likely. But if it is held, we must conclude that an appeal to pagan authorities would not be considered inappropriate

---

[81] *Ib.*, vi [*MPL*, CCX, p. 123]. Cf. Antisthenes's speech, translated in *PIA*, p. 126.
[82] *Anticlaudianus*, I, vi [*MPL*, CCX, p. 492].
[83] The title comes from *Romans*, ix, 28, *Verbum enim consummans, et abrevians in aequitate: quia verbum breviatum faciet Dominus super terram.*

in the Cantor's time and that his interpretation of Biblical verses was modified by his reading of pagan philosophy.

Thus discussing "superfluous and highly decorated [*curiositatem*] clothing, foods, and buildings," [84] he quotes *I Timothy*, vi, 8, " Having food and raiment, let us be therewith content" and remarks that the Apostle says, " food " and not " pleasure " [*oblectamenta*], " raiment " and not " ornaments." Quoting *I Corinthians*, ix, 13, " They which wait at the altar are partakers with the altar," he notes that the Apostle writes *vivat*, not *lasciviat*. Should a modern reader wonder why the Cantor should have found any problem in this choice of words, he is answered by the rest of the chapter, which is a quotation from Seneca's *60th Epistle*, followed by Boethius's verses on the Golden Age.

Guigo, the Carthusian

More typically Christian is a letter of Guigo, the Carthusian, who lived into the first third of the twelfth century. This letter is addressed to the monks of Mons Dei and extols poverty. He recalls to his readers their hermit ancestors, with their life of hard work and abstinence. He is obviously impressed by the communism of the primitive Church and the sacrifice of possessions. Yet, as was fitting for a Christian, the motive is self-humiliation, an acknowledgment of our complete dependence on God, rather than an appeal to conform to Nature.

> You who are spiritual men, like the Hebrews—that is, nomads, having no permanent city here but seeking a future home—build for yourselves, as you have begun to do, tabernacles in which you may dwell. For in tabernacles dwelt our fathers, living in the Land of Promise as in a foreign country, awaiting with their fellow heirs of the promise a city which hath foundations whose builder and maker is God, not having received the things promised but seeing them from afar and being persuaded of them and confessing that they are strangers and pilgrims on earth. For he who says this signifies that he is seeking a better country, that is, a heavenly [*Hebrews*, xi, 9-16]. Therefore our fathers in Egypt and the Thebaid [were] most ardent followers of this holy life, dwelling in deserts, most circumscribed and wretched, of whom the world was not worthy. They built cells for themselves in which, barely roofed over and sheltered, they used to be protected from storm and rain, in which, rich in the delights of a hermit's frugality, they, though in need themselves, enriched many. By what name I might more worthily call them I do not know, celestial men or terrestrial angels, living on earth but having communion with the heavens. They worked with their hands and they fed the poor by their labor; hungry themselves, they nourished out of the wastes of the desert those who had escaped from the urban prison and the weak, and they sustained them, however needy they might chance to be, living by their labor and by the work of their hands.

[84] *Verb. abbrev.*, ch. lxxxii.

What shall we say to this, who are not animate but animals, clinging to earth and to our carnal senses, walking in carnal sensuality and depending on the labor of others? Although He may console us for this in some measure, Who in spite of His riches made Himself poor for our sakes [*II Cor.*, viii, 9], and Who set the example of voluntary poverty, He Himself deemed it worthy to show us the form of poverty in Himself. For in order that the poor Evangelists might know their duty, He Himself wished to be fed by the faithful and sometimes, but only in order to bring them to the faith, He did not refuse to accept the necessities of life from infidels. But even in the primitive Church those holy poor who had endured for Christ's sake the theft of their goods, or according to the counsel of perfection had abandoned and sold all their possessions and shared them with their brothers in the faith, with how great solicitude, with how great piety the Holy Apostles preached that they be fed by the faithful, both the book of the Acts of the Apostles and Paul in his Epistles clearly show. But if it will be conceded more freely, though the Lord prescribes and ordains this very thing, that the announcers of the Gospel so live according to the Gospel, yet it is not denied by the authority of the Apostles, even to those living according to the Gospel, as those holy poor who then were in Jerusalem; for they were called the holy poor for this reason, that they had enlisted in the profession of sanctity and of a common life and had made themselves poor of their own free-will [*Luke*, xviii, 22; *Acts,* ii, 44, 45; iv, 34, 35; *Rom.*, xv; *I Cor.*, ix; *II Cor.*, viii]. When the Apostle by his most severe authority declares to certain men that he who will not work must not eat, to show at once of whom he is speaking, he adds the words, " For we hear that there are some which walk among you disorderly, working not at all, but are busybodies. Now them that are such we command and exhort by our Lord Jesus Christ that with quietness they work, and eat their own bread " [*II Thess.*, iii, 11, 12]. " Their own," that is, that which was prepared and acquired by their own labor. And yet, lest he might seem to have turned out and rejected, as it were, those, though disorderly, working not at all, and busybodies, yet having the name of the Lord called down upon them, he immediately raises them up, saying, " But ye, brethren, be not weary in well doing in Christ Jesus our Lord " [*Ib.*, 13]. As if he were saying, " And if they persevere in their evil-doing, or in their negligence, do you nevertheless be not weary in sustaining them by your benefactions."

Since, therefore, he had commanded earlier in most severe terms that those who are unwilling to work should not eat, but later to those who are willing to work yet do nothing, he has shown himself somewhat more kindly, we can say according to the text of his words— nor does he stray from the truth—that his severity was meant for those not willing though able; his indulgence for those willing though not able. But since he commands and beseeches even them in the Lord Jesus Christ to eat their bread with quietness, they seem not to eat their own bread, unless they make it theirs by working in so far as they can work by the witness of God and their conscience. Forgive us, Lord, forgive us. We make excuses, we tergiversate, but he does not exist who can hide from the light of Thy truth; for just as it illuminates the converted, so it strikes the averted . . .[85]

c. *The vanity of the arts and sciences*

The doctrine that the desire for a certain kind of knowledge was the ultimate cause of man's downfall, the companion doctrine that Adam before the Fall was intellectually an infant, as well as the interpretation of Nature and its laws as the instinctive rather than the acquired, all combined, or might have been expected to combine, to produce a kind of religious anti-intellectualism in some of the Christians. As the Cynic sometimes maintained that human beings had only to follow the light of nature in order to achieve personal *autarky*, so the Christian at times turned away from the impedimenta of civilization to the innocence of childhood.

Yet, when one considers the criticism leveled against the Church as the instrument of ignorance and the disparager of knowledge, one finds that the anti-intellectualistic tradition in Catholic Europe was surprisingly weak. Aside from the better known, and often misinterpreted, documents which will be cited below, there is nothing outstanding in religious literature which would justify such criticism. The Christian perhaps ought to have been an anti-intellectualist if he had decided to be consistent with certain Biblical texts and ecclesiastical practices, but the fact remains that he usually was not.

Tertullian

The Greek fathers, immersed as they were in Athenian philosophy, were less inclined to disparage the arts and sciences than their Latin colleagues. Tertullian is especially noted for a supposed antipathy to rationality. But it may very well be that this famous Father maintained simply that man could not completely humiliate himself before God, so long as he retained his reasoning powers. The belief in the absurd is a belief in the Incarnation and Resurrection, and the words, so frequently quoted, " *Certum est quia impossibile est,*" and *Prorsus credibile est quia ineptum est,*[86] may be taken as a sacrifice of human reason analogous to the sacrifices demanded by the vows of chastity and obedience. When one refers this back to the doctrine that Adam was an infant and forward to the *docta ignorantia*, one realizes that, however submerged it may have been throughout the centuries, nevertheless this type of anti-intellectualism had a long and influential history. But when it springs from a deep-seated contempt of self and when from an impatience with the rules of logic, it is next to impossible to say.[87]

---

[85] *Epistle to the Brothers*, xiii [*MPL*, CLX XIV, pp. 332 f.]. For the Gospel of Work in ancient cynicism, see *PIA*, p. 122, 131.

[86] *De carne Christi*, 5.

[87] This type of anti-intellectualism runs parallel to that of the Wise Fool in folklore and literature. It would take us too far afield to attempt to trace the ramifica-

Gregory the Great

Thus Gregory, in the much quoted dedicatory epistle to his *Moralia*, when he denies that the words of the " celestial oracle "—that is, the Holy Ghost— can be bound by the rules of Donatus, may be simply refusing to take the trouble to write grammatically and in traditional style. He was, after all, the Pope; he had tremendous demands upon his time; his business was primarily religious and he may have seen no reason why that which distracted him from his religious duties was to be taken even seriously.[88] But at the same time he had a genuine contempt for the pride that comes from learning and for those " who revere more the talents of the learned than the simple life of the innocent." [89]

Pope John XIII

A similar type of anti-intellectualism appears in the words of another Pope, John XIII, who living under Theodora and Marozia knew intimately the pleasures of ignorance. When the synod of Gallic bishops meeting in Rheims in the tenth century protested against the ignorance of the Vatican, His Holiness replied through Leo, the Apostolic Legate, " The vicars of Peter and his disciples refuse to take as their masters either Plato or Vergil or Terence or the crowd of philosophers who, flying high like birds have described the air, or diving deep like fish the sea, or grazing like cattle the earth. From the beginning of the world God has not chosen orators and philosophers, but men without either letters or polish." [90] This was but the echo of a philosophy; it would be absurd to see more in it. And yet it was an echo of notes which were to be struck again by more serious hands, when learning itself had increased.

Saint Anselm

In the meantime Saint Anselm who was far from being a *rusticus* wrote some lines which repeat the words and sentiments of John XIII as if they were a literary commonplace.

> And Christ rewards the just, not the philosophers. You are a farmer: be just and you will be happy. Varro was a philosopher, Peter a fisherman. And lo, Peter dwells in heaven; Tartarus holds Varro captive.[91]

---

tions of the latter, but a study by Enid Welsford, *The Fool, His Social and Literary History*, London, 1935, with its full bibliography and notes, provides much of the necessary information.

[88] Cf. his *Epist.*, xi, 54, to the Bishop of Venice [*MPL*, LXXVII, p. 1171].

[89] *Moralia*, xxiii, ch. 4 [*MPL*, LXXVI, p. 257].

[90] Translated from the Latin as given in Gregorovius's *History of the City of Rome*, Eng. tr., London, 1903, Vol. III, p. 498. Cf. St. Bernard, p. 124, below.

[91] *De contemptu mundi*, 701 C [*MPL*, CLVIII, p. 687].

Bernard of Clairvaux

It was not until the twelfth century that pious anti-intellectualism reached its height. Saint Bernard put intellectual curiosity into the same category as Eve's sin. There is a kind of knowledge—self-knowledge—which he believes to be of fundamental importance, but it is to be found entirely within the human soul. Let one but look abroad and one will fall not only into error, but also into sin. One cannot always tell whether he is attacking sensual or intellectual curiosity, but the following text would seem to put them both in the same class.

> The first degree of pride is curiosity. You may know it by these marks. If you see a monk in whom you previously had confidence, who in his standing and walking and sitting begins to let his eyes wander, to carry his head erect and ears alert, you may know from the fact that a wicked man winketh with his eyes, speaketh with his feet, teacheth with his finger [*Prov.*, vi, 13]. And from the insolent motions of his body one can apprehend that a new disease has fallen upon his soul, which, as he grows slack in self-scrutiny, his carelessness of his own affairs makes curious about others. For since he does not know himself, he goes abroad to feel his kids [*Cantic.*, i, 7]. Rightly should I call his eyes and ears his kids, which symbolize sin; for just as death entered the world through sin, so it enters the mind through these windows. Thus in feeding these is the curious man occupied, while he cares not to know what sort of self he has abandoned within. And in truth, man, if you reach inward vigilantly towards yourself, it will be astonishing that you ever again reach outward towards anything else. Hear, man of curiosity, the word of Solomon; hear, fool, the Sage. "Keep thy heart," he says, "with all diligence," [*Prov.*, iv, 23], that all thy senses may vigilantly keep guard over that out of which are the issues of life. For whither do you withdraw from yourself, man of curiosity? To whom do you commit yourself while withdrawn? How do you dare raise your eyes to heaven, you who have sinned against heaven? Look rather upon earth, that you may know yourself. She will show you to yourself, for you are earth and will return to earth. . . .
>
> You . . . Eve, were set down in Paradise to work and tend it with your husband. If you had carried out the commandment, you would have gone on to a better place where there would have been no need for you to be occupied in any work whatsoever, nor to be worried with keeping guard. Every tree of the Garden was given you to eat, save only that which is called the tree of the knowledge of good and evil. If the others are good and taste good, what need is there to eat of the tree whose very taste is bad? "One should know no more than one ought to know" [*Rom.*, xii, 3].[92] For to know evil is not to know but to be void of knowledge.[93] Therefore, keep what

[92] The Vulgate does not follow literally the Greek Testament at this point. St. Bernard's point would be lost, if we quoted the English Bible, which follows the Greek.

[93] We have made no effort to reproduce the punning on *sapere* and its derivatives with their double meaning of "to taste" and "to know."

is committed to you, await what is promised; fear the forbidden, lest you lose the conceded. Why do you consider your death so intently? Why do you cast roving eyes so repeatedly upon it? What pleasure is there in gazing upon forbidden fruit? I stretch forth my eyes, you say, not my hand. I am not forbidden to look but to eat. . . Even if it is not a fault, yet it is the occasion of a fault, and the sign of one committed and the cause of committing one. For with you intent on other things, the serpent slips quietly into your heart, gently speaks . . . Finally he offers what is forbidden and snatches away what is permitted; he holds out the apple and carries Paradise away . . .

You too, the seal of God's likeness, were set down not in Paradise but in the delights of God's garden [*Ezekiel*, xxviii, 12, 13]. What more ought you to ask? Full of wisdom, perfect in beauty, seek nothing higher than yourself, search for nothing stronger. Remain within yourself lest you fall from your heights, if you walk in the high places and among the marvels which are above you . . .[94]

This passage in itself might not be conclusive evidence of doctrinal anti-intellectualism, but it can be reinforced with others. Among them is one which is peculiarly interesting in that it admits the necessity of self-knowledge and knowledge of God, but insists that they may be acquired without technological or scientific training. He is thus clearly in the tradition of Tertullian as cited above and seems indeed to be quoting the words of some of its members.

You are not unaware that we proposed to-day to speak on ignorance, or rather on the kinds of ignorance, for, if you remember, two kinds were suggested, one of ourselves, the other of God, which, we also advised you, were both to be shunned, since both are to be condemned. That I may make this clearer, it remains to go into it at greater length. But first I think we should ask whether all ignorance is to be condemned. And I believe it is not. For not all ignorance damns a man, but there are many, indeed countless things, which one may be ignorant of without lessening one's chance of salvation. For example, if you are ignorant of the mechanical arts, carpentry or masonry and whatever other arts there are of this kind, which men engage in for the utility of this present life, how would that impede one's salvation? One may even be ignorant of all those arts which are called liberal—however much they may be taught and engaged in for nobler and more useful studies—for very many men have been saved without them, because they were satisfactory in their morals as well as their deeds. They are enumerated by the Apostle in his *Epistle to the Hebrews*, and were beloved by the Lord, not because of their knowledge of letters, but because of their pure conscience and unfeigned faith [*Hebr.*, xi]. All were pleasing to God in their life, in the merits of their life not of their knowledge. Peter and Andrew and the sons of Zebedee and all their fellow disciples were not taken from the schools of rhetoricians and philosophers, and none the

---

[94] *De gradibus humilitatis et superbiae*, ii, 10 [*MPL*, CLXXXII, p. 957].

less the Savior through them wrought salvation upon the earth. Not in wisdom, which in them was more than in all the living . . . but in their faith and meekness did He save them and make them saints and masters. Finally, they made known to the world the ways to life and that not in the sublimity of their speech or in the learned words of human wisdom, but as it pleased God by the foolishness of their preaching He saved them who believed, for the world in its wisdom did not know Him [*I Cor.*, i, 17, 21; ii, 1].

Helinandus

The same emphasis upon self-knowledge as a prerequisite to salvation is found in Helinandus, whose classical background was richer than that of many of his fellows. He, too, feels that one can know oneself without knowing much of anything else, so that, though the word "knowledge" is used by him in the name which he gives to the highest good, it means something so different from what it usually means, that Helinandus may without injustice be classified with the anti-intellectualists. The quotation from Juvenal in the passage below is particularly significant, for Juvenal, when in the mood which inspired the *Eleventh Satire*, was a staunch admirer of the Cynic's way of life.

> In Delphi it is said that there was once inscribed upon the ancient tripod of Apollo a very well-known oracle, given to one who had come to ask the god how he might attain felicity, *gnothi seauton*, i. e., *Know thyself*. One should not believe that Apollo was the author of this expression, nor even its discoverer, but rather its thief. For he stole it from where it is at present. It is the same thing to know oneself as to look upon one's face. But surely that is meant in the passage of the *Song of Songs* wherein it is said, "If thou know not thyself, O thou fairest among women, go thy way forth, etc." [*Cant.*, i, 8].[95] Now this expression or rather this theft of Apollo, our satirist Juvenal calls a divine and heavenly phrase because of the great utility contained in it. For he says,

> > " Whip me the fool, who marks how Atlas soars
> > O'er every hill on Mauritania's shores,
> > Yet sees no difference 'twixt the coffer's hoards
> > And the poor pittance a small purse affords!
> > Heaven sent us, ' Know thyself.' " [96]

Which is to say, Foolish is science and stupid is the knowledge of superfluities when necessities are unknown. For what does it profit a man to know how to measure the world and to be ignorant of

---

[95] The English Bible reads simply, "If thou know not, O thou fairest, etc."; the Vulgate, "Si ignoras te, O pulcherrima." Helinandus's Latin which is not from the Vulgate, is in literal correspondence with the Septuagint. The Hebrew text is ambiguous, for though it might authorize the *te*, yet the pronoun, we are informed, might be merely a dative of reference.

[96] Translation by William Gifford, 1802.

himself? Apart from this knowledge, nothing is useful to mortals, nothing can save mankind. This is the primal necessity and it is enough if it alone exist. For it teaches man to fear God, to beware of sin, to love his neighbor, to despise earthly things and to love heavenly.[97]

The Venerable Guibertus

In the Venerable Guibertus the *cultus ignorantiae* becomes a revulsion against all " external " and practical knowledge, a submission of one's will and intellect to God. Guibertus attributes this sacrifice of personal reason to Saint Paul's teachings, which in his eyes induce a man to believe in religious dogmas not in spite of their illogicality but because of it. One may argue that this is not anti-intellectualism, but merely anti-utili-tarianism. Nevertheless the kind of knowledge which one attains through " divine folly " is not that demonstrable through the usual intellectual pro-cesses, but that known through an inner light which is closely allied to " the law of Nature." We do not argue that it is identical with it for the obvious reason that the place which Nature and Faith occupied in the lives of the men who appealed to them were by no means the same. No Cynic would live the life of a twelfth century mystic, however indiscernible were the systematic differences which their fundamental concepts displayed.

" And he said, Lord, wilt thou also slay a righteous nation? Said he not unto me, She is my sister? and she, even she herself said, He is my brother " [*Genesis*, xx, 4, 5].

Our stubborness touched by the fear of the Lord, is restrained and broken against itself. It is restrained, I say, when it withdraws from worldly wisdom, which seeks only praise and utility, and what is distributed in the outer world, to a confession of happy ignorance which justice brings about. When he said, Lord, whatever I knew presumptuously, I have breathed out when you inspired me, and like the Apostle I wish to be made a fool for Christ's sake [*I Cor.*, iv, 10] that by the cult of this ignorance, which is, however, of worldly things, I may share in the supernal wisdom which is the height of justice, when, I say, I shall have done this, shall I not, ignorant in this way, and thus just at last, deserve to be slain by Thee, Who art justice? For if I have been wanting and do not disavow my fault, this befalls me from the confusion of my mind wherein neither the intellect prevailed nor was the will ready, but rather not only had it become like the reason by a certain unworthy brotherhood, but the reason contrariwise was too subservient to it. " In the simplicity of my heart and innocence of my hands have I done this." " Sim-plicity " is commonly used for " folly," but if, he says, I have fallen into error in the dullness of my heart, that is, of my reason, yet have I a clean hand with Thee preventing me from doing a vile deed.[98]

---

[97] *De cognitione sui*, ii [*MPL*, CCXII, p. 723].
[98] *Moralia in Genesim*, VI, vers. 5 [*MPL*, CLVI, p. 157].

The Venerable Hildebert

The utilitarian nature of *scientia* appears clearly in some lines from a sermon by the Venerable Hildebert.

> *Scientia* is the lower part of the reason by which men can correctly manage their earthly affairs and secular business, and arrange to live rightly in this depraved world which everyone knows to be mortal.[99]

Innocent III

But the culmination of this tradition, as far as the Middle Ages are concerned, is to be found in Innocent III. His *De contemptu mundi,* with its famous passage on the superiority of even plants to man, contains a diatribe on knowledge which was to find its modern echo in certain of the Renaissance sceptics. A new strain resounds in this passage and completes the cycle of thought which begins in Greek cynicism. Pleading for a rejection of riches and even of necessaries, the Pope makes no appeal to the need of self-abnegation, of humility before God, of sacrifice. The plea is simply that of Diogenes, that unnecessary things cause more trouble than they are worth. What is worth while is peace of mind which, though it could only be attained through God, was nevertheless precisely what the Cynics and most other pagan moralists had desired above all else.

> Let scholars scrutinize, let them investigate the heights of heaven, the stretches of the earth, the depths of the sea, and let them dispute over each particular, and explore whole subjects, let them spend their time in learning and teaching. For what shall they discover from this occupation but labor and pain and affliction of spirit? He knew this by experience who said, "I gave my heart to know wisdom, and to know madness and folly: I perceived that this also is vexation of spirit. For in much wisdom is much grief: and he that increaseth knowledge increaseth sorrow" [*Eccl.,* i, 17, 18]. For although the investigator ought both to sweat at his many vigils and to spend wakeful nights in labor and sweat, yet there is scarcely anything so low, so easy, that a man can wholly understand it and comprehend it clearly, except perhaps that he knows perfectly that he knows nothing perfectly, though from this an incontestable proof follows that "the corruptible body is a load upon the soul, and the earthly habitation presseth down the mind that museth upon many things" [*Wisdom,* ix, 15].[100] Hear what Solomon thinks about this, "All things are full of labor; man cannot utter it" [*Eccl.,* i, 8]. "There is that neither day nor night seeth sleep with his eyes, and cannot find the reason of the works of God. Because though a man labor to seek it out, yet shall he not find it" [*Eccl.,* viii, 16, 17].[101] "They search out iniquities; they accomplish a diligent search: both the inward thought of every one of them and the heart is deep and God

[99] *1st Sermon on Palm Sunday* [*MPL,* CLXXI, p. 478].
[100] Douay version.
[101] Modified to conform to the Latin text.

will be exalted" [*Ps.*, lxiv, 6, 7]. "For men to search their own glory is not glory" [*Prov.*, xxv, 27]. For the more a man knows, the more he doubts; and he seems to himself to know most who knows least. The part of wisdom therefore is to know that one knows not. "God hath made man upright; but they have sought out many inventions" [*Eccl.*, vii, 29].[102]

There follows a diatribe on the vanity of the arts and sciences which was to become typical of pious scepticism.

Men scurry about through hedges and by-ways, they climb mountains, cross hills, leap over rocks, dart through crags, scramble out of pits, penetrate caverns, tear up the bowels of the earth, the depths of the sea, secret rivers, forest shades, trackless solitudes, expose themselves to winds and rains, thunders and lightnings, floods and tempests, avalanches and landslides. They hammer and fuse metals, they carve and polish stones, cut and hew wood, spin yarn and weave garments, rip and sew, build houses, plant gardens, cultivate their fields, tend vineyards, heat ovens, build mills, fish, hunt, and go fowling. They meditate, they cogitate, take counsel, give orders, quarrel, go to law, ravage and steal, cheat and bargain, fight and battle and do number-less things of like nature to accumulate wealth, to multiply gain, to pursue profit, to acquire honors, to raise their rank, to extend their power, and this too is labor and vexation of spirit. If you do not believe me, let Solomon be believed who said, "I made me great works; I builded me houses; I planted me vineyards; I made me gardens and orchards, and I planted trees in them of all kinds of fruits: I made me pools of water, to water therewith the wood that bringeth forth trees: I got me servants and maidens, and had ser-vants born in my house; also I had great possessions of great and small cattle above all that were in Jerusalem before me. . . . And whatsoever mine eyes desired I kept not from them, I withheld not my heart from any joy; for my heart rejoiced in all my labor: and this was my portion of all my labor. Then I looked on all the works that my hands had wrought, and on the labor that I had labored to do: and, behold, all was vanity and vexation of spirit, and there was no profit under the sun." [*Eccl.*, ii, 4-11].[103]

---

[102] *De contemptu mundi*, I, xiii [*MPL*, CCXVII, p. 707].
[103] *De contemptu mundi*, I, xiv [*MPL*, CCXVII, p. 708].

THE NOBLE SAVAGE

The existence of non-Hebraic peoples furnished a problem to the early Christians, whereas to the Pagans ethnic diversity was, in general, simply a fact. For the Pagan had no sacred text which led him to believe that all human beings were members of one family with a common ancestor. The separation of the world into Greeks and Barbarians required no explanation and no one thought of a catholic religion until the time of the Roman Stoics when the world as a whole was brought under one system of law. The Christian, however, had to reconcile ethnic diversity with the story of the First Man. This was usually done by going back to the Old Testament story of the Flood and the resettlement of the earth after its waters had subsided. According to this story, it will be recalled, the sons of Noah, Ham, Shem, and Japhet, were the progenitors of the various nations [*Gen.* ix, x] and, though the Bible gives but the faintest clues to just what territorial distribution was made among them, the Fathers were not slow to trace the genealogy of various nations back to these three. In this way history was completed, and whatever benefit accrued to a modern nation from the knowledge of a Biblical ancestor was conferred upon it. At times the national founder could be presented in the guise of King Saturn, the inventor or introducer of the useful arts, a kind of culture-hero, at times simply as a primitive king under whom the nation lived a life similar to that of the Golden Age.

How much of this tradition derived from the legend of Aeneas, it would be difficult to say without a detailed study of the texts, which is not possible. It would seem likely, however, that later writers based the general scheme of their brief sketches upon the Roman model.

An early and influential example of such genealogies is to be found in Josephus who was frequently imitated,[1] and who never hesitated to embroider a colorful picture over the bare scriptural background. He thus assigns to the seven sons of Japhet seven well known nations of the western world: to Gomar the Galatians, to Magog the Scythians, to Javan the Ionians and Greeks, to Mados the Medes, to Tubal the Iberians, to Meschèch the Cappadocians, to Tiras the Thracians.[2] There was thus preserved an ethnic homogeneity throughout the world and observed fact was reconciled with Biblical legend.

But it was also noticed that savages were not likely to live in accordance with Scripture. The Pagans, having no sacred text, were in no way logically forced to condemn them for this. If they admired savages, they could base

---

[1] By among others, St. Jerome, *Lib. hebr. quaest. in Gen.*, ch. x, verse 2; and later Cosmos Indicopleustes, *Top. christ.* II, 131 (Montfaucon).

[2] *Ant. jud.*, I, 122 ff.

129

their admiration for them on their proximity to Nature. But the Christian
found it more difficult to admire them, even when their rigorous life was in
harmony with the self-denial of the hermits or monks. Thus Tertullian
could find nothing too bad to say about the Scythians [3] and Saint Basil
refers to their lack of education with contempt.[4] So in the West, Sidonius
speaks of " Scythian conversation " in terms which recall the " Scythian
speech " of certain Greek writers,[5] and Lactantius, discussing idolatry among
the Romans, finds that it would be excusable among barbarians *quorum
religio cum moribus congruit*,[6] but presumably only excusable among them.
Returning to the East, we find Origen, attacking Celsus's tolerance of
various national religious customs, who lists a number which in his eyes are
absurd.[7] This attack is imitated in expanded form by Saint Jerome. He is
discussing food-taboos, the locusts of Saint John the Baptist, the customs of
various Pagans, and the Egyptian worship of animals.

> These few things we have laid down about the Scriptures so that we
> might show the harmony of our doctrines with those of the philoso-
> phers. But who does not know that each people is accustomed to
> eat, not according to a universal law of nature, but according to what
> things are found abundantly in their habitat. Thus the Arabs and
> Saracens and all the barbarians of the desert live on the milk and
> flesh of camels because this sort of animal is easily bred and fed in
> such regions' barren climate. These people think it is wrong to eat
> the flesh of swine. For swine which are accustomed to feed on acorns,

[3] *Adv. Marc.*, I, 1. The passage is given at length at *PIA*, pp. 243 f.

[4] See *Ep.* lxxiv. In general Basil does not idealize the savages, as the founder of a
monastic order might have been expected to do. On the contrary, their mode of
life is contrasted most unfavorably with that of civilized man. The only elements
of the idea of the Noble Savage discernible in this Father are (a) the assumption
that there are certain moral truths known by all men at all times, and therefore by
implication by savages; (b) the admission that, along with their lack of self-
control and their cruelty, some of the primitive folk, specifically the Scythians,
manifest some traits of genuine humanity and kindliness; (c) the attitude of
leniency towards the faults of the savages precisely because of their lack of the
advantages resulting from moral education and discipline; (d) the attempt to incite
the civilized to well-doing by pointing to such (undeniably scanty) virtues as the
savages possess, against the background of which the moral depravity of civilized
men deserves severer punishment, because of their greater opportunities to learn
the truths of morals and religion. For Saint Basil's use of the argument from the
savage's ignorance of morality and religion, see his *Homily on Psalm VII*, 102 C-D
[*MPG*, XXIX, p. 240]. For a clearly unfavorable view of savages, see his *Epist.
CCLIX*, the passage on the Magusaeans. Cf. Eusebius, *Praep. Ev.*, vi, 275; Epi-
phanius, *Exp. cath. fid.*

[5] See his *Epistles*, V, 7 [Ed. Luetjohann, *MHG*, 1887]. Cf. his *Carmina*, XII, *Quid
me, etsi valeam*, etc. For the term, " Scythian speech," see *PIA*, p. 323, n. 65.

[6] *Div. inst.*, I, ch. 21 [*CSEL*, XIX, p. 79].

[7] *Contr. Cels.*, V, 34. It is curious that he quotes with apparent approval a passage from Herodotus which advocates the same type of tolerance which he is attempting to attack. See *Hist.*, III, 38.

chestnuts, roots of ferns, and barley are either very rarely found [in deserts] or not at all. And even if they should be found, they would have no food, which is what we have said above. If you compel people from the North to eat asses and camels, they will think the same of eating their flesh as if they were forced to eat wolves and crows. In Pontus and Phrygia the paterfamilias demands a great price for the fat white worms which have a black head and are born in rotting wood, and, as among us the heath-cock and fig-pecker are counted as delicacies, so among them to eat grubs is a luxury. Again, it is the custom of Easterners and the peoples of Libya to eat locusts, because through the wilderness and the hot wastes of the desert clouds of locusts are found. [The case of] John the Baptist proves this to be true. Yet compel a Phrygian or a Pontan to eat a locust and he will think it wrong. Force a Syrian, African, or Arabian to eat a Pontan worm and he will look down upon it as upon flies, centipedes, and lizards, although the Syrians are accustomed to eat the land-crocodile and the African even to eat green lizards. In Egypt and Palestine, because of the rarity of cattle, no one will eat a cow, and they confine their meats to the flesh of bulls, oxen, and bull-calves. But in our province, they think it wicked to eat veal, wherefore the Emperor Valens recently promulgated a law throughout the Orient that no one should eat veal, with a view to [conserving] the agricultural utility of calves and changing the very bad customs of the judaizing mob who consume calves instead of fattened poultry and suckling pigs. The Nomads and Troglodytes and Scythians and the new savages, the Huns, eat half-raw meat. Moreover the Ichthyophagi, a nomadic tribe on the shores of the Red Sea, broil fish on stones heated by the sun and live on this food alone. The Sarmatians, Quadi, Vandals, and innumerable other people, delight in the flesh of horses and foxes. What shall I say of the other heathen, since as a boy in Gaul I saw the Attacoti, a British people, eat human flesh; when they come upon herds of swine and cattle and sheep, they slice off the buttocks of the herdsmen and the breasts of the women and esteem them the most delicious of foods. The Scottish nation does not practice monogamy; but, as if they had read the *Republic* of Plato and were following the example of Cato, there is no individual wife among them, but as each pleases, they satisfy lust in the manner of the brutes. The Persians, Medes, Indians, and Ethiopians—kingdoms by no means small, but equal to the Roman Empire in size—mate with their mothers and grandmothers, with their daughters and nieces. The Massagetae and Derbices consider them who die of disease very unfortunate, and they devour their slaughtered parents, kinsmen, neighbors when they reach old age, saying that it is better that they be eaten by them than by the worms. The Tibareni hang the old men whom they have selected on gibbets. The Hircanians cast them while half alive to the birds and dogs. The Caspians give them dead to the very beasts. The Scythians bury alive those who have been loved by the deceased with the bones of the dead. The Bactrians throw the aged to dogs who are fed in this way. And when the Prefect of Alexander, Stasanor, wished to change this custom, he almost lost the province. Force an Egyptian to drink ewe's milk; compel, if you can, a Pelusiote to eat an onion. Nearly every city in Egypt venerates its own beast and monster, and whatsoever they worship, this they think inviolate and holy.[8]

The value of this passage from St. Jerome to our study is simply the long list of savages known to him in none of whom does he find anything to admire. Among them were peoples, the Scythians and Ethiopians, for instance, who had been established as Nature's Sages in Pagan literature. And yet Jerome is able to speak of them along with less respectable savages without apparently feeling the need to mention their extenuating nobility. It is, moreover, rare in Christian Latin authors of this time to find the Barbarians spoken of with anything other than horror. Saint Jerome's contemporary, Salvianus, uses them, however, in a somewhat new fashion. They are, he admits, shameless and vicious; but their evil-nature is to be expected of men who have not received the Word of God. One may pardon the vicious man who is ignorant of virtue; the man who knows what virtue is and yet does not reform, is inexcusable. The savages are thus presented as in no sense "noble"; their proximity to nature is not mentioned; they are merely horrible examples of what to avoid.[9]

Comparing the life of Christians with that of savages he says,

> The barbarians are unjust, and so are we; they are avaricious, and we are; they are faithless, and we are; they are greedy, and we are; they are shameless, and we are; in fine, the barbarians are full of all kinds of wickedness and foulness, and we are too. But perhaps it will be replied, " If we are on a par with the barbarians in viciousness, our wickedness is similar and we stand accused of the same offences, why are we not likewise on a par with them in strength?" For since either we ought to be as strong as they are, or surely they ought to be as weak as we are. That is true, and it still remains to be told how they are the more guilty who are the weaker. How do we prove this? By the very fact that, as we have said above, we have shown that God does all things as a judge. For if, as is written, " The eyes of the Lord are in every place, beholding the evil and the good," (*Prov.* XV, 3) and, as the Apostle adds, " The judgment of God is according to truth against all evil-doers," (*Rom.* II, 2) [10] we see that we who do not desist from doing evil sustain the punishment of evil-doing from the judgment of the just God. But, you say, the barbarians do the same evil, and yet they are not so wretched as we, yet we are the more offending sinners. For our vices and the Barbarians' may be equal, but yet in these vices our sin is the graver. For since all the barbarians are, as we have already said, either pagans or heretics, let me speak first of the pagans, since their guilt is first: the Saxons are cruel, the Franks faithless, the Gepidae inhuman, the Chuni shameless, in short, the life of all barbarian tribes is vice. But should their vices meet the same charge as ours; is the

---

[8] *Adversus Jovianum*, II, ch. vii. [*MPL*, XXIII, pp. 307-309].

[9] Cf. *De gubernatione Dei*, V, iv; VI, vii.

[10] Translation adjusted to the text of Salvianus.

shamelessness of the Chuni as criminal as ours; is the perfidy of the
Franks as blameworthy as ours; is the drunkenness of an Alanian as
reprehensible as that of a Christian, or the rapacity of an Albanian
as damnable as that of a Christian? If a Chunian or Gepidan lies,
what wonder is it, since in his heart he does not know the guilt of
falsehood? If a Frank swear falsely, what strange thing does he do,
since he thinks his very perjury to be a kind of oath, not a crime?
And what wonder if barbarians so believe, barbarians who know not
God, since the greater part of those who bear the Roman name so
think, although they know that they are sinning? For I need not
speak of another race of men. Let us consider solely the crowd of
businessmen and merchants who occupy in force the greater part of
all the countries of the world, if their life is anything other than
meditation upon fraud and a grinding out of lies, or if they do not
believe those words should not utterly perish which are of no personal
advantage to the speaker. So great among them is their honor of
God who prohibits false-swearing, that they think the fruit of all
perjury peculiarly savory. Why wonder, then, that barbarians lie
who do not know the crime of lying? They do not act in contempt
of celestial laws, ignorant as they are of the laws of the Lord, for he
does nothing contrary to the law who is ignorant of the law. Therefore our special charge is that we know the divine law and violate it
always; we say that we know God, and tread His orders and precepts
under foot; and therefore since we spurn Him whom we believe
boastfully to cherish, that very thing which seems to be worship of
God, is an insult to Him.[11]

There is, however, a passage in Salvianus where he feels differently about
the savages, admitting their superiority to civilized Christians. In this
passage he finds no solution to the problem and attributes their condition to
a secret plan of God.

It is asked, since these things are so, if everything in this world is
done through the care and governance and judgment of God, why the
condition of the barbarians is so much better than ours, why among
us too the lot of good men is harder than that of bad? Why are the
honest cast down and the dishonest strong? Why do all things fall
before specially wicked powers? I can reasonably and firmly say, I
do not know. For I am in ignorance of the secret counsels of the
Deity. It is enough for me to consult the oracle of the Divine Word
for a solution of this problem. God, as we have already proved in
the preceding chapters, says that all is surveyed, all is ruled, all is
judged by Himself. If you wish to know what should be believed,
you have the Holy Scriptures; perfect reason is to believe what you
have read in them.[12]

It is precisely the superiority of at least one group of savages, the Goths,
which explains their victories over the Romans, he maintains in another
passage. The Romans have sinned against chastity; the Goths are pure.

[11] De gub. Dei, IV, xiv [Ed. C. Halm, Berlin, 1877, pp. 49-50].
[12] De gub. Dei, III, i, 2 [Ed. Halm, p. 24].

10

[What makes our immodesty the worse is that] among modest barbarians we are immodest. Moreover, I say, the barbarians themselves are offended by our impurity. Among the Goths, a Goth is not permitted to be a fornicator; alone among them, by prejudgment of the nation and the name, are Romans permitted to be impure. And what hope, I ask, is there for us before God? We delight in shamelessness, the Goths execrate it. We flee from purity, they love it. Fornication among them is a crime and perilous, among us it is an honor. And do we think that we can stand before God, do we think that we can be saved, when every sin of impurity, every shameless turpitude, is permitted by the Romans and punished by the barbarians? Here now I ask them who believe that we are better than the barbarians what things very few of the Goths would do and what every Roman, or practically everyone, would not do. Do we wonder if the lands of the Aquitanians or of all of our subjects have been given by God to the barbarians, since those lands which the Romans have polluted with fornication, the barbarians now clean with chastity? [13]

The use of the savages as evidence either of nobility or baseness kept alive the various traditions of their customs which had been influential in classical Greek thought and which were to reappear later in the Renaissance. We have cited some of the Latin Fathers who made this ambiguous use of the legends; we shall now return to an earlier period and quote some of their Greek predecessors.

Clement of Alexandria is a good example of a Greek Father who while admiring some of the traits of the savages, yet does not hesitate to use them as bad examples. He contrasts, for instance (*Paed.*, II, ii) the Scythians, Celts, Iberians, and Thracians, who are warlike drunkards, with his fellow Christians, who are moderate drinkers and lovers of peace. He notes the Sauromatian worship of the sword and of fire (*Protrepticus*, ch. V) as an instance of absurd idolatry, an idolatry of which he says that Heraclitus was the philosophic spokesman. Indeed, he devotes a whole chapter of his *Stromata* (I, xv) to showing that Greek philosophy was derived from the barbarians and was, on that account, of no great value; and he follows it with another to show that the barbarians were the inventors of most of the arts. Yet this very attempt to depreciate the achievemens of the Greeks makes it easy for him to slip into eulogy of the barbarians, as when he contrasts the deeds of that pre-eminent Noble Savage, Anacharsis, with the words of the Greeks (*Strom.* I, xvi). Or again (*Paed.* III, iii), when he is inveighing against men's using their hair for adornment,

---

[13] *De gub. Dei*, VII, vi, 23-26 [Ed. Halm, p. 88]. Similar ideas are expressed in *De gub. Dei*, VII, xxiii. By the next century the Goths were firmly entrenched in the Roman Empire and thus lost their status as savages. It is amusing to find Cassiodorus writing in a letter, *ut . . . Gothorum posses demonstrare iustitiam: qui sic semper fuerunt in laudum medio constitui, ut et Romanorum prudentiam caperent, et virtutem gentium possiderent.* *Epistles*, Bk. III, *ep.* 23 [Ed. Mommsen, *MGH*].

he cites the Germans and Scythians as luxury-hating tribes. Thus he too keeps the legends of the Noble Savage in circulation and consequently ran the risk of suggesting to his readers that if savages could reach material and even moral greatness without Christianity, perhaps Christianity was not so necessary as its proponents felt themselves bound to believe.

The greatest creditor of the Greeks was, of course, the Jews, who were supposed to be the parent stock of Greek and barbarian as well, and of whose religion and general civilization the pagan nations were believed to retain only a weak image. If as Numenius had said—and Clement quotes him with approval (*Strom.* I, xxii)—Plato was only Moses speaking Attic, why not turn to Moses and waste no more time over his imitator? [14] His purpose was, it may be assumed, to induce his fellows, whose education has been almost entirely Greek, to turn away from their traditional sources of wisdom for that of the people who were the ancestors of the primitive Christians. Thus when he wished to humiliate the Greeks, he called to their attention the legendary nobility of their savage contemporaries. When, on the contrary, he wished to praise the Christians, he contrasted their life with the horrors of savagery. His opinions varied with his rhetorical needs, and since rhetoric was so largely an affair of stereotyped phrases and literary references, the introduction of the Noble Savage into a Christian Father's discourse need not be taken as evidence of any thorough-going admiration for the uncivilized life. The following passage is typical of Clement's use of this commonplace.

> Lions, it is true, are proud of their bushy names, but they are protected by their hair in battle, and boars too are given a certain majesty by their crests as well as frightening hunters when they stiffen them.
>
> "And fleecy sheep are weighed down with their wool," but our Father, who loves man, has made their wool copious for your use, O man, and has taught you to shear their fleeces. Of the heathens, the Celts and Scythians wear their hair long, but they do not embellish it. The long hair of the barbarian is somewhat terrifying and his reddish locks threaten war. Its color is akin to that of blood. Both these barbarian tribes hate luxury. The German will summon as a clear witness to this the River Rhine, the Scythian will summon his wagon. Sometimes the Scythian makes light even of his wagon— its size seems to the barbarian a sign of wealth—and, abandoning luxury, he leads a simple life. The Scythian takes his horse, a sufficient home and less cumbersome than his wagon, and mounting it, is borne wherever he wishes. When distressed with hunger, he asks his horse for food, and the animal offers his veins and gives his master his only possession, his blood. Thus the horse is the nomad's mount and his food. [15]

[14] Here, though Clement deprecates imitation, he proceeds to write a life of Moses, which he takes almost bodily from Philo's. See *MPG*, VIII, p. 896, note 96.

[15] *Paedagogus*, III [Ed. Staehlin, Leipzig, 1905, p. 250].

This passage, whether sincere or not, is in the manner of the pagan cultural primitivists. The contempt for luxury, the admiration for not only a simple, but a hard, life (the rejection of a wagon, if a horse will do as well) are reminiscent of the philosophy of Diogenes. It is likely that, had the savages been Christian, the tradition of the Noble Savage might have been stronger in early Christian writings. For the savage way of living, as represented in legend, had much that would have pleased a primitive Christian. The savages, however, not only were not Christian, but had become the bitter opponents and persecutors of those Christians who had come among them to preach the Word. The stories of the martyred evangelists date from the early Christian period and consequently, the early Christian writers, even when dealing with the Scythians, tended to emphasize their evil traits and to forget their good.

Thus Clement's pupil, Origen, defending the Christians for breaking the Roman law against secret meetings, compares Roman laws to Scythian, arguing that they are unholy (*Contra Cels.,* I, i). He calls the laws of Rome which Christians violate "Scythian and tyrannical," as if the two terms were synonymous. Now the Scythians had been charged with the martyrdom of Saint Andrew who had been sent to evangelize them.[16] Such a charge was too serious to be counter-balanced by a frugal life or abstemious manners and may have given plausibility to the belief of Jordanes that it was the Getae, not the Scythians, who had excited the admiration of the Pagan writers.[17]

It was not then strange that the cruel rather than the noble Scythian survived in early medieval literature. Both Latin and Greek fathers had contributed their influence to this. When then one reads such a writer as Solinus (*Polyhistor,* xvi) one sees nothing of their good traits and finds them described as cruel and cannibalistic. Isidore of Seville, whose writings were the source of so much that was of a later date, gives us the following account of them.

> Scythia, like Gothia, was given this name from Magog, the son of Japhet. The Scythian land was once huge, for it reached on the East from India and on the North through the Moesian [Bulgarian?] swamps along the Danube, and Ocean, to the ends of Germany. Afterwards it was cut off, on the East where the Seric Ocean reaches

[16] For the life of Saint Andrew, see Ordericus Vitalis, *Hist. eccles.,* Pt. I, bk. ii, 9, 10 [*MPL*, Vol. 188, p. 139 ff.]; Freculphus Lexoviensis, *Chronicon*, II, ii, 4 [*Id.* 106, p. 1147]. In Flavius Lucius, Saint Philip, rather than Saint Andrew, spread the Gospel in Scythia [*Id.* Vol. 21, p. 87 f.]. In any event the Scythians were held guilty of martyring an evangelist and hence lost inevitably a good share of the nobility which they had previously enjoyed.

[17] *De Getarum origine,* ch. V. Jordanes believed that the Getae came to Scythia from the island of Scanzia and were the early Goths. In the XVIIIth century (1787), John Pinkerton revived these ideas in his "A Dissertation on the Origin and Progress of the Scythians or Goths," Preface, p. viii. See also Bayer, *Dissertatio de Scythia,* etc. [*Act. Acad. Petrop.,* I, ch. 1].

to the Caspian Sea, which is to its west; thence from the South it shrank to the Caucasus range. Hyrcania bounds it, having on the West many people, likewise nomadic because of the sterility of the soil.

Some of these people cultivate the land; some, monstrous and savage, live on human flesh and blood. The Scythian lands are in part very rich; some, however, are uninhabitable; for while in several places there is an abundance of gold and precious jewels, men seldom enter them because of the ferocity of the griffins. This is, however, the land of the finest emeralds. There is also a dark-blue stone and a very pure crystal in Scythia. And its rivers are the Moschorus, the Phasis, and the Araxes.[18]

When the reading of classical texts was revived in the XIIth century, we find that the older idea of the Scythians was revived as well. An example of this is found in Hugo of Saint Victor, who writes of them in imitation of Trogus, reproducing in fact many of Trogus's expressions.[19]

The Scythians, a very ancient people, located to the north, have no less illustrious origins than empire, and are not more famous for the virtues of their men than for that of their women. Accustomed to wander through untilled spaces, the Scythians do not cultivate their fields, but convey their wives and children with them in wagons, protected from the rain and the severity of winter by hides. And they drive their flocks and herds along with them. They live on milk and honey; a people strong in work and in war, of huge corporeal strength. The kingdom of the Scythians is believed to have arisen under Ragan.[20]

We have thus two traditions concerning the lives of the Scythians in medieval writings, one of which depicted them as admirable, the other as detestable. The two traditions, in fact, were carried into modern literature as well. Writers who were educated in the classics and had a leaning towards primitivism of one type or another, like Rousseau in some of his moods, found the Scythians an ancient model for civilized man to copy.[21] Writers who were in general anti-primitivistic, like Jean Bouchet, author of the famous *Annales d'Aquitaine* [22] saw less desirable traits in them.

II

The Christian contribution to the life of the Noble Savage is found above all in descriptions of certain more or less imaginary peoples living in the

[18] *Etymol.*, lib. XIV, ch. iii. [*MPL*, Vol. 82, pp. 500 f.].

[19] For the passage from Trogus, see *PIA*, pp. 327 ff.

[20] *Excerptiones priores*, V, ii. Ragan would appear to be purely legendary and where the legend started is doubtful. The name does not occur in any of the classical authors or onomastica consulted by me, nor in the index to Mimms, *Scythians and Greeks.*

[21] See the *Premier Discours* [*Oeuvres Complètes*, ed. Auguis, 1825, Vol. I, p. 16].

[22] The *Annales* were published at Poitiers in 1557. See p. 3.

Orient. It will be recalled that one tradition located the Earthly Paradise in the East. Moreover, it was there that the Essenes were found as well and, though they were in reality a religious and not racial community, were described by both Pliny and Solinus as a people. Whereas the Pagans in general depicted the savages whom they admired as living a simple life, even when it was soft, the Christian had a tendency to depict them as living a life compounded of details from Pagan accounts of Noble Savages and from the Apocalyptic literature. Thus even when the Pagans were dealing with an imaginary tribe, like the Hyperboreans, they gave them none of the paraphernalia of civilization, none of the luxuries and superfluities of urban culture, although they did make them miraculously happy. In strict contrast with this is the Christian treatment of such a people as the Camerini, who are first found in the *Liber Junioris Philosophi*.[23] The Camerini receive their food as a gift from heaven and earth; live in a juristic state of nature; know no evil; do not work; and die happily, lying down in their coffins and breathing their last. At the same time, their country, like Saint John's heaven, is full of precious stones, emeralds, pearls, jacinths, agates, and sapphires. Whether the author added this detail because of a vulgar love of jewels or because of the supposed ethical virtues of these stones, we have no way of telling. But they were to appear constantly in Christian stories of Earthly Paradises throughout the Middle Ages. There is no need of extended comment here on the contrast which this makes with pre-Christian primitivism, but it is perhaps worth pointing out that when explorers in search of fabulously wealthy lands in the western ocean meet the savage inhabitants of these places, they find it normal to describe them in terms of cultural primitivism. The passage on the Camerini which follows, then, may be thought of in a class with accounts of the country of Prester John and the Island of Saint Brendan.

It is said that the people of the Camerini live in the East. Moses called their country Eden. From it a very great stream is said to flow and to be divided into four rivers, whose names are Geon, Phison, Tigris, and Euphrates. The men who live in the said country are extremely pious and good and among them is to be found no evil either of body or soul. If, however, you should wish to learn more details about them, it is said that they use neither our ordinary bread nor any similar food, nor even the fire which we use, but they say that a kind of bread rains down on them day by day, and that they drink wild honey and pepper. The fire of their sun is reported to be so hot that, as soon as it is poured down upon the land from heaven, all the people might be burned, did they not throw themselves quickly

[23] This would appear to be a Latin translation of a Greek original composed at Antioch and Alexandria about the middle of the fourth century. It was first printed in Geneva in 1628. For the name "Camerini," see Mueller, *Geographi Graeci Minores*, Paris, 1882, Vol. II, p. 513, n. 4. Cf., however, Hecataeus, fragm. 263, in Mueller, *Fragm. Hist. Graec.*, Vol. I, p. 17.

into the river, in which they linger until such time as the fire returns
to its own place again.

They are, moreover, without government, ruling themselves. As no
evil is found among them, so they have neither fleas nor lice nor
bedbugs, nor anything else which is harmful. Their clothes cannot
become soiled; but if it should happen, they wait for a cleaning by
the sun's fire, for burning makes things better. They have also
various precious stones, emeralds, pearls, jacinths, agates, and sapphires in the hills, from which they are taken as follows. The river,
rushing down both day and night, wears away the hillside and by the
force of the water carries earth off its surface. The people's ingenuity
has discovered a way of taking what is thus produced. Making nets
and placing them in the narrow parts of the stream, they catch easily
what comes down from the upper reaches.

Living, therefore, in such great happiness, they know not how to labor
nor are they wearied by any weakness of disease, except this alone—
that they leave the body. But they know in advance of death the
day of their departure. For all die at the age of one hundred and
twenty years, and the elder does not see this death of his junior nor
do parents mourn for their children. When, then, the day of death
begins to approach, each makes for himself a sarcophagus of various
aromatic woods, for there are many aromatic trees in their country.
And when his last hour of life has come for him, saluting all and
bidding all farewell, he places himself in his sarcophagus and so
repays his debt to nature with the greatest freedom from care.[24]

The Camerini do not appear to have survived in medieval literature, but
the place which they might have occupied was amply filled by a less imaginary people, the Brahmins. The Brahmins were known to the Pagan world
in the fourth century B. C. through the works of the historians of Alexander's wars, Onesicritus, Nearchus, Aristobulus, of whom passages on the
Gymnosophists have been preserved, as well as in all probability in Anaxi-
menes and Marsyas. Arrian, too, in his *Anabasis* (Bk. vii, ch. 5 and 6)
relates anecdotes about them and in his *Historia Indica* (ch. xi) gives an
account of seven castes, basing his remarks on the work of Nearchus. To
these authors must be added Philostratus, whose life of Appolonius of Tyana
contained stories which would have enhanced the more marvelous features
of the legends. Consequently there was no doubt general acquaintance with
these people in the first Christian century.

But perhaps the most influential series of documents in this tradition
was the *Gesta Alexandri* of Pseudo-Callisthenes, apparently the first link
in the long chain of romances which constituted later the *Roman d'Alexandre*. The date of this work is uncertain and its frequent repetitions,
indeed, make it appear to be a compilation of older stories pieced together

[24] Junior Philosophus, *Totius orbis descriptio*, 4-7. [Mueller, *Georg. Graec. Min.*,
Vol. II, p. 514] The longevity of the Camerini and their mode of death recalls somewhat similar features in the life of the Hyperboreans. The latter die, however, by a
kind of joyful suicide.

in more or less haphazard fashion. The portions which interest us can be given rough *termini post quos*. The use of the name of the month, August, for instance, would put one section at the earliest in the second half of the first century A. D.; the Christian expression, " made in the image of God," would indicate a second century date in all probability; there is a definite reminiscence of Saint Paul (or possibly of some work of which Saint Paul is reminiscent) in certain eschatological passages, which would date it in the second century; the reference to monks, however, would date the opening passage much later.[25] At the same time, many of the ideas contained in this document are of much earlier origin. This is certainly true of the Cynic passages, the emphasis upon vegetarianism, the exclusive drinking of water, nudity, the technological state of nature and the like.

The document consequently gives us a Christian version of cultural primitivism, preserving throughout Catholic Europe the legend of a non-Christian people living in Asia whose way of life was essentially Christian. It is perhaps not an exaggeration nor over-simplification to maintain that because of the legend of Alexander, the Brahmin took the place which in Greek thought was occupied by the Scythians.[26]

> He said that the Brahmins are not a people withdrawn from the world by choice, like monks, but have received this way of living from on high and from the judgment of God. They dwell by a river in a state of nature, living in nakedness. There is no four-footed beast among them, no agriculture, no iron, no building, no fire, no bread, no wine, no clothing, nor anything pertaining to the productive arts or to pleasure. But they have a climate which is brisk and invigorating and in all respects very fair. Worshipping God and possessing wisdom (*gnosis*)— and this to no small degree—and though they are not able to comprehend the reasons of Providence, yet they pray unceasingly. And when they pray, they look to Heaven, instead of to the East. And they eat the fruits of the trees upon which they happen and wild vegetables, and they drink water, being wanderers in the woods, and they sleep on beds of leaves. They have much

[25] Liddell and Scott give an epigram of Pallades (4th c.) as the source of the earliest occurrence of μοναχός.

[26] E. A. Wallis Budge, in his translation of the Ethiopic text of the life of Alexander, maintains that the text of Pseudo-Callisthenes is " probably not later than A. D. 200." The Ethiopic text, based according to Budge on an Arabic version of the story, metamorphoses Alexander into a Christian king, monotheistic, temperate, continent, especially in sexual matters. It identifies the Brahmins with the Israelites who lived in the time of Elijah " and who had not bowed the knee to Baal." For the non-Greek versions of the legends and its mutations, see Budge's *The Life and Exploits of Alexander the Great*, 2 vols., London, 1896, esp. pp. xix ff. The Brahmins in the Ethiopic version are " naked men, and poor and miserable," " and their women and children and aged folk fed upon the herb of the field like animals " (Budge, vol. II, p. 131). Their conversation with Alexander is in no way condemnatory of him or of his way of life; he is rather a representative of the highest form of civilization. It is the survival of this which apparently influenced the version of Leo which follows in our text the passage from Pseudo-Callisthenes.

persynon [27] and the so-called acanthus. And the land produces still other fruits upon which they live.

The men inhabit the ocean-side of the river Ganges. For this river flows into the Ocean. And their wives are on the other side of the Ganges, towards India. And the men cross over to their wives in the months of July and August. These are their colder months, since at that time the sun is high above us and over the North. And these months are said to be more temperate and stimulating to procreation. When they have spent forty days with their wives, they return to their dwellings. When a woman has borne two children, the man no longer crosses the river nor consorts with his wife. They appoint substitutes for each other [28] and pass the rest of their lives in continence. But if it should happen that a barren woman be found among them, the husband goes to lie with her for the space of five years. And if she still does not conceive, he no longer approaches her. For these reasons, the nation is never very populous, both because of the difficult conditions of life in that country and the natural control over birth. This is the polity of the Brahmins.

[Alexander asks the Brahmins to explain their philosophy to him.]

And the Brahmins of India spoke as follows to Alexander the King.

Desiring wisdom, Alexander, have you come to us. Wherefore we Brahmins grant your request, the more willingly as wisdom is the kingly power in our life. [29] You have desired to learn this, King Alexander. The philosopher is not ruled, but he rules. For no man has power over him. But since up to now you have refused to believe the slanders you have heard about us, you have come to taste the truth. For Calanus, an evil man, once lived among us, and through Calanus you men of Hellas have learned of the Brahmins, but you have not known them. For that man was not really one of us, for he deserted virtue for riches. It was not enough for him to drink the waters of temperance of the Tiberoboam River and to eat things made of milk, by which the mind grows fit for a god, but he hated the riches of the soul. And so a dreadful fire blazed within him and he turned away from wisdom to pleasure. But none of us is rolled upon the coals nor do our bodies suffer any pain, but our food is the medicine of health. We live without wealth in accordance with nature, and death is the termination of our life as it is of all. But if some mortals, having learned false doctrines, shoot at us with vain arrows, they do not hinder our freedom. It is the same thing to lie and to believe too rapidly. For the liar who persuades does

---

[27] This is perhaps the *persea*, an Egyptian fruit tree. See Hippocrates, *De morbis mulierum*, I, 90 (ed. Ermerins, vol. II, p. 641).

[28] Just what this means, we do not know, for the rest of the sentence shows that a new couple takes the place of that of which the wife has borne two children. *Commonitorium Paladii* in the passage corresponding to this simply says, " If during five years she has not conceived, he immediately divorces her for this reason" (*Kleine Texte zum Alexanderroman*, ed. Fr. Pfister, Heidelberg, 1910, p. 4).

[29] Cf. Philostratus, *Life of Apollonius*, II, xxvii, . . . τὸ γὰρ βασιλικώτερον σοφία ἔχει.

wrong and he who believes and gives heed to the liar before he learns the truth does wrong. Slander is the mother of War and gives birth to Passion, because of which men fight and make war. Courage, however, is not the slaying of man. That is the work of bandits. But courage is to combat the rigors of the climate with naked body and to destroy the desires of the belly and to win battles rather on that field and not to be conquered by desire in the hunger for reputation and wealth and pleasure. Conquer these first, Alexander, slay these. For should you conquer these, you will have no need to fight against external foes. For you fight external foes to pay tribute to those within. Do you not see that by conquering those without you, you have been conquered by those within? How many kings of folly seem to you to reign in the witless? Taste, hearing, smell, sight, touch, the belly, the genitals, all the body. And many inner desires too, like cruel mistresses and insatiable tyrants, give one an infinity of orders—Love of Money, Love of Pleasure, Death by Treachery, Fornication, Murder, Wrangling. By all those and many others are mortals enslaved; because of them they slay and are slain.

But we Brahmins, since we have won the inner battles, do not fight in external war. We rest in view of the trees and of heaven and we listen to the melodious voices of the birds and to the eagle's call, and we are roofed over with leaves and we live in the open air and we eat fruits and drink water. We sing hymns to God and we gladly accept the future and we listen to none who are not of profit to us. Such is the life of us Brahmins, not speaking many words, but keeping silent.[30] But you say what should not be done and do what should not be said. Among you no one is considered a philosopher if he cannot talk. Your intelligence is the tongue and your wits are on your lips. You strive for gold and silver and you need slaves and great houses; you pursue power, you eat and drink like cattle; you do not perceive for yourselves. You wrap soft clothes about you, for you have become like silk-worms. You do everything without scruple and you take thought too late in what you do; you babble about yourselves as about your enemies; having the power of speech, you are fought by it. Stronger than you are the silent, even if they do not question themselves. You borrow wool from sheep, like prisoners of war;[31] you wear your glory on your fingers like an ornament; you wear jewelry like women and you are proud of these things. Made in the image of the Creator, you have a temper like that of a wild beast. When you have heaped up many possessions, you glory in them, and you long for them because nothing can help you towards the attainment of truth. Gold does not elevate the soul nor fatten the body, but, quite the contrary, it darkens the soul and causes the body to waste away. But we, pressing onwards towards truth, that is, nature, and the

---

[30] For the importance of silence, cf. Philostratus, *op. cit.*, VI, xi.

[31] The meaning of this simile escapes us. Later on Dandamis urges Alexander to tear off his sheep's wool, i. e., to go naked, so that here he may mean that a man is a prisoner of his clothes. The prohibition of woolen garments in Western philosophy was to be found in Neo-pythagoreanism. See Philostratus, *op. cit.*, VI, xi; VIII, vi; VIII, vii, the speech of Apollonius to the Ethiopian gymnosophists.

things alloted by nature, have forethought for these things also. When hunger approaches, we dispel it with nuts and vegetables furnished by Providence. And when thirst approaches, we go to the river, trampling gold underfoot, and we drink water and relieve our thirst. But gold does not quench thirst nor still hunger nor heal a wound nor cure an illness nor satisfy desire, but rather it stimulates this yearning for things which are foreign to nature. It is evident that a thirsty man yearns to drink and, taking water, quenches his thirst. The hungry man naturally seeks food and, eating, is satisfied, and he ceases to desire. Consequently it is clear to all that to desire gold is foreign to nature. For every desire of man ceases when he takes his fill, since this is in accordance with nature. But the love of money is insatiable, because it is contrary to nature. Then, too, you array yourself in this and glory in it, lording it over other men. And therefore you make your own the common possessions of all, since avarice has made many distinctions in the one nature which is similar for all. Now Calanus, your false friend, had this opinion, but is spurned by us and thus the cause of many evils to all is held in honor among you and is honored by you. But being profitless to us, he was exiled by us in ridicule, and whatever things we despise, these the avaricious Calanus admired, Calanus the fool, your friend, not ours. Trifling and more pitiable than the most wretched men, he has destroyed his soul by love of money. And therefore he did not appear to be worthy of us or worthy of the love of God. Nor did he repose in the security of the woods, living in the forests, since he destroyed his wretched soul with love of money.[32]

> [The next chapter relates Alexander's desire to see the sage, Dandamis, a sort of Indian Diogenes. The King sends Onesicrates, his legate, to invite him to appear before him. Onesicrates finds the Sage reposing on a bed of leaves. He tells him that Alexander, the "Son of God," "Lord of all Men," will reward him richly if he will come to see him, but that if he will not, the King will decapitate him. The Sage replies as follows.]

God, the great king, never generates insolence [hybris] but light, peace, life, and water, the bodies of men and their souls, and these He receives again when fate looses them after they have conquered desire.[33] Lord and God is He alone. He prevents murders and does not wage war. But Alexander is not God, for he too must die. And how can he be Lord of All who has not crossed the Tiberoboam River (nor has he set up his dominion over the whole cosmos) and again, he has not been borne across the girdle of the Gades, nor has he seen the middle course of the sun. And in the northern marches, grassy Scythia does not even know his name. And if that country has no room for him, let him cross the Ganges River and he will find

---

[32] In Onesicritus, as reported by Strabo (XV, 64 ff.), the hostility between Dandamis and Calanus is attenuated. Calanus acts the part of Diogenes of Sinope, with extreme programmatic rudeness, whereas Dandamis rebukes him, praising Alexander as a "philosopher in arms." His attitude in general is one of respect; his sole criticism of the Greeks being their preference for custom to nature.

[33] The Buddhistic element is obvious.

a land capable of bearing men, even if their country is not waiting for him to capture it. Whatever promises Alexander is making to me and whatever gifts he may send me are useless to me. But this is what is pleasing and useful and valuable to me—as home, these leaves, and as fat food, the flowering herbs, and water to drink. Money and things brought together with care . . . can produce nothing but grief, of which all mankind is full.

Now I am going to lie down on my bed of leaves and, closing my eyes, look at nothing. If I should wish to search for gold, I should lose my sleep. Earth produces all things for me, as a mother produces milk for her child.[34] Whithersoever I wish, I go; what I do not care to notice, I need not. Even if Alexander should cut off my head, he will not destroy my soul, but the head remains silent while my soul will go into the hands of the Lord, leaving my body like a ragged garment on the ground, whence it was taken. But I, become a spirit, shall ascend to my God, Who has enclosed us in the flesh and sent us down to earth, to see whether when we have descended we shall live for Him as He has ordered. He will demand of them going to Him a reckoning, being judge of all acts of pride. For the groans of those sinned against become the punishment of sinners. Let Alexander make these threats to those who wish the gold of wealth and fear death. For he has wasted his two weapons on us. The Brahmins neither love gold nor fear death. Therefore depart, and say to Alexander, " Dandamis does not need your possessions and therefore he will not go to you. But if you have need of Dandamis, come to him." [35]

> [Alexander, instead of being angered by such unconventionality, comes to the Sage and asks to be shown in what respect Dandamis and the Brahmins are superior to the Greeks.]

Dandamis answered him, I too wish to give you the words of God's wisdom and to teach you to make your mind divine. But you have no room in your soul to hold the gift of God presented to you by me. For insatiate desires have filled your soul and unquenchable love of money and devilish lust for power, which are fighting with me now because I have enticed you hither, and you are not putting nations to death, pouring out the blood of many peoples. And they are aggrieved at me to-day, because they see a city which is still standing and men who are safe. And you may say that you will continue your march to the Ocean and after that to another land, and after that to still another, and that you will grieve mightily when you have no more men to conquer. How then can I show you the words of God's wisdom, when your mind is so filled with boasting and unmeasured desire that the whole world doing your bidding has not given you sweet satisfaction? You were born small and naked and you came into the world a man alone, and you have grown. Why do you slaughter everyone? That you may take over their property? And when you have conquered everyone and gained possession of every

---

[34] This idea is as early as Hesiod. See *PIA*, p. 25.

[35] Cf. Arrian, *Anabasis*, VII, ii, 2.

inhabited country, you will sit down on only that much ground as I am lying on or you are sitting on. We shall move about, masters of just so much land as we occupy. Hence we, the despised, without battle or warfare, have all things equal to you, earth, water, and air. And all the things which I own, I own by right, and I desire nothing more. But you, making war and shedding blood and slaughtering many men, even if you should possess every river in the world, would drink only so much water as I. Therefore, Alexander, learn this bit of wisdom from me; wish to own nothing, like a pauper, and all things will be yours and you shall lack for nothing.[36] For desire is the mother of poverty (and poverty the child of disorder) appeasing pain with an evil drug, never finding what it seeks, never being satisfied with what it has, but always racked by desire for what it has not. But you will be wealthy in as pleasant a fashion as I, if you are willing to live with me, and if you hearken to me attentively, you will also share my goods. For God is my friend and I share with delight in His works, and He is alive within me. I am turned away from evil men. Heaven is my roof, the whole earth my bed, the woods my table, the fruits my delicious food, the rivers furnish me with drink. I do not eat meat like a lion; the flesh of animals does not rot in my bowels; I have not become a grave for dead beasts. Providence gives me food, as a loving mother gives milk to her babe.

But you are seeking to learn from me, Alexander, what I possess above other men and how much greater wisdom I have than most. As you see me, so have I lived from birth; I live as I came forth from my mother's womb, naked, without wealth or trouble. Therefore I know the ways of God and I understand the necessary sequence of things. But you wonder when you have revealed to you what happens before your eyes every day, not understanding that the things shown to you hour by hour are the works of God. Famines, plagues, wars, thunderbolts, droughts, rains, harvests, do I prognosticate, and how and whence and why these things occur. For Providence gives me knowledge. And it delights me greatly that God with His own works had made His righteousness a counselor for me. If fear of wars, or other vehement emotion should come to a king, he would seek me as a messenger of God. And I, in converse with God's Providence, persuade Him to give some benefaction to those present before me. And, having loosed his fear, I send him away with courage. What is better, tell me, to hurt men and have an evil reputation, or to watch over them and to be known to them as their benefactor? And which better becomes the sons of God, to make war and destroy the creations of Providence, or to make peace and help rebuild the things which have been broken and cast out, as the Creator's servant? Your power will not avail you, King Alexander, nor your heaps of gold, nor your many elephants, nor your garments, many and diverse, nor the army which is camped about you, nor the goldbridled horses and the spear-bearers, and all the other things which you have captured in wars and battles. But you will be served by the greatest things, if you obey my words and hearken to my voice. But even if you slay me, Alexander, I shall

---

[36] See *PIA*, p. 119, for this theme in early Cynicism.

not be afraid to tell you the things which may help you. For I shall
go to my God, Who has made all things. For He knows that I am
just and nothing is hidden from Him Whose eyes are all the stars,
the sun, and the moon. He judges also sinners. Him you cannot
escape, nor have you any place to flee to, to stand up against Him.
Nor shall you avoid His judgment. Hence, King Alexander, do not
destroy what God wishes to build up; do not force into concealment
what He wishes to make resplendent. Do not pour forth the blood of
cities nor walk over the legions of the dead. It is better to live for
oneself than to drive others to death, and to bless others while alive
and to know that to steal is a loss rather than a gain. Why, being
one soul, do you wish to destroy so many peoples? . . . Remember
me in the wilderness, me naked and poor, and profit thereby, and
ceasing to make war, cleave to peace, the beloved of Providence. Seek
not courage in evil, but lead a life free from care among us. Cast off
from yourself the sheep's wool; take not refuge in the clothes of a
corpse. Then will you do honor to yourself, imitating us, by having
become such a one as you were when you were born. For the soul is
tested for virtue in the wilderness. Choose therefore, O King Alexander, to lead our immaterial life . . .[37]

> [The passage terminates in the same vein, playing largely on the
> viciousness of material power and the emptiness of worldly honors.
> The counsel seems to have had but little effect on Alexander, for, after
> a few hypocritical remarks, he again offers his presents to the Sage.
> Dandamis again refuses them, saying that all the gifts of God are his
> already and he needs nothing more. Alexander is finally persuaded that
> he cannot induce the Sage to leave his forest and retires. There follows
> another speech by Dandamis, which we shall omit here, since in the
> main it reproduces ideas already voiced by him: the life in accordance
> with Nature, vegetarianism, autarky, simplicity of living.]

There seem to have been two sources of later medieval information about
this supposed meeting of Alexander and the Brahmin Sage, Dandamis: the
first, the *Res Gestae Alexandri* of Julius, which is probably a fourth century
work; the second, a lost Byzantine, or at any rate oriental rhetorical work,
called by some such title as the *Letters of Alexander and Dindimus*. Julius
Valerius appears to have been popularized in an *Epitome* of the ninth century at which time a Latin version of the letters by Pseudo-Alcuin were
also in circulation. The letters as we have them come from Leo, a tenth
century figure, and were apparently the source for such poetic versions of the
correspondence as those of Godfrey of Viterbo (*ca.* 1185) and Wilkinus
of Spoleto (*ca.* 1236), as well as of certain prose versions, such as that edited
by Skeat in 1878 for the Early English Text Society,[38] the date of which,

---

[37] Ps-Callisthenes, *Gesta Alexandri*, III, ix-xiv [Ed. Muller, Paris, 1877, p. 104 ff.].
It is not our purpose to trace the growth of the Alexander-Romance through the
Middle Ages, but simply to indicate how one element in it, Alexander's meeting with
the Gymnosophists, could have spread throughout Europe. The episode, it goes
without saying, is no part of serious history, and one would look for it in vain in
such a book as Quintus Curtius's *Historiae Alexandri Magni*.

[38] See *Alexander and Dindimus*, EETS, extra series, no. 21, 1878.

according to Skeat, was during the fourteenth century. The correspondence of Leo and the *Epitome* of Julius Valerius were fused into a single compilation by Vincent de Beauvais and included in the *Speculum historiale*. In the meantime some attempt was made in the more critical period of the twelfth century to inform the public of the truth of the Alexander-story. A compilation appeared at that time, which Paul Meyer called the *compilation de Saint Alban,* based on Trogus, Solinus, Josephus, Isidore of Seville, the Bible, Saint Augustine, and other sources which would have seemed to a reader of the period as sober history rather than fantasty. It seems to have had very little influence but does indicate a tendency of the time towards the purgation of the story's less credible incidents.[39] The first *roman d'Alexandre* is now believed to have been that of Albéric of Besançon of the twelfth century.[39a] The romances, however, do not concern us here since they do not reproduce the episodes in question.

The legend of the Brahmins was thus definitely established in Christian literature as early as the fourth century and possibly earlier.[40] As the story grew, the Brahmins were made more and more Christian. They became in fact instinctive Christians, the true type of Noble Savage, exhibiting in their untutored lives all the traits of the saint and philosopher. Leo's tenth century Latin version of the legend illustrates this clearly in the pages containing the correspondence of Alexander and Dindimus. The impudent Cynic tone has disappeared. Dindimus does not berate the King, the King is as " philosophic " in his way as his correspondent is in his. We shall close this section with some excerpts from this version of the story.

The first letter of Alexander is a request for information about the Brahmin way of life. From infancy, says the King, he has had a zeal for learning in order to improve his life. He should now like to learn how the Brahmins live " for no man ever comes to grief from his goodness if he makes another man as good as he is." Dindimus's answer is in the traditional primitivistic tone. Emphasis is placed upon the " natural " in the sense of " that which arises without human effort or contrivance," [41] upon the simple life, vegetarianism, and the usual features of cultural primitivism. This passage is followed by one on the beauty of the cosmic scene which is in the tradition of Seneca's Ninetieth Epistle.[42] Coupled

[39] See Paul Meyer's *Alexandre le Grand dans la littérature du Moyen-Age,* 1886, T. II, ch. iv.

[39a] See *The Medieval French Roman d'Alexandre,* Vol. II, intro. by E. C. Armstrong, in Elliott Monographs, XXVII, p. x.

[40] We say "possibly" because in the Clementine *Recognitiones,* IX, 20, the date of which is uncertain, there is a reference to them as a people *qui et ipsi ex traditione majorum, moribus legibusque concordibus, neque homicidium neque adulterium committunt, neque simulacra colunt neque animantia edere in usu habent, numquam inebriantur, numquam malitiose aliquid gerunt sed Deum semper timent.*

[41] See *PIA,* p. 449, definition 17.

[42] See especially section 34. For translation, see *PIA,* p. 273. Cf. Ps.-Cyprian, *De spectaculis,* 9.

with it is a strain of anti-intellectualism found not only in certain parts of Seneca, but also in some Christian writers of the Middle Ages. At this point a definitely Christian note is struck, in the identity of God and the Word, which introduces a typically Patristic satire upon polytheism.

The reply of Alexander gives an economic interpretation of Brahmin cultural primitivism. The Brahmins, it charges, have been making a virtue out of a necessity. They lack the material basis of civilization and pretend that they are better off without the blessings which it might confer. The concluding passage on the legitimate sensory pleasures is not unlike one to be found in Saint Augustine, *City of God* (XI, xxii) and there may be, indeed, some historical affiliation between them. Passages of interest follow.

> We Brahmins lead a life which is simple and pure; we commit no sins; we are unwilling to possess more than the law (*ratio*) of our nature requires. We suffer and support all things. We call that necessary which is not superfluous, for we have abundant supplies. We seek no other supplies for eating than what Mother Earth produces without labor. We set our tables with such foods as do us no harm and consequently we are without any sickness, and we are healthy throughout our lives. We prepare no drugs for ourselves; we seek no aid for the health of our bodies. Riches we do not love; among us there is no envy. No one of us is stronger than the other. And the poverty which we have, through it we are rich, for we all possess it in common. We have no law-courts, because we do no evil on account of which we might have to go to court. One law is contrary to our nature, for we have pity for none, doing none of those things which ought to inspire us with pity. We forgive no one's transgressions, so that God may forgive ours nor do we give up our riches in penance for our sins. We do not work which leads to avarice. We do not give over our members to lust; we commit no adulteries, nor do we do any vicious act because of which we ought to do penance. It is unlawful among us to plough a field with the ploughshare and to yoke oxen to the wagon. We do not fill our bellies with quantities of food nor do we spread nets in the sea to catch fish. . . . We hold no man in servitude. We do not rule over men who are our similars. It is, moreover, cruel to reduce man to servitude, since nature herself has given him to us as our brothers and he was created by the one Heavenly Father just as we were. We do not crush stones into lime to build dwelling houses, nor do we make pottery out of the earth nor tiles. We lay no foundations on which to build palaces, for we dwell either in trenches or in mountain caves, where the howling of the wind is never heard and where we fear no rain . . . Our women do not deck themselves out to be pleasing; they consider ornaments a burden. They are unwilling to be beautiful through adornment, preferring the natural condition in which they were born. For who can change a work of nature? . . . We do not quarrel, we bear no arms; we have peace through custom, not through virtue . . . We suffer death only at the proper time, because we all equally know how to die . . .

We Brahmins do not suffer sudden death, because we do not corrupt the air with foul deeds whence pestilence is apt to arise. We do not enjoy sports; if, indeed, we wish something humorous, we read of your deeds and of your predecessors', and though we ought to laugh at them, we weep instead. But we see other things to admire and take delight in; we see the heavens brilliantly agleam with stars, the sun ruddy in his chariot, illuminating the whole world with his beams. We see the purple sea and when the tempest stirs it, it does not shatter the beach on which it falls but embraces it as if it were its sister . . . This source of wonder we always have. For our nature has this custom and, if you should be unwilling to follow it, it is your own fault. We do not sail the sea for business, nor do we send emissaries to foreign lands where perils galore will meet them who go there . . . We do not teach the art of eloquence, but we are naturally eloquent . . . We do not frequent the schools of the philosophers, in whose doctrines is discord and no sure and stable distinctions, but always falsehood. But we do frequent those schools in which we learn the good life, and which prove the law which they teach and which do not teach us to harm our fellows but rather to do good according to real justice . . . God loves nothing other than good works, as He hearkens to a man praying to Him with words, for by the word is man like God, since God is the Word. And that Word created the world and by the Word all things live . . . You worship as many gods as a man has bodily members. You say that Juno is goddess of the heart, she who is said to be the goddess of wrath; Mars, because he was the god of battle, you say is god of the chest; Mercury, because he talked much, you say is god of the tongue; Hercules, because he did twelve wonderful deeds of courage, you say is god of the arms; Bacchus, because he was the god of drunkenness, you say is god of the gullet and stands above man's gullet as over a cellar full of wine; Ceres, because she was goddess of grain, you say is goddess of the stomach; Venus, who was goddess of fornication, you say is goddess of the genitals; Jupiter, however, you say is god of the nostrils, because you say he governed the spirit of the air; Apollo, because he first invented music and medicine, you say is god of the hands. You divide man's body among the gods and you do not hold that one God, Who is in Heaven, created your bodies . . .

> [Alexander replies that Dindimus, with his denunciation of all art and custom, is on the side of stupidity, rather than wisdom, and that the Brahmins must either think themselves gods, or have ill-will towards the gods. Dindimis, in turn, answers that it is rather the Greeks who might be suspected of such thoughts. Alexander terminates the correspondence with the following critique of cultural primitivism.]

So, Dindimus, you say that you are happy because you have your natural abode in this part of the world where nothing from without is permitted to reach you nor is anything exported by you. But, as if locked within this region, so you remain, and since you cannot get rid of your country, you praise it, and the privations which you suffer, you say you suffer through continence. Thus, according to your doctrine, those men who have been imprisoned should be called happy, because they lead a life of punishment in prison until old age. For your doctrine is not unlike such an opinion. The good things which

11

you say you have are like the tortures of prisoners, and that which our
law metes out to wicked men, you suffer naturally. Because of this,
it happens that he who is called wise among you, is pronounced a
convict by us. And surely it is fitting that we weep for your miseries
and heave deep sighs over your great misfortunes. For what worse
affliction can a man have than to be denied the power to live in freedom? God has not wished to keep you eternally punished, but has
ordered you while alive to sustain great dangers. Although you say
that you are philosophers, you have no mead of praise for this.

Truly then do I say that your life is not happiness but castigation,
and, if you please, let us speak of some details of your order of living.
You say that the Brahmins do not have the custom of sowing nor of
planting vines against trees nor of making beautiful houses. The
obvious reason for all this is that you have no iron with which you
could do the things which we have mentioned. In the second place,
you do not know how to navigate; it is therefore necessary that you
eat vegetables and lead the hard life of cattle. Do not the wolves do
this too? When they cannot find meat to eat, they fill themselves
with earth to cheat their hunger. But if you were permitted to come
to our country, I should not question your wisdom in supporting
penury; but your penury would have remained within your frontiers.
Or, if we could have brought it along too, we should have been
poverty-stricken. A man is not to be praised for living in meanness
and poverty, but for living temperately in the midst of riches. For
blindness and poverty have their unique reputation, blindness because
it does not see what it desires, poverty because it does not have the
wherewithal to do things. You say that your wives are unadorned
and that among you are no fornication and adultery. It would be a
marvelous thing if you had brought this about by will-power; but the
real reason is that your wives' appearance is not pleasing to you
simply because they are not adorned. And therefore you remain
chaste. You say that you have no zeal for learning and neither seek
nor confer pity. All this you have in common with the beasts, who
act thus because of natural causes and do not delight in any good.
Nature, however, has herself in many ways enticed us rational men
towards good living, for we have free will. For it is impossible that
so large a world should not have a balance of moderation in it, so
that gladness might come after unhappiness. If the human will is
diverse, for it changes with the mutations of the heavens, similarly
the mind of man is itself diverse, and when the day is bright, both the
will and the mind are joyful, and when the day has been cloudy, they
are sad. Similarly, man's senses pass through different stages. Thus
it is that infancy rejoices in simplicity, youth in hardihood, old age is
slowed down in stability.[42a] For who seeks cleverness in a boy, or
constancy in a youth, or mobility in an old man? There are many
delightful things which fall to our use, some to our vision, some to
our hearing, some to our sense of smell, or touch or taste. Now we
have pleasure in dances, now in songs, sometimes in soothing odors,
or sweet tastes or soft textures. If we have all the good fruits of the

---

[42a] Reading *tardatur in stabilitate* in place of *tardatur instabilitate.*

earth and an abundance of fish from the sea and the pleasures of the birds of the sky, should you wish us to abstain from all these things, you would be criticized either as proud, because you look down upon such gifts, or envious, because you think that they have been given to me as a better man than you.[43]

III

Such must suffice as a sample of medieval thought about the Brahmins. We shall terminate this paper with some indications of what the Middle Ages felt about Germans and other Nordics. These peoples, it should be remembered, who were remote and mysterious to the Ancients, were the very stock of many medieval writers and hence lost their exotic aura. They had acquired a certain reputation in Tacitus, but like the Scythians and many other Noble Savages, they gained nothing upon close acquaintance. As early as Isidore of Seville, who was one of the most erudite men of his time and hence certainly had read his predecessors, and who had the characteristic medieval respect for the written word, we find the Germans described in the most unflattering terms.

> [Central Europe] is called *Barbary* because of the barbarous people who inhabit it . . . Germany . . . is a land rich in men who are plentiful and savage. Whence, and because of its fertility, it is called Germany.[44]

The passage, extremely brief, concludes with mention of the wild animals of the German forests and the precious stones.

In the eleventh century Aymon introduced his *History of the Franks* with a long excerpt from Caesar's *Gallic Wars*[45] describing the Germans as a warlike people, continent in their youth, having no agriculture nor private property. This excerpt in itself would not evoke great sympathy for the people it describes, but it was the kind of thing which hard primitivists could use for their purposes.

Adam of Bremen, Aymon's contemporary, is the best known of such writers. It was he who praised the Nordic in terms which have survived to our day. Adam presents a curious combination of Christian and Primitivist. He admires what the Pagans had admired centuries before his time, the simple life, communism, the " natural," and so on. But, as might be expected, he regrets that the savages whom he is describing are not Christians. There was probably a merely literary reason behind his admiration for the Northmen. For he believed that they were identical with the

---

[43] *Kleine Texte zum Alexanderroman*, ed. Fr. Pfister, Heidelberg, 1910. [*Sammlung Vulgaerlateinischer Texte.*]

[44] *Etymol.*, Bk. xiv [MPL, LXXXII, p. 504.]

[45] The passage is quoted in full in *PIA*, p. 362 f. For Aymon, see *MPL*, CXXXIX, p. 630.

Hyperboreans, of whom he had read in Martianus Capella [46] and since Martianus Capella extolled them *multis laudibus*, Adam's interest in them is the greater. His attitude is well examplified in his treatment of the Sueones, whom he considers to be a tribe of Hyperboreans.

> Although all the Hyperboreans are noted for their hospitality, our Sueones are outstanding. To them the worst sin is to deny hospitality to passers-by, so that they have a sort of competition among them to see who is worthy to entertain a guest. To him the winner extends all the rights of humanity, for as long as he wishes to tarry, and takes him eagerly to his friends, from house to house. They have these good traits in their customs. The preachers, however, of the Truth, if they are chaste and prudent as well as capable, they favor with great love, so that they do not forbid the bishops to be present at the people's common council, which they call the *warh*. There they frequently listen to sermons on Christ and the Christian religion without reluctance. And no doubt they would be converted to our faith by easy argument, were it not that evil preachers, seeking their own advantage, not that of Jesus Christ [*Phil*. II, 21], scandalize those who might be saved. [47]

The Sembians, or Prussians, are described by Adam as particularly noble because of their condemnation of wealth which they treat as the people in Voltaire's El Dorado treated gold. They are, however, pagans and they become drunk on a mixture of mare's milk and blood. [48] Like so many other writers, of antiquity as well as of our own time, the more remote the people whom Adam is describing, the more noble. Thus the Icelanders have the palm among his island tribes for virtue.

> The island is so great that it holds within its borders many peoples who live on the young of their flocks alone and are clothed in their skins. There are no vegetables there, and a very small number of trees, wherefore they live in underground caves, enjoying a roof and bed in common with their flocks. Thus, leading a life holy in its simplicity, since they ask for no more than nature yields, they can gladly say with the Apostle, "Having food and raiment, let us be therewith content" [I *Tim.*, vi, 8]. And they have their mountains for towns and their springs for pleasure. A happy people, I say, whose poverty no one envies, and in this most happy, that they have now all accepted Christianity. They have many noteworthy ways of life, above all, that of charity, wherefore all things are held in common among them, as well for foreigners as for natives. [49]

Elsewhere, Adam of Bremen is more willing to mention the less praise-

---

[46] See his *Descriptio insularum aquilonis*, ch. 12 [*MPL*, CXLVI, p. 630]. It is this work which contains the earliest mention of Vineland. See ch. 38 [*MPL*, CXLVI, p. 656].

[47] *Descript. insular. aquilonis*, ch. 21 [*MPL*, CXLVI, p. 638].

[48] *Ibid.*, ch. 18.

[49] *Ib.*, 35 [*MPL*, CXLVI, p. 653].

worthy traits of the Northmen. A typical passage concerns the Saxons about whom he quotes at length from Einhard. Though Einhard mentions some flattering characteristics of this people, he does not hesitate to include the unflattering as well. Though they have good laws, they apply too rigorous punishment for violating them; they practise human sacrifice; " like almost all the inhabitants of Germany [they are] both fierce by nature and given to the worship of demons "; they are opposed to true religion and do not think it " dishonorable to defile or violate either divine or human rights "; their war with Charlemagne was prolonged by their perfidy.[50] Their life is therefore no model for civilized man.

Though the abundance of medieval literature which remains does not permit as complete a survey as is possible in the case of Greek and Roman writings, it is probably that most significant passages bearing on savages have been examined by us and that those which praise or condemn their manner of living have been mentioned in this paper. It will be observed that medieval man did not have the same interest in savages that the Ancients had, probably because medieval man was the savages whom the Ancients had seen fit to eulogize. In the second place, as was observed at the opening of this essay, there were two strong objections to savages in the Middle Ages, one that they were not Christians, and second that many of them who had been praised by the Ancients most highly were responsible for the martyrdom of the Evangelists. But it will also be observed that if the savages were not in general a cause of wonder for their admirable morals, their countries were very frequently lands of natural marvels. They contain extraordinary jewels, gold and other metals, which were believed to have symbolic moral potency, and of course those fantastic beasts of which medieval legend was full. The study of the Noble Savage during this period, therefore, should be accompanied by a second study, that of earthly paradises and wonderful islands. There will then be found a literary tradition which runs from the Fifth Century Greeks unbroken to the time of the explorers of the Fourteenth Century. If the accounts of these explorers are written in primitivistic language, it is in great part due to this unbroken tradition.

---

[50] *Ib.* ch. 5 [*MPL*, CXLVI, p. 463 ff.].

EARTHLY PARADISES

In Pagan legend the nearest approach to the Earthly Paradise was the Islands of the Blessed. To these islands were translated the living bodies of heroes who lived upon them a life free from care and full of noble pleasure. The location of the Islands of the Blessed was a matter of dispute, but in general it came to be believed that they were in the Atlantic. By a natural confusion, they were identified with the Fortunate Islands, and as early as Isidore of Seville, if not earlier, it was believed that they were the Pagan counterpart of the Earthly Paradise.[1] Neither the Old Testament nor the New gives any clue to the fate of the Garden of Eden after the Fall. All that was known was that after the expulsion of the first couple, God " placed at the east of the garden of Eden Cherubim, and a flaming sword which turned every way, to keep the way of the tree of life " [*Gen.*, iii, 24]. But that it still existed somewhere was almost universally believed. The only exceptions to this are to be found in the works of those writers who interpreted Paradise in a purely allegorical fashion.[2] To others it was but one of the marvelous lands which might possibly be found by adventurous explorers. We find indeed no period without its legends of wonderful undiscovered countries—usually islands—in some of which certain features of the Golden Age survived, and it is plausible that were the literature of the first thirteen centuries after Christ complete, the tradition would appear unbroken.

As in Pagan stories, there was interwoven with the stories of wonderful countries other stories of wonderful people. We are interested here only in the preservation of those details of peoples and lands which would have perpetuated primitivistic or anti-primitivistic notions.

Lands beyond the Ocean

One of the earliest passages in Christian literature mentioning lands beyond the Ocean is to be found in the Clementine *Epistle to the Corinthians* (ch. xx, 8) which comments on cosmic harmony and peace. The passage, which is but a sentence, reads, " The Ocean, impassible to man, and the worlds [*kosmoi*] beyond it are subject to the same commands of the Lord." Though this is, at least in appearance, merely a literary flourish, it furnished Origen with authority for the belief in the spatial existence of worlds un-

---

[1] See *PIA*, p. 297.

[2] So Augustine in some of his moods; see e. g., *De genesi contra Manichaeos*, II, ch. ix [*MPL*, XXXIV, 202-203]; Hugo of Saint Victor, *Allegoriae in Vetus Testamentum*, I, ch. vi [*MPL*, CLXXV, 638], where Paradise is the Church, the Fountain is Christ, the four rivers are the Gospels, and so on; Innocent III, *Sermones*, III [*MPL*, CCXVII, 605-610]. Cf. St. Jerome, *Lib. Hebr. quaest.* in Genes., ch. ii, verse 8 [*MPL*, XXIII, 688]. In the twelfth century Rupert of Deutz discussed this question in his *In Genesim*, II, cap. xxiv, xxv, [*MPL*, CLXVII, 269].

known to us, into which the saints might have right of entrance. It thus stands as the ancestor of such tales as that of Saint Brendan's voyage. It must have been supported in Origen's mind by his master, Clement of Alexandria, for we find Clement asserting dogmatically that the Heaven of Christianity was the counter-earth of the Pythagoreans,[3] so that it had as corporeal an existence as this earth. Origen is very forceful about this. He is anxious for his readers to believe that Heaven has not simply " ideal " existence, but real.

> We have said above that it is difficult for us to give an account of this world, lest some people be perhaps given ground for believing that we assert the existence of certain *ideas*, as the Greeks call them. This is far from our intention. How to speak of an incorporeal world existing only in the fancy of the mind or the flux of thoughts and yet to assert that the Saviour is from that world or that the saints will go there, I do not see. Nevertheless, that there is something more beautiful and splendid than this present world is beyond doubt indicated by the Saviour, a world whither He calls and urges those believing in Him to strive for. But whether that world which He wishes us to know is separate from this one and far away, either in place or quality or glory, or whether it excells in glory and quality and yet is contained within the limits of this world, which, as far as I am concerned, seems more probable, is uncertain, and, as I think, is unfitted for human thinking and mentality as they are now. But from what Clement seemed to mean when he said, " The Ocean is impassible to men as well as those worlds which are beyond it," speaking of worlds in the plural beyond this one, which, moreover, he suggests are controlled and rulled by the same providence of the most high God, he seems to sow certain seeds of an idea for us of this sort, that the whole world of those things which are and subsist—celestial and super-celestial, terrestrial and infernal—are called, as a whole, one perfect world, within which or by which the others—if there are any—must be thought to be contained. Wherefore he wished the sphere of the moon and the sun, and of the other bodies which they call " planets " to be each given the name of " world." But that uppermost sphere which they call " fixed," they wish nevertheless [in spite of its stability] to be called a world in its own right. Finally they even call the book of the prophet Baruch to witness of this assertion, because in it there is a clearer description of the seven worlds or heavens. Yet they wish another sphere to be above that which they call the " fixed," and, as in our world the sky contains everything which is below the sky, so they say it embraces by its immense size and indescribable expanse the spaces of all the spheres in its more magnificent stretch, so that all things are within it, as this world of ours is under the sky. That sphere in the Holy Scriptures is called the good land and the land of the living, having as its heaven that which is higher, in which heaven they say the names of the saints are written, or have been written, by the Saviour. By

[3] *Stromata*, V. Cosmas Indicopleustes held a similar belief. See his *Topographia Christiana*, Bk. II, 131 [Montfaucon].

that heaven is that land contained and bounded, which the Saviour has promised to the meek and the merciful [*Matth.* v, 4].[4]

Though Origen in this passage states simply his belief in the possibility of the existence of Heaven *intra huius mundi circumscriptionem,* yet in another he makes it perfectly clear that the saints, when they leave this life, will go to another earthly country where they will receive a preparation for immortality. This country is called " Paradise," which retained its Greek meaning for Origen, and is not Heaven.

> I think that the saints, when they depart from this life, will remain in some place situated on the earth, which the Divine Scriptures call Paradise, as if in some place of learning, a lecture hall, so to speak, or school for souls, in which they will be taught [the significance] of all that they have seen on earth and receive also certain information about things to follow in the future, just as in this life, too, they had been given certain signs of future events, though through a glass and in enigmas, yet conceived them somehow, and these things are revealed more clearly and brightly to the saints in the world of time and place. If anyone has been especially clean in heart and pure in mind and keener in sense, making rapid progress he will mount quickly into the region of air and reach the Kingdom of Heaven through the mansions of each place in succession, so to speak. These mansions the Greeks call *spheres,* that is globes, but the divine Scriptures call them " heavens." In each of these he will first see what is done there, then he will know the reason why it is done, and so in order he will pass through each, following Him who passed through them to the heavens, Jesus, Son of God, who said, " I will that they also be with me where I am " [*John,* xvii, 24]. But concerning these different places he says, " In my Father's house are many mansions " [*John,* xiv, 2]. He Himself is nevertheless everywhere and has traversed the whole world. No longer are we to believe that He is within those boundaries in which He was confined because of us; that is, in that circumscribed space, like our body, which He had when He was placed upon earth among men, wherefore He might be thought to be confined as if in some one place.
>
> When then, for example, the saints shall have reached the heavenly regions, they will see the nature of each star, and comprehend whether they are animate or whatever they are. And they will understand the other reasons for God's works which He Himself will reveal to them. For He will show them, as if they were His sons, the causes of things and the excellence of His own condition; and He will teach them why that star has been placed in that region of heaven and why it is separated from another by so great an intervening space, as, for instance, what would have been the future effect if it had been nearer; if, however, farther, what would have happened; or if this star had been larger than that, how the universe would not have been preserved as it is but all things would have changed into some other form. Thus when they have run through all

---

[4] *De principiis*, II, iii. 6 [Ed. Paul Koetschau, Leipzig, 1913] In *Opera*, V, 121-123.

things which concern the theory of the stars and their revolutions, which are in heaven, they will then come to those things which are not seen, and to those whose names alone we have now heard, and to the invisibles, which the Apostle Paul has taught are indeed many. What they are, however, or how they may differ, we cannot even guess with our narrow intellects. And so the rational nature, growing step by step, not as it grew in this life in flesh or body and soul, but increased in mind and perception, is led to perfect knowledge, a mind now made perfect, no more impeded there by carnal senses, but increased by intellectual growth, always looking to the pure and, so to speak, face to face with the causes of things. It thus attains perfection, first, by that by which it ascends to that level, second by that by which it remains there, having as food by which it is fed, theorems and the understanding of things and the nature of the causes.[5]

The details of the life in Paradise, however corporeal the place may be, is refined to the point where man's bodily vestment requires no sustenance and where his main preoccupation is knowledge. It will be noted that this is a picture of what Philo described as man's nature before the Fall. There is nothing in common between this conception and that of the Pagan primitivists. But oddly enough as Christianity developed, its writers began to introduce into their accounts of the Earthly Paradise several of the primitivistic features of Pagan literature. Thus in one of the earliest descriptions of its wonder, that found in the poem on the Phoenix, long ascribed to Lactantius,[6] one finds many of the terms used in Pagan literature to describe life in the Golden Age.

Distant in the far-east is a happy land where the great gate of the eternal heavens lies open, yet not near the Sun's summer rising nor his winter, but where he pours forth his light at the turn of spring. There a plain spreads wide its open spaces; no hill rises, no hollow valley yawns; but mountains whose peaks are thought by us to be lofty top that land by twice six ells. Here is the grove of the sun and a wood planted with many trees, blooming with the beauty of perpetual foliage. When the heavens blazed with the fires of Phaeton, that land was untouched by flames. And when the Deluge submerged the earth with its waves, this place stood above Deucalion's waters. Hither no bloodless Disease, no feeble Senility, no cruel Death, no Bitter Fear approaches; here are neither unspeakable Sin nor insane Love of Riches, nor Fear nor Fury burning with the love of slaughter. Bitter Grief is absent and Need clothed in rags and sleepless Cares and violent Hunger. There neither the tempest nor the horrid force of the wind rages, nor does the frost cover earth with frozen dew. No cloud spreads its fleece above the fields nor do troubled rains fall from on high. But a fountain is in the middle, called by the name of Life,

---

[5] *De principiis*, II, xi, 6-7 [Ed. Koetschau], *Opera*, V, 190-192.
[6] On the authorship of this famous poem, see F. J. E. Raby, *History of Christian-Latin Poetry*, Oxford, 1927, p. 15, n. 2.

transparent, gentle, rich with sweet waters, which gushing once a month, waters the whole grove with its stream.[7]

It is neither possible nor necessary to trace the fortunes of this poem. It was read throughout the Middle Ages, not only in the original Latin, but in a variety of vernacular imitations. Among these is one in Anglo-Saxon in which Paradise is an island, whose weather is always temperate, whose topography is a plane, whose trees are ever green, where there is neither enmity, death, disease, toil, nor wealth.[8] It was to this kind of land that St. Brendan traveled.

St. Brendan was an Irish monk of the sixth century, who, among other adventures, was supposed to have reached the Earthly Paradise, an island in the Western Ocean. This island, a source of wonder to medieval geographers, actually appeared on maps, moving westward and then northward with the growth of oceanic exploration, and not disappearing until after the sixteenth century.[9] In the tenth century at the latest, possibly during the ninth,[10] the legend was written down in a Latin version which would appear to be the earliest account which we have. There is a possibility that it in turn is derived from an Irish *imram*, the *Imram Maelduin*.[11] Though the wall about Paradise is described in terms which are obviously reminiscent of the Apocalypse, the land itself is pictured with more fidelity to the tradition of soft primitivism.

> With his friend as a companion, all gloom departed, and gladly they started towards the eastern regions. For forty days they were blown by helpful winds, so that nothing except sea and air fell upon their sight. Then, however, by the grace of our Lord Jesus Christ, they approached that belt of darkness which surrounds Paradise. Clouds produced a thick obscurity to keep out the descendants of Adam. The darkness was so thick that anyone in it would think himself deprived of sight. The friend, however, said to them, " Spread the sail, that it may be filled with wind." When they approached the darkness, the clouds parted, and a certain space was cleared like a sheet. Through this they entered when the clouds were condensed on either side, as if along a road, and safely did they advance in their friend's com-

[7] Ps-Lactantius, *De ave phoenice*, lines 1-28, in *Anthologia latina*, Pt. I, no. 731 [Ed. A. Riese, Leipzig, 1869, pp. 188-189]. Cf. Sidonius, *Carmina*, II, lines 407-417 [Ed. Luetjohann, Berlin, 1887].

[8] See the text in the appendix to Wright's *St. Patrick's Purgatory*, London 1844.

[9] W. H. Babcock, in his *Legendary Islands of the Atlantic*, N. Y., 1922, gives 1275 as the earliest appearance of the island on a map (p. 381). The latest map which he mentions as bearing the island is dated 1570 (p. 48). People believed in its existence until the eighteenth century at least.

[10] See E. G. R. Waters, *The Anglo-Norman Voyage of St. Brendan*, Oxford, 1928, p. lxxxii.

[11] See Waters, *loc. cit.* But Whitley Stokes, the editor and translator of the *Imram*, seems to believe that it derives from the *Navigatio*, which he traces back to the ninth century. See his *The Voyage of Mael Duin*, *Revue celtique*, IX, p. 450.

pany. Following that road, they passed three days, and on the fourth day they emerged and were filled with great joy. For they saw land which with all the longing of their minds they wished to see and which with sweat and ineffable toil they had long sought. About it a wall appeared to them, which, reaching to the clouds, was exceedingly high. Its material was unknown to the travelers. Its whiteness, brighter than that of snow, gave witness that it had been made by that Architect who made all things from nothing. It was free of all sculpture, but shone on all sides with precious stones. Chrysolites set in lumps of gold threw off great radiance. With topaz and chrysoprase, jacinth and chalcedony, emerald and sardonyx, jasper and amethyst, onyx and crystal, with beryls and with other precious stones the wall shone equally on all sides, as if the stones had been set with great art and industry. That wall surrounding Paradise was built upon a high mountain, whose summit was of gold and whose base, which came down to the sea, was of marble. The sea, far from the wall, reverberated with the beating of its waves. A huge gate was the entrance. But arriving there, they found the way in most difficult. For savage dragons, shining with a fiery glow, guarded the gate. Beside them a lance hung over the entrance, which threatened death to those who would go in. Its point looked to the earth, its hilt to heaven. They had to pass under this. No kind of metal, nor even adamant, could resist the steel of its point. But God gave them His aid. For behold, a youth most fair, a servant of God, ordered them to approach the shore and he received them as they landed and embraced them one by one, calling them by name. When the dragons were calmed and lay quietly on the ground, and the lance was held back by an angel, they joyfully entered the gates of Paradise. Passing through the outer boundaries of Paradise, with the youth as guide, they looked upon a land fertile in watered groves, with orchards and meadows unceasingly in bloom. Flowers of a wonderful kind and sweet perfumed the air, as is proper in the habitation of the just. Beautiful trees and delightful flowers, precious fruits and pleasing odors, gave forth the greatest pleasure. The trees and flowers in that part of the zodiac where the sun may be do not fade, but always produce their fruits. An everpresent gentle summer provides a ready supply of fruits. The groves are full of animals and the streams of fish. The rivers there flowed with milk and the dew, lightly dropping from heaven, was the sweetest honey. The mountains were purest gold, and the sand the most precious gems. The sun shone there unceasingly, nor was one's hair ever stirred by wind or breeze. The clouds never gathered there to shade the brightness of the sun. The inhabitants of this place will never suffer from heat, cold, sadness, hunger, thirst, poverty, nor other adversity. They will have a supply of all good things; but what is more, their will will be done in all things.[12]

St. Brendan's success in finding the Earthly Paradise stimulated others to seek it. Their efforts naturally proved vain and the island which the saint

[12] *Navigatio Sancti Brendani*, as given in Waters, *The Anglo-Norman Voyage of St. Brendan by Benedeit*, Oxford, 1928, note, pp. 84-94.

was believed to have found became the Lost Island, or Perdita. This island is briefly mentioned by Honoré d'Autun.

> There is a certain island in the ocean called Perdita, which is by far the most outstanding in its delightfulness and the general fertility of all its lands. Once found by accident, it was therefore never found when sought, and is therefore called Perdita. To this island Brendan is said to have come.[13]

That the island was a popular subject of dispute is proved in a curious way by Gaunilo's famous reply to St. Anselm's ontological proof of the existence of God. St. Anselm had argued that the idea of a perfect being implied the existence of the being; Gaunilo answered that similarly the idea of a perfect island would imply its existence. But his selection of an island is obviously not an affair of chance, for he prefaced his argument with a description of Perdita. We may reasonably conclude that unless people were discussing Perdita, he would not have chosen it as an example. We may further conclude, with perhaps less certainty, that his use of the island gained in rhetorical force because in his circle, at any rate, its existence had been questioned. This passage of the late eleventh century probably antedates that of Honoré d'Autun.

> Some say that somewhere in the Ocean is an island, which because of the difficulty, or rather the impossibility of discovering what does not exist, some call *Perdita*. And they speak more fully of it than they do of the Fortunate Islands, that it abounds in an inestimable richness of all kinds of wealth and delights, and without proprietor or inhabitant excells all other lands so far discovered which men inhabit in the abundance of its possessions.[14]

The twelfth century is the great age of legendary voyages to the Earthly Paradise. Sometimes the legends are written with a didactic purpose and are cast in the form of visions, but at other times the didactic intention is not emphasized. The accounts had a certain added power because the Earthly Paradise was supposed to be physically existent and also because a number of reports of wonderful countries, given in apocalyptic terms, were believed in full seriousness. Hugo of Saint Victor locates Paradise in the East and describes it as if he were describing any other country. The variety of vegetable life, the equable climate, the tree of life, are mentioned as they were always to be mentioned, though sometimes the tree of life is replaced by the fountain of life, which in turn became in later accounts of mysterious and wonderful lands, the fountain of youth.

> Asia has many provinces and regions whose names and location I shall set forth briefly, beginning with Paradise. Paradise is a place in the East, planted with every kind of timber and fruit trees. It

[13] *De imagine mundi*, lib. I, cap. 36 [*MPL*, CLXXII, p. 132].
[14] *Liber pro insipiente*, par. 6 [*MPL*, CLVIII, p. 246].

contains the tree of life. No cold is there nor excessive heat, but a constantly mild climate. It contains a fountain which runs off in four rivers. It is called *Paradise* in Greek, *Eden* in Hebrew, both of which words in our language mean a *Garden of Delight*.[15]

The Country of Prester John

One of the most famous legends, which seems to have arisen in the twelfth century, is that of Prester John.[16] This mysterious figure is first mentioned in the chronicle of Otto, Bishop of Freisingen, under the date of 1145, according to which entry the Bishop of Gabal—Jibal in Syria—met the Priest. About 1165 appeared the Latin text of a letter of Prester John to Manuel, Emperor of Byzantium, of which we have about a hundred manuscripts. It is from this letter, which would appear to be the earliest extended account of his kingdom, that we quote relevant portions.

The document is a hodge-podge of fantastic details, some reminiscences of the Book of Revelations and Pseudo-Callisthenes, others scraps from lapidaries and bestiaries, the whole a combination of both primitivistic and anti-primitivistic strains. Thus Prester John is modest, charitable, and chaste; his people are honest, straightforward, and faithful. At the same time his menial servants are kings and dignitaries of the Church; his wealth is unbelievably great; his power is mightier than that of any other ruler. His country too is a combination of the Fortunate Islands and Heaven; it flows in milk and honey, it contains no poisonous beasts, the fountain of perpetual youth is located in it; but it is also especially rich in precious stones and metals which many Pagans believed should never be removed from the earth.[17] This peculiar combination of simplicity and luxuriousness was seldom found in the soft primitivism of the Ancients. But the Christians were confronted with the text of the Apocalypse in which precious stones and metals seemed to have the favor of the Deity. Indeed the lapidaries of the Middle Ages frequently begin with a description of the " twelve precious stones " from *Revelations*, xxi, 19, 20.[18] With those verses as a precedent, it would have been difficult for a Christian to deny the decency of jewels.

> 1. Prester John, by the power and virtue of God and our Lord, Jesus Christ, lord of lords, to Manuel, governor of the Romans, hail, etc. . . .
>
> 9. If you wish to know the magnitude and excellence of our highness and in what lands our power has sway, know and believe without doubting that I, Prester John, am lord of lords, and surpass in all the

---

[15] *Excerptiones priores*, III, cap. ii [*MPL*, CLXXVII, p. 209].

[16] Only a specialist could do full justice to this legend. There is an excellent succinct account of it in Lynn Thorndike's *History of Magic and Experimental Science*, N. Y., 1929, Vol. II, pp. 236 ff.

[17] See *PIA*, Index, under *Metallurgy*.

[18] See among others the beginning of the 11th c. OE lapidary, published as MS A, in Evans and Serjeantson, *English Mediaeval Lapidaries*, London (EETS), 1933, p. 13.

wealth which is under heaven all the kings of the world in my virtue and power. Seventy two kings pay us tribute.

10. I am a devout Christian, and everywhere do we defend poor Christians whom the empire of our clemency rules, and we sustain them with alms . . .

21. Our land flows with honey and abounds in milk. In some parts of our land, " no poisons harm nor garrulous frogs croak, no scorpion is there nor serpent winding through the grass." Poisonous beasts cannot live in that place nor harm anyone.

22. In the country through one of our provinces flows a river which is called Ydonus. This river, flowing out of Paradise, winds through the whole province at various speeds and there are found in it natural jewels, emeralds, sapphires, carbuncles, topazes, chrysolites, onyx, beryls, amethysts, carnelians, and several other precious stones.

23. In the same place grows a plant which is called *assidios,* the root of which, when carried, puts to flight unclean spirits and forces one to say who he may be and whence and what his name is. Wherefore unclean spirits never dare to enter into anyone in that country.

24. In another province of ours whole pepper grows and is gathered; it is exchanged for wheat and corn and hides and cloth . . .

27. This grove is situated near the foot of Mount Olympus, whence a transparent spring arises, possessing every kind of taste. The flavor varies, however, each hour of the day and night, and lasts a three days journey, not far from Paradise from which Adam was expelled.

28. If anyone, even if he has fasted for three days, tastes of that spring, he will suffer no weakness from that day on, and will always be as a man thirty two years old, however long he may live.

29. There are stones there which are called *midriosi,*[19] which eagles often are accustomed to carry off to our land, by which they rejuvenate and restore their sight.

30. If anyone should wear one on his finger, his sight would not fail, and, if diminished, it is restored, and the more he uses his eyes, the sharper his vision becomes. Blessed by the right charm, it makes a man invisible, banishes hatred, prepares the way for peace, routs envy . . .

42. In certain other provinces near the torrid zone are reptiles which in our tongue are called salamanders. These reptiles live only in fire, and they produce a sort of membrane about them as other worms do, which make silk.

43. These membranes are carefully worked by the ladies of our palace, and from them we have garments and cloths for every service of our excellency. These cloths are washed only in a strong fire.

---

[19] We have not been able to find this stone in the medieval lapidaries. The author of this letter seems to have confused two legends, (1) that eagles can look directly at the sun and (2) that swallows cure the defective eyesight of their young by applying a stone—originally a plant called *celidonia*—to their lids.

44. Our serene highness has an abundance of gold and silver and previous stones, elephants, dromedaries, camels and hounds.

45. Our clemency welcomes all travelers from abroad and pilgrims. There are no paupers among our people.

46. Neither thief nor plunderer is found among us; no flatterer finds a place there, nor does avarice. There is no division among us. Our men have an abundance of all kinds of wealth. We have few horses and those of little value. We believe that no people has riches nor a population equal to ours. . . .

51. None of us lie, nor can anyone lie. But if anyone should begin to lie there, straightway would he die, that is, he would be considered to be as if dead among us and no mention would be made of him among us, that is, he would receive no further honor.

52. We all follow truth and we love one another. There is no adulterer among us. We have no ruling vice.

53. Each year we visit the body of the holy prophet Daniel with a great army in the Babylonian desert, and all are armed because of the *tyri* and other frightful serpents . . . [There follows a description of his sumptuous palace, all gold, precious stones, and rare woods.]

63. Our bed is of sapphire, because of that stone's virtue in preserving chastity.

64. We have the most handsome women, but they come to us only to procreate children, four times a year, and thus sanctified by us, as Bathsheba by David,[20] each returns to her home.

65. Once a day our court eats together. At our table there eat daily thirty thousand, besides those entering and leaving. And all these receive their expenses daily from our vaults, not only their horses [21] but their other expenses.

66. This table is of precious emerald, held up by two columns of amethyst. The power of this stone keeps anyone sitting at the table from becoming drunk . . .

97. If now you ask why, since the creator of all made us the most powerful and glorious of mortals, our sublimity does not permit itself to be called by a nobler name than that of priest, your prudence should not wonder.

98. For we have many servants in our court who have been endowed with nobler name and function, as far as ecclesiastical honors are concerned, and even with greater than ours in divine service. For our waiter at table is a primate and king, our cup-bearer an arch-bishop and king, our chamberlain a bishop and king, our marshal a king and abbot, our first cook a king and abbot. And therefore our highness has not suffered that it be named by the same names or distinguished

---

[20] The text gives *Beersheba*, the name of a city. It is difficult to see just what Bathsheba's sanctification consisted in, but if we retain *Beersheba*, we have an even greater difficulty.

[21] But see par. 46.

by the same ranks of which our court is seen to be full, and therefore has chosen to be called by a lesser name and lower grade for the sake of humility.[22]

The Purgatory of Saint Patrick

Another of the influential visions of Paradise was given in the *Tractatus de Purgatorio Sancti Patricii*, by Henry of Saltrey, which was imitated by Marie de France.[23] The number of Latin transcripts and versions is very large.[24] No critical edition of the Latin text exists, but numerous manuscripts have been found and described, dating from the twelfth to the fifteenth century. Since the thirteenth century, the story they tell has enjoyed a wide popularity as a whole, as well as in fragments inserted in various *Chronica* and lives of saints. Different themes of it were used in later legends, principally descriptions of torments in Hell, scenes in Purgatory, and so on.[25]

The first English translation of the legend is believed to have been made towards the end of the thirteenth century. Its insertion in the *Early South English Legendary* secured for it a wide distribution and repeated copying. It became known also in other countries and is said to be one of the sources of the *Divine Comedy*. The resemblances between the passage given below and that from the *Voyage of Saint Brendan* are too obvious to require indication here.

> The unconquered soldier, now freed from the plague of unclean spirits, saw before him a high wall, elevated in the air. It was a wonderful wall of incomparable beauty and marvelous architecture, in which he perceived but one gate, and that closed, which, adorned with divers metals and precious stones, shone with a wonderful gleam. When the soldier approached this, but was still distant by the space of half a mile, the gate was opened before him and an odor of such sweetness came through it that—so it seemed to him—if the whole world were turned to perfume, it would not surpass that abundant sweetness. And he received such strength from it that he thought he could now sustain the trials and threats which he had previously endured. And looking beyond the gate, he saw a door, surpassing the brightness of the sun in its radiance.
>
> 55. When he had proceeded a little distance, there came to meet him with crosses, tapers, and banners, as well as with branches of golden palms, as it were, such a procession, so great and so ordered,

---

[22] *Letter of Prester John*, par. as indicated [Ed. Zarnoke, in *Abhandlungen d. Saechsischen Gesellschaft d. Wissenschaften, Philol.-Histor. Classe*, VII, 1879, p. 909 ff].

[23] See the edition of T. A. Jenkins, 1903, p. 11, 1485-1708 esp.

[24] See G. P. Krapp, *The Legend of St. Patrick's Purgatory: Its Literary History*, 1900.

[25] For the popularity of the legend in France, from the twelfth to the nineteenth century, see Krapp, *op. cit.*, pp. 24-30.

as had never been seen in this world to his way of thinking. There
followed in this procession people of both sexes, of different ages, and
of each and every rank, some as archbishops, others as bishops, others
as abbots, monks, canons, priests, and ministers of each grade of the
church, clothed in the sacred robes fitting to their orders. In fact,
all, both clerics and laymen, were seen to be dressed in the same
form of garment there as that in which they would serve God in this
world. Now all welcomed the soldier with great veneration and
jocund gladness and they joyfully conducted him within the gate
with a chant more harmonious than any heard in this world.

56. When the song was ended and the procession dissolved, each
going his own way, two like archbishops took the soldier into their
company and led him away with them, as if they were going to
show him their country and its delights. Speaking with him, they
first blessed God who had strengthened his soul with such constancy
in the trials through which he had passed and which he had endured.
While they were leading the soldier through their delightful country,
here and there he saw many more pleasing and joyful things than
he or the most skillful of men could set forth by tongue or pen.
That country was lit by so great brightness that, as the light of a
lamp is obscured by the radiance of the sun, so the noon-day brightness of the sun seemed to be cast into shadow by the marvelous
effulgence of the light there. Night never darkened it, because the
splendor of the pure heaven illuminated it with everlasting brightness. The whole country, like a sweetly verdant field, was adorned
with divers flowers and fruits, with various herbs and trees, by the
odor of which, he says, he would have lived forever, had he been
permitted to live there. The boundary of the country he was not
able to learn, because of its too great size, except for that part through
which he passed by the gate. He saw there as great a number of
people of both sexes as he thought no one had ever seen in this life
or he believed the rest of the world to contain, some of whom remained
apart in groups in various places. Yet as they wished, they walked
about joyfully, some to this group, others to that, and it was so
done that they took pleasure in one another's company. Choir joined
choir here and there, and praises to God resounded in a union of sweet
harmony. And as star differs from star in brightness, so there was
a certain harmonious difference in the clear beauty of their garments
and their faces. Some were clothed in robes of gold, others in green,
purple, hyacinthine, blue, white; yet the form of their raiment was
the same as each had had in this world, which in this way indicated
to the soldier of what rank or order each had been. Their clothes,
of various colors, seemed to shine with different degrees of brightness.
Some walked crowned as if they were kings, others carried golden
palms in their hands. So the appearance of such and so many just
men in that place of rest was delightful to the soldier and not less
delightful was the soft and ineffably sweet sound of their harmonies.
From all sides he heard the singing of the saints, chanting praises of
God; each rejoiced in his own felicity and each exulted in the joy of
the others. But all who saw the soldier praised the Lord for his
coming . . . and it seemed as if a new cause for exultation had arisen

12

from his arrival. He felt neither excessive heat nor cold there, nor anything which could offend or harm him; for all things were at peace, all calm, all agreeable. He saw many more things in that place of rest than any man could speak of or describe.

57. When these things had taken place, the pontiffs said to the soldier, " Lo, brother, with God's help you have seen what you desired to see, for coming hither you have seen the torments of sinners and here you have seen the repose of the just. Blessed be the Creator and Redeemer of all Who has given you such resolution, Whose grace you have constantly needed as you passed through your trials. Now, however, we wish you to know what are those places of torment which you have seen and what is this land of so great blessedness.

58. This country is the earthly paradise, from which Adam, the first made, was expelled for the fault of disobedience. For since he disdained submission in disobedience to God, he could no longer see what you see, nay, incomparably greater joys. . . ."

The Vision of Tnugdal

A third vision of Paradise is that of Tnugdal, of which it has been said that it was " perhaps the best known, as it is undoubtedly the most elaborate, of all the medieval visions." [26] The identity of the author, who calls himself " Pater Marcus," is not known. The date at which the vision is supposed to have occurred is 1149, which is four years after the first mention of Prester John. Fifty-four Latin manuscripts are reported by Wagner, all belonging to the period between the twelfth and fifteenth centuries, as well as numerous translations into the vernaculars. The portion which we quote has obvious affiliations with *The Phoenix* and must have been a means of perpetuating older details about the Earthly Paradise.

Going on a little they came to a gate which was then opened to them. When they had passed through, they saw a beautiful meadow, sweet smelling, studded with flowers, fresh and lovely, in which was a multitude of souls which none would be able to count. And there was a host of men and women exulting and there was no night there, nor did the sun ever set, and there is a fountain there of living water. The soul after such great trouble which it had sustained, when it came to this beautiful field of delightful sweetness, broke into these words with great devotion: Blessed be the name of the Lord, from now henceforth and to everlasting, Who has freed me from the gates of Hell according to His great compassion and led me to share the lot of the saints. Now I know that the Holy Scriptures are most true. What eye has not seen nor ear heard, that hath God prepared for them that love Him. And he added, Of what souls, I pray, is this the place of rest, and that fountain, what is its name? Replying, the angel said to him, Here dwell the moderately good, who snatched from the torments of Hell, do not yet deserve to be joined to the company of the saints. And this fountain which you see is called the

[26] Ernest J. Becker, *The Medieval Visions of Heaven and Hell*, Baltimore, 1882, p. 82. Cf. A. Wagner's study, *Visio Tnugdali*, Erlangen, 1882.

Fountain of Life; if anyone tastes of this water, he will live forever nor thirst thenceforth.

Roger de Wendover

The last of the visions which we shall quote is peculiar in that it combines the legend of the Earthly Paradise with an allegorical description of human progress. The grotesque figure of Adam in it suggests the gradual rehabilitation of the human race through the just deeds of his descendants. It will be noted that this is an echo of the Philonic interpretation of human history, as given on a smaller scale, and was not dissimilar to a theory deriving from Origen and eventuating into the eschatological doctrines of the Universalists. The document dates from about a century after those just quoted.

> Turning towards the east of the temple of which we have been speaking, they came to a very lovely spot, glowing with various plants, full of the fragrance of trees and fruits, where he, when he was led out, saw a very clear fountain which poured forth from itself four rivulets of varied fluids and colors. Over this fountain grew a very beautiful tree of wondrous size and immense height, which was rich in its abundance of all kinds of fruit, as well as in the odor of its flowers. Under this tree near the fountain reclined a man of fair form and gigantic body, who from breast to feet was clothed in a garment of many colors and woven with wondrous beauty. With one eye he seemed to smile and with the other to mourn.
> "This man," said Saint Michael, "is the original parent of the human race, Adam, who hints with his smiling eye at the gladness which he has from the ineffable glory of saving his children, and with his weeping eye shows the sadness which he has from the rejection of certain of his children and their damnation by God's just sentence. The garment in which he is clad, but not yet entirely, is the stole of immortality and the robe of glory, of which he was despoiled by his original sin. For from Abel the Just, his son, until the present, he began to recover this robe passing through the entire succession of his just children, and, as the elect shine by their various virtues, so this robe is dyed in various colors; when the number of the elect shall be complete, then will Adam be entirely clothed with the stole of immortality and glory and the world will come to its end." [27]

The passage ends with the visionary's awakening. He is a simple peasant whose customary inarticulateness is changed by his experience and he converts all his listeners by the eloquence and force of his tale.

The Land of Cocaigne

Such visions, with their marvels, stimulated the same satiric reaction as did the legends of the Age of Cronus in Greece.[28] Just as the writers of the

[27] Roger de Wendover, *The Flowers of History,* "De Paradiso et Adam primo parente" [Ed. H. Hewlett, London, 1887, p. 33].

[28] See *PIA,* pp. 38 ff., for parodies of the Golden Age in Greek comic poets.

Old Comedy saw the absurdities in an age in which no one worked and earth bore food spontaneously, so the inventors of the Land of Cocaigne could not resist the humor in legends telling of rivers of milk and honey, heaps of precious stones, fountains of youth. The *fabliaux* dealing with this wonderful country are too long to be reprinted and are easily found in the various collections of such poems.[29] One discovers many of the same details as were characteristic of the Old Comedy, with such changes as would be appropriate to a Christian culture. Thus the more one sleeps, the more one earns; food all cooked is free; there is a river of Burgundy; there are four Easters a year, four harvests, and so on, but only one Lent every twenty years; the women are promiscuous; there is a fountain of youth which, like that of Prester John, keeps a man thirty years old as long as he drinks of it. The most famous pictorial representation of the Land Cocaigne is no doubt that of Breughel the Elder, which retains for posterity the main features of this legend. But enough has been quoted to suggest the popularity of the belief that the Earthly Paradise still existed, that it had traits of a miraculous nature, and that some people at least thought the whole conception ridiculous.

Our purpose now is to indicate briefly certain passages which bear witness to a belief that real lands existed in the Western Ocean which, if not so marvelous as the Earthly Paradise, yet had some features which would have stimulated adventurers to seek for them.

The Fortunate Islands

The legend of Saint Brendan's Island was paralleled by that of the Fortunate Islands. In Pliny, who first mentions this archipelago, they are fortunate in name only; in Isidore of Seville, they begin to have marvelous features; by the time of Rabanus Maurus (ca. 776-856) they have come to resemble the spontaneously fertile land of the Cyclopes.[30]

> The Fortunate Islands are so called because they produce all sorts of good things, as if they were happy and blessed in the copiousness of their products. For by their very nature they produce fruits of the most precious trees; the slopes of their hills are covered with unplanted vines; there is grain in place of grass and kitchen vegetables everywhere. Whence the error of the Gentiles and the songs of the pagan poets who thought that these islands were Paradise, because of the fertility of their soil. They are located in the Ocean to the west

---

[29] See, for instance, *Fabliaus de Coquaigne* in *Fabliaux et Contes de poètes françois des XI, XII, XIII, XIV et XVe siècles*, Ed. Barbazan, Vol. IV, Paris 1808, pp. 175-181.

[30] See *PIA*, pp. 303 ff. Their existence, curiously enough, must have been doubted by Christian writers as early as the third century. See Eumenius's Panegyric of Constantine, in the seventh chapter of which appears the words, " ipsas, *si quae sunt*, Fortunatorum insulas " [*MPL*, VIII, p. 627]. The genitive plural may indicate a confusion in the mind of the writer between the Fortunate Islands and the Islands of the Blest.

of Mauritania, close to the setting sun, and are separated from one another by the sea.[31]

The spontaneous fertility of the Fortunate Islands appears again in the twelfth century in the *Vita Merlini*. An added element of wonder is the longevity of their inhabitants.

> The Isle of Fruits, which is called the Fortunate Island, has its name from its peculiar fertility. Its fields have no need of the farmer's plow; they are utterly uncared for except as Nature tends them. It brings forth grain of rare fertility and grapes and fruits ripened on its trees with spreading boughs. The soil bears everything as if it were grass, by spontaneous production. Man lives there a hundred years or more.[32]

The descriptions of Isidore of Seville and Rabanus Maurus are repeated with but slight verbal changes in the *Imago mundi* (ch. xli) and in Vincent de Beauvais's *Speculum historiale* (II, 79). This carries us into the thirteenth century. But as late as the fifteenth century, the legendary island of Brazil was ranked as one of the Fortunate Islands on the map of Fra Mauro [33] and a legend on the Catalan Atlas of the *Bibliothèque Nationale* continues the tradition with a substitution of the Indians for the Pagans of Isidore and Rabanus Maurus.

Ireland

It was perhaps inevitable that distant lands should be described with something of the air of mystery that surrounded imaginary islands and Earthly Paradises. Ireland, being one of the outposts of the western world, was given a character little short of magical. In the classical geographers, it is spoken of without enthusiasm. Strabo describes its people as incestuous cannibals (IV, 201) and Mela as ignorant and uncouth (III, vi, 53). Yet by the time of Bede (8th century) Ireland has become a place to wonder about. Its climate was described as so mild as to cause no need for stabling cattle in winter; it was rich in milk and honey; it had no snakes nor poisonous insects; and a leaf from one of its trees when steeped in water, would cure snake bite.[34]

One of the details which seems especially to have captivated the imagination of these people is the Fountain of Life or of Youth. People dwelt upon it since it was believed by some that if Adam had not sinned, man would have been immortal. There was nothing in the Bible to induce them to believe that any race or group of individuals had escaped the doom brought on by Adam's sin, but nevertheless they still continued to believe that in some outlying corner of the earth there was a magical escape from it. Peter

---

[31] Rabanus Maurus, *De universo*, Bk. XII, ch. 5 [*MPL*, CXI, p. 354].

[32] From Geoffrey of Monmouth's *Vita Merlini*, verses 908-915, in *La légende Arthurienne,* by E. Faral, Paris, 1929, vol. III, p. 334.

[33] See W. H. Babcock, *Legendary Islands in the Atlantic*, p. 52.

[34] *Historia ecclesiastica*, I, i [*MPL*, XCV, p. 26 f.].

Comestor thus mentions " certain islands " in which no one ever dies,[35] and contemporaries of his identified these islands with Ireland. Why Ireland should have been selected is a matter of conjecture, but we find as early as Plutarch the story of a mysterious island to the west of Britain in which Cronus is imprisoned in unending sleep. The climate there is unusually mild and the air is pervaded with fragrance.[36] It should also be recalled that the Hyperboreans were believed to be very long-lived as early as Callimachus, and Mela maintains that they terminate their life by joyful suicide when they have had enough of it. This, we may add, was about the only way in which they could die, since, like most people whose lives duplicated that of the Golden Age, they were free from disease.[37] It is possible that memories of such legends disposed men's minds to believe in the extraordinary vitality of Irish soil, for Ireland as one of the remotest points of Europe was real enough to command respect and yet distant enough to be marvelous.

At any rate the legend was definitely established by the twelfth century. Thus Giraldus Cambrensis (?1146-1220), utilizing Peter Comestor, speaks of two small islands in a lake in Munster, on one of which no one dies. It is called the Island of the Living.[38] Interestingly enough, Giraldus does not think this adds much to the happiness of the inhabitants.

> There is a lake in northern Munster with two islands in it, one larger than the other . . . On the smaller no one has ever died, or could die of a natural death. Wherefore it is called the Island of the Living. Nevertheless the [people] there are sometimes sorely afflicted with a lethal disease and are reduced in wretchedness to their last breath. When there is no more hope, they feel that life holds nothing more for them; and when, with waning strength, they are brought to the door of death, as they prefer to die rather than drag out a living death, they have themselves carried over to the larger island in a boat. As soon as they reach its shores, they give up the ghost.
>
> This seems to me worthy of note, because in the first book of the *Historia scholastica*, near the beginning, there is mention of islands of the living of this kind. There the tree of the sun is spoken of. They who eat of its fruit, as King Alexander wrote to Aristotle, extend their life very greatly.[39]

By the fourteenth century Ireland is less marvelous, for it was of course better known at first hand, but its climate and certain magical properties

---

[35] See his *Historia scholastica*, ch. xxiv [*MPL*, CXCVIII, p. 1075].

[36] The passage is given at length in *PIA*, p. 297 f. It is from *De fac. in orbe lun.*, xxvi.

[37] See *PIA*, pp. 310 ff.

[38] The *Atlas Catalan* of the *Bibliothèque Nationale* says in a legend on Ireland, " En Hibernie il y a beaucoup d'îles qu'on peut croire merveilleuses, parmi lesquelles il s'en trouve une petite où les hommes ne meurent jamais, mais quand ils sont assez vieux pour devoir mourir, on les porte hors de l'île." See Buron's edition of the *Imago Mundi*, Paris 1930, T. II, p. 386, n. 240.

[39] *Topographia hibernica*, II, ch. iv [Ed. Dimock, Lond., 1867, in *Rer. brit. med. aev. script.*, vol. XXI.]

of its soil are still like those of the Earthly Paradise.[40] Thus John of
Fordun emphasizes the peculiar power of the Irish climate to counteract
poisons, the fertility of the soil, the absence of excessive heat and cold, a
feature which is common to all Earthly Paradises.

> After Britain Ireland is the greatest of all islands, and is situated to
> the west of it. But as Britain is narrower towards its northern end,
> so it too has its greatest width towards the south and reaches a point
> opposite the north of Spain, although a great body of water lies
> between them. Ireland, however, both in breadth and salubrity as
> well as in its serene climate, surpasses Britain by far. Hence it is
> rare that snow stays on the ground there for more than three days;
> no one because of the winter would either mow his hay in summer or
> build a stable for his cattle. No reptile is ever seen there; no serpent
> could ever live there. For if a serpent should go there from elsewhere,
> as soon as it would smell the odor of its air, it would die. The more
> so, since practically everything which comes from this island prevails
> against poison. The island is rich in milk and honey, not devoid of
> vineyards and birds, but famous for its deer and goat hunting.[41]
>
> *Chronicle.* Ireland is an island in the ocean in Europe, next to
> island of Britain, smaller in extent but more fertile. It runs in a
> northern-southerly direction; its regions which are nearer to Spain
> reach the Bay of Biscay. It is, moreover, an island very rich in grain-
> bearing fields, watered by springs and rivers, agreeable because of its
> meadows and woods, rich in metals and gems. For there is found the
> hexagonal stone, the iris, which when placed in the sun forms a
> rainbow in the air.[42] As for the salubrity of the climate, the region
> of Ireland is peculiarly temperate. For both summer and winter are
> moderate there. There is no excess of heat or cold. It is a place
> where there is no serpent, where birds are rare, and there are no
> bees,[43] so that swarms desert the combs if anyone puts in the hive
> pebbles or sand taken from Ireland. There are no snakes there, no
> frogs, no poisonous spiders, for the earth of the whole country is anti-
> dotal to poisons. Hence soil taken from there and scattered about
> kills snakes and toads. In fact, Irish wool and the hides of Irish
> animals keep out poisons. There are wonderful springs and lakes
> there, which are not pertinent to the present discussion. But in that
> land are many other marvels the properties of which I shall not
> describe, since they would, I believe, bore the reader.[44]

Columbus and the West Indies

The Atlantic continued to be held to be a sea of wonderful islands approaching the marvelousness of the Earthly Paradise, until the period of

[40] Cf. with the passage which follow in the text, the description of Kent in the
Vita S. Augustini (11th century?), printed as an appendix to Lanfranc's work in
MPL, CL, pp. 747-748.

[41] This is quoted from Bede's *Historia ecclesiastica*, I. i.

[42] This is obviously some hexagonal crystal which acts as a prism. That it was
known fairly early is shown by Pliny, XXXVII, ix, 52.

[43] The honey mentioned in the previous section must be symbolical.

[44] *Chronica*, I, xviii [Ed. W. F. Skene, Edinburgh, 1871, pp. 16 f.].

explorations was over. In fact, so strong was this belief that the very explorers began to describe the lands which they had found in legendary terms. The most dramatic case of this is to be found in the reports of Columbus. In his Narrative of the Third Voyage, he points out that the site of the Earthly Paradise must lie near the stem of the pear-shaped earth. In its vicinity are the islands which he has discovered. Their temperature is mild, their people gentle, generous and beautiful. They have no metals nor weapons. Now much of this was probably true, but, curiously enough, it was also in part confirmation of the legends, as Columbus himself realized. It was small wonder then that America began to appear to be a heavenly country, the fulfillment of man's earthly hopes.[45] We shall close this chapter with selections from Columbus's reports.

1. *The Site of the Earthly Paradise*

> . . . I have now seen so much irregularity, that I have come to another conclusion respecting the earth, namely, that it is not round as they describe, but of the form of a pear, which is very round except where the stalk grows, at which part it is most prominent; or like a round ball, upon one part of which is a prominence like a woman's nipple, this protrusion being the highest and nearest the sky, situated under the equinoctial line, and at the eastern extremity of the sea. . . . Ptolemy and the others who have written upon the globe, had no information respecting this part of the world, which was then unexplored; they only established their arguments with respect to their own hemisphere, which, as I have already said, is half of a perfect sphere. And now that your Highnesses have commissioned me to make this voyage of discovery, the truths which I have stated are evidently proved, because in this voyage when I was off the island of Gargin, and its vicinity, which is twenty degrees to the north of the equinoctial line, I found that the people are black, and the land very much burnt; and when after that I went to the Cape Verde islands, I found the people there much darker still, and the more southward we went, the more they approach the extreme of blackness; so that when I reached the parallel of Sierra Leone, where, as night came on, the north star rose five degrees, the people there were excessively black; and as I sailed westward, the heat became extreme. But after I had passed the meridian, or line which I have already described, I found the climate became gradually more temperate; so that when I reached the island of Trinidad, where the north star rose five degrees as night came on, there, and in the land of Gracia, I found the temperature mild; the fields and the foliage likewise were remarkably fresh and green, and as beautiful as the gardens of Valencia in April. The people there are very graceful in form, less dark than those whom I had before seen in the Indies, and wear their hair long and smooth; they are also more shrewd, intelligent, and courageous . . .

[45] The rest of this story has been sufficiently told by G. Chinard in his studies of *l'Exotisme américain*. See especially his first book on the subject, *L'exotisme américain dans la littérature française au 16e siècle*, Paris, 1911. His first chapter shows how quickly men were to identify the West Indies with the Fortunate Islands and other marvelous lands.

I do not find, nor have ever found, any account by the Romans or Greeks, which fixes in a positive manner the site of the terrestrial paradise, neither have I seen it given in any mappe-monde, laid down from authentic sources. Some placed it in Ethiopia, at the sources of the Nile, but others, traversing all these countries, found neither the temperature nor the altitude of the sun correspond with their ideas respecting it; nor did it appear that the overwhelming waters of the deluge had been there. Some pagans pretended to adduce arguments to establish that it was in the Fortunate Islands, now called the Canaries, etc.

St. Isidore, Bede, Strabo, and the Master of the Scholastic History [Peter Comestor], with St. Ambrose, and Scotus, and all the learned theologians, agree that the earthly paradise is in the east, etc.

I have already described my ideas concerning this hemisphere and its form, and I have no doubt, that if I could pass below the equinoctial line . . . I should find a much milder temperature, and a variation in the stars and in the water; not that I suppose that elevated point to be navigable, nor even that there is water there; indeed, I believe it is impossible to ascend thither, because I am convinced that it is the spot of the earthly paradise, whither no one can go but by God's permission; but this land which your Highnesses have now sent me to explore, is very extensive, and I think there are many other countries in the south, of which the world has never had any knowledge. I do not suppose that the earthly paradise is in the form of a rugged mountain, as the descriptions of it have made it appear, but that it is on the summit of the spot, which I have described as being in the form of the stalk of a pear; the approach to it from a distance must be by a constant and gradual ascent; but I believe that, as I have already said, no one could ever reach the top; I think also, that the water I have described may proceed from it, though it be far off, and that stopping at the place which I have just left, it forms this lake. There are great indications of this being the terrestrial paradise, for its site coincides with the opinion of the holy and wise theologians whom I have mentioned; and moreover the other evidences agree with this supposition, for I have never either read nor heard of fresh water coming in so large a quantity, in close conjunction with the water of the sea; the idea is also corroborated by the blandness of the temperature; and if the water of which I speak, does not proceed from the earthly paradise, it seems to be a still greater wonder, for I do not believe that there is any river in the world so large or so deep.[46]

2. *The Indians of Hispaniola*

. . . This island, like all the others, is most extensive, and richly wooded. It has many ports along the sea-coast—incomparably more than others I know of in Christendom—and marvelously fine, large, flowing rivers. The land there is elevated, with many mountains and

[46] *Select Letters of Christopher Columbus*, with Original Documents relating to his Four Voyages to the New World; trans. and edited by R. H. Major, 2d ed., London, 1870, pp. 134-139, 140-143. Cf. *Journal of Christopher Columbus* (During his First Voyage, 1492-93), trans. by C. R. Markham, London, 1893, p. 184.

peaks incomparably higher than in the centre isle. They are most beautiful, of a thousand varied forms, accessible, and full of trees of endless varieties, so high that they seem to touch the sky; and I have been told that they never lose their foliage. I can affirm that I saw them as green and lovely as trees are in Spain in May, and some of them were in flower, some with fruit, and some in other conditions, according to their kind. The nightingale and other small birds of a thousand kinds were singing in the month of November when I was there; and there were palms of six or eight varieties, the graceful peculiarities of each one of them being worthy of admiration. But besides the other trees, fruits, and grasses, there are wonderful pine-woods, and very extensive ranges of meadow land. There is honey, and there are many kinds of birds, and a great variety of fruits. Inland there are numerous mines of metals, and considerable numbers of people. *Spanōla* is a wonder, with its hills and mountains, fine *plains*, open country, and land rich and fertile for planting and sowing, to bring in profit of all sorts; for *building* towns and villages. The seaports there are incredibly fine, as also the magnificent rivers, most of which bear gold. The trees, fruits, and grasses, differ widely from those in *Juana*. There are many spices, and vast mines of gold and other metals. The people of all the islands I have discovered and taken, and those of whom I have heard, both men and women, go about naked as when they were born, except that some of the women cover one part of themselves with a single leaf of grass, or a cotton thing that they make for this purpose. They have no iron, nor steel, nor weapons, nor are they fit for them, because although they are well-made men of commanding stature, they appear extraordinarily timid. The only arms they have are sticks of cane, cut when in seed, *with a sharpened stick at the end, and they are afraid to use these. Often I have sent two or three men ashore* to some town to hold converse with them, and the natives came out in great numbers, and as soon as they saw our men arrive, fled without a moment's delay.

I protected them from all injury, and at every point where I landed and succeeded in talking with them, I gave them some of the clothing I had—cloth and many other things—without receiving anything in return, but they are hopelessly timid people. It is true that since they have gained more confidence, and are losing this fear, they are so unsuspicious and so generous with what they possess, that no one who had not seen it would believe it, never refusing anything that is asked for, and they also offer themselves, and show so much love that they would give their very hearts. Whether it be anything of great or small value, with any trifle of whatever kind, they are satisfied.[47]

[47] *The Letter in Spanish of Christopher Columbus (1st voyage) to Luis de Sant Angel*, 15 Feb.–14 March, 1493. From the Brayton Ives copy, only English translation, London, 1889, pp. 33-37. Cf. C. R. Markham's edition of the *The Journal of Christopher Columbus* [Hakluyt Society], London, 1893, p. 112, "The Admiral . . . says, 'for they are the best people in the world, and the gentlest.'" In the *Journal* of Columbus's first voyage, there are numerous references and brief descriptions of these Indians and their lands, duplicating the sentiments expressed in the quotations given above. See pp. 37-41, 46-47, 49, 50, 54-55, 60, 61-62, 65, 68, 71-73, 90, 106-109, 123-125, 127, 131-132, 135. See also R. H. Major's edition of *Select Letters of Christopher Columbus*, 2d. ed. (1870), for further references to Indian peoples in subsequent narratives, pp. 23-24, 62-70, 119-121, 181-182, 201-203, 212-218, 226-227.

ANTIPRIMITIVISM IN THE MIDDLE AGES

The authority of antiquity

It was, of course, part of the dominant Christian tradition to accept unquestionably certain opinions as authoritative, and it came to be believed that an authority gained in importance in proportion to its age. This was paralleled in pagan thought by the occasional identification of the *consensus gentium*, which never erred, with the ideas of primitive man,[1] by the frequent appeal to Homer and Hesiod as almost sacred terts, and in fact by the argument from etymology as found in Aristotle, by means of which the supposed original meaning of a word was held to have probative value. The Bible's authority rested fundamentally upon its supernatural origin, but parts of the Old Testament were of the greatest antiquity and the New Testament was the most ancient of Christian writings. If, however, the age of an authority were emphasized, the question of the authority of the pagan philosophers would be bound to arise, for all of them whose prestige was important antedated Christianity. The Christian philosopher knew that, however old the roots of his religion might be, his philosophy was not so old as that of the Greeks, and he had to resort either to the theory that the Greeks had taken their ideas bodily from Moses or that age in itself was not a criterion of truth.

Arnobius

Arnobius chose the latter alternative, and, frankly admitting the novelty of Christian dogma, saw no reason to disparage it on that account. He utilized the legend of the rise of primitive man from a state in which he lived on a diet of acorns and inhabited caves to a better condition as an argument in favor of a new religion. He did not maintain that every innovation was good, but saw no evidence of evil in novelty.

> As for the objection which you are accustomed to make, that our religion is new and arose only a few days ago, so to speak, and that we ought not to have abandoned the ancient faith of our fathers and gone over to barbarous and foreign rites, it is supported by no rational argument. For what if in the same way we should choose to blame those earlier, indeed the most ancient, ages because when the growing of grains was discovered, they despised acorns and repudiated the wild strawberry, because they ceased to be covered with the bark of trees and to be clothed in pelts, when woven garments were devised, more useful and convenient, or because when houses were built and more comfortable dwellings established, they did not cling to their ancient shelters nor prefer to remain like beasts in rocky caves? It is common to all and a thing taught to us almost in infancy to prefer

[1] See *PIA*, pp. 255 f.

good things to bad, to set the useful above the useless, to pursue and seek more gladly that which has been considered to be more precious and in it to fix our hope of welfare and of advantageous conditions.[2]

Lactantius

A similar point of view was taken by Lactantius in a passage frequently cited by seventeenth century writers. He seems to have confined his remarks, however, to the field of philosophy, for had he applied it to religion, as Tertullian did, he would have fallen into Montanism.

> Wherefore each man ought, especially in those affairs with which the business of living is concerned, to have confidence in himself and to strive with the aid of his own judgment and senses towards the discovery and testing of the truth, rather than to be deceived by belief in the errors of others, as if he himself were devoid of reason. God has given wisdom to all as their manly portion, that they might be able to investigate the things they have not experienced and weigh the things they have experienced. Nor is it true that because certain philosophers have preceded us in time they have also surpassed us in wisdom which, if it is given equally to all, cannot be monopolized by our predecessors. Wisdom is inexhaustible, like the light and clarity of the sun, for as the sun is the illumination of the eyes, so wisdom is of the human heart. Wherefore, since to know, that is, to seek the truth, is inborn in us all, they deprive themselves of wisdom who uncritically approve the discoveries of their elders and are led along by others like cattle. But they are ignorant of this fact that, although some have been given the name of " elder," they do not think it can possibly occur that they themselves should know more because they are called " juniors," or that their ancestors should be fools who have been called " elders." What then hinders us from following their own example, so that like them who handed over to posterity their false discoveries, we who have discovered the truth should pass on to our children a better legacy?[3]

Montanism

Texts of the Montanist heresy have disappeared, but from what we know of it through its adversaries and through its one surviving defender, Tertullian, we know that it maintained one thesis which is relevant to a doctrine of religious progress. All Christians had to believe that at least the New Testament contained a truth more important for mankind than its predecessor. The great question that remained was whether its revelation was the last which man would have. The Montanists maintained that their founder and certain other seers and seeresses had also been divinely inspired and hence they were forced into a defense of the position that even in religion the most ancient authority was not necessarily the best. Although the Montanist

---

[2] *Adversus nationes*, Bk. II, 66 [Ed. A. Reifferscheid, Vienna, 1875, in *Corpus scriptorum ecclesiasticorum latinorum*, vol. IV, pp. 101 f.].

[3] *Divine Institutions*, Bk. II, ch. vii [Ed. Samuel Brandt, in *CSEL*, XIX, pp. 124 f.]

heresy was suppressed, traces of it lingered on and we find the theory of religious progress being revived in the late twelfth century by Joachim of Florus, who will be discussed below.

Ages of the World

Pagan writers had played with the idea that the world was growing old and tired and that its fertility was waning. In that idea lies concealed the analogy between cosmic and individual history. In Saint Augustine a triple parallelism is worked out between the seven days of creation, the seven ages of men, and the seven ages of the cosmos—a sort of Great Week, similar to the Great Year of the Stoics.

Normally one might expect that Saint Augustine would consider the period of infancy to be the best and to picture a steady decline in goodness from Adam's loss of his childlike innocence. But, on the contrary, the best age is the fourth, the age of youth, the day on which the stars were made, the beginning in human history of the reign of David. In the sixth age, when senility sets in, a new man is born—the spiritual man—made fit to receive the teachings of Christ. Thus the course of history is compounded of a phase of amelioration, a phase of decline, and a phase of rebirth.[4]

1st Age. But why God rested on the seventh day must, I think, be considered more carefully. I perceive that throughout the whole text of the Divine Scriptures six ages of work have been distinguished within fixed limits, so that rest may be hoped for in the seventh. And I perceive that the same six ages are like those six days during which those things were done which the Scriptures say God did. For the beginnings of humanity, in which it began to enjoy that light, may be well compared to the first day when God made light. This age must be thought of as the infancy of the universal period itself, which we ought to think of as the life of a single man. Because each man, when he is first born and goes forth into the light spends his first age in infancy. This stretches from Adam to Noah, for ten generations. The Deluge was as the evening of this day, for our infancy is wiped out as by the deluge of oblivion.

2d Age. And there begins on the morrow, after the time of Noah, a second age, like childhood, and this age reaches to Abraham, for another ten generations. And it may be fittingly compared to the second day on which the firmament was made between the waters, because the ark in which were Noah and his family was the firmament between the lower waters on which it was floating and the upper which were raining down upon it. This age was not wiped out by a deluge, because our childhood is not erased from memory by oblivion. We remember to have been children, but we do not remember to have

---

[8] Commentaries on the seven days of creation were of course common before the time of Saint Augustine, and in fact his master, Saint Ambrose, was the author of one of the most famous of them. But no one before him seems to have thought to make the parallel between the seven days and the seven ages. See Frank Egleston Robbins, *The Hexaemeral Literature*, Chicago, 1912, p. 72.

been infants. The evening of this day is the confusion of tongues among those who built the Tower of Babel and it fell after Abraham. But that second age did not beget the people of God, for childhood is not able to beget.

3rd Age. Immediately after Abraham the third age followed, like adolescence. And it may be well compared to the third day, on which the earth was separated from the waters. For the people of God was separated from all whose error was unfixed and shifting with vain doctrines of appearances, as if tossed by every wind that blew, who might properly be called by the name of the sea. The people of God was separated from the vanity of these people and the waves of this period by Abraham, like the earth when it seems dry, that is, thirsting for the heavenly shower of divine commandments. This people by worshipping the one God, like the watered earth, in order to produce useful fruits, received the Holy Scriptures and the Prophecies. For this age could now beget a people for God, because the third age, that is, adolescence, is capable of having children. And therefore it was said to Abraham, " A father of many nations have I made thee. And I will make thee exceeding fruitful, and I will make nations of thee and kings shall come out of thee. And I will establish my covenant between me and thee and thy seed after thee in their generations, for an everlasting covenant, to be a God unto thee and to thy seed after thee. And I will give unto thee, and to thy seed after thee, the land wherein thou art a stranger, all the land of Canaan, for an everlasting possession; and I will be their God " [*Gen.*, XVII, 5-8]. This age extended from Abraham to David, for fourteen generations. Its evening fell with the sins of the people by which the divine commandments were forgotten, and lasted until the sins of the wicked king, Saul.

4th Age. And then began the reign of David. This age is like youth. And in truth youth rules among all ages, and is itself the sure adornment of all ages. And therefore it may be properly compared to the fourth day on which the stars were made in the heavenly firmament. For how could the splendor of a reign be more clearly symbolized than by the perfection of the sun? And the light of the moon means the people obedient to its kingdom, like the synagogue itself, and the stars mean the princes, and all things established as if in the firmament in the stability of the kingdom. Its evening fell with the sins of the kings for which that people deserved to be taken captive and to serve in slavery.

5th Age. There was next the immigration into Babylon, when in that captivity the people spent their time in mild idleness in a foreign land. And this age reached until the advent of Our Lord Jesus Christ, the fifth age, to wit, the decline from youth to old age, not yet old age, no longer youth. This age of older people is what the Greeks call *presbytes*. For an old man in Greek is not called a *presbyter* but a *geron*. And in truth that age was weakened and broken from the strength of the kingdom among the Jews, as a man grows old from his youth. And it may be well compared to the fifth day when animals were made in the waters and birds in the air, after which those men began to live among gentiles, as in the sea, and to have an unfixed and unstable home, as the birds who fly. That clearly there were great whales there, that is, those great men who were able to conquer the waves of the period rather than serve as slaves in captivity. For they were not corrupted to the worship of idols by fear. Wherein must be observed how God blessed those animals, saying, " Be fruitful and multiply, and fill the waters in the seas, and let fowl multiply in the earth " [*Gen.* I, 22]. For in truth the Jews, from the fact that they were scattered among the gentiles, were truly multiplied. The evening of this day, that is of this age, is the multiplication of sins among the Jews, for they were so blinded that they could not recognize the Lord Jesus Christ.

6th Age. This age began with the preaching of the Gospel through Our Lord Jesus Christ, and the fifth age was over. The sixth began, in which old age appears. For it is in this age that carnal rule was violently attacked and the temple was destroyed and its sacrifices brought to an end. And now that people attained the limits of its power, as if it were approaching the end of life. Yet in that age, as in the old age of a man, a new man is born who now lives spiritually. For on the sixth day it was said, " Let the earth bring forth the living creatures." But on the fifth day it was said, " Let the waters bring forth," not living creatures but " creeping things that have life." For bodies are creeping things and up to now that people had been serving the Law with bodily circumcision and sacrifices, as if in the sea of the Gentiles. It says that those creatures are alive, because in this life eternal things began to be desired. For serpents and beasts which the earth brings forth, mean the people who were about to believe firmly in the Gospel. Concerning these it is said, regarding that vessel which was shown to Peter, in the *Acts of the Apostles,* " Kill and eat." And when he declared them to be unclean, the answer was, " What God hath cleansed, that call thou not unclean " [*Acts,* X, 16]. Then man was made in the image and likeness of God, as Our Lord was in that sixth age born in the flesh, concerning Whom it was said by the prophet, " And He is a man and who will acknowledge Him ? " and as on that day there were male and female, so in this age there were Christ and the Church. And as man on that day was set over the beasts and creeping things and birds of the sky, so in that age Christ rules the souls obedient to Him, who have come to His Church, partly from the Gentiles, partly from the Jews. Hence men are tamed by Him and made tractable, both those given to carnal concupiscence like beasts, or darkened by shadowy curiosity like serpents, or born aloft by pride like birds. And just as on that day man and the animals which were with him were fed on grains and fruits and green herbs, so in this age spiritual man, whenever he is a good minister of Christ, and does as He did to the best of his powers, is fed spiritually with his people on the nourishment of the Holy Scriptures and the divine law; partly to conceive fecundity of reason and speech, as with grains; partly for the utility of the customs of human intercourse, as with fruits; partly for the vigor of faith, hope, and charity in eternal life, as with green herbs, that is, with growing things which cannot be parched by any blast of tribulation. But he is thus fed spiritually with those foods that he may know many things; he is, however, carnal, that is, a child in Christ although of God's flock, that he may believe many things which he cannot yet know. Yet all have the same food.

7th Age. The evening of this age, which we would be glad not to have fall upon us, if it has not yet set in, is that of which God says, "When the Son of Man cometh, shall he find faith on the earth?" [*Luke*, XVIII, 8]. After that evening there shall come a dawn when the Lord Himself shall come in splendor. Then shall they rest with Christ from all work, those of whom it is said, "Be ye perfect, even as your Father which is in Heaven is perfect" [*Matth.*, V, 48]. For such do really good works. And after such works rest may be hoped for upon the seventh day which has no evening. Therefore in no wise can it be said in words how God made and established heaven and earth and every creature which He established. But this exposition by the order of the days indicates as it were the history of the things done, so that one may above all see a prediction of the future.[5]

One might imagine that with this pattern of history before him, Saint Augustine would have modeled his universal history, *The City of God*, upon it. But as a matter of fact, though he reproduces the notion of historical ages in that work,[6] he makes no use of it to interpret historical events, but bases the changes in national fortunes upon obedience and disobedience to God's commandments.[7] He does, however, utilize the notion of nations participating in the sin of their rulers, as in what he says of the fourth age above as well as of the termination of most of the ages through sin in general.

The tradition thus begun by Saint Augustine had great popularity in the Middle Ages, many authors simply repeating his words or adding literary embellishments of no doctrinal interest. To avoid such repetition, we give herewith a list of such passages.

> Eugippus, *Thesaurus*, ch. lvii [*MPL*, LXII, p. 668]
> Isidore of Seville, *Etymologies*, V, ch. xxxviii, 5 [*MPL*, LXXXII, p. 223]
> Taio, *Sententiae*, III, iv [*MPL*, LXXX, p. 362]
> Bede, *De temporibus*, ch. xvi ff. [*MPL*, XC, p. 288]
> Alcuin, *Disputatio puerorum*, ch. v [*MPL*, CI, p. 1112]
> Claudius Taurinensis, *Brevis chronica* [*MPL*, CIV, p. 917]
> Rabanus Maurus, *Liber de computo*, ch. xcvi [*MPL*, CIV, p. 726]
> Honoré d'Autun, *De imagine mundi*, II, ch. lxxv [*MPL*, CLXXII, p. 156; CLXXVIII, p. 771]
> St. Julian of Toledo, *De comprobatione aetatis sextae*, III, Introduction, 1-4 [*MPL*, XCVI, p. 569]
> Abelard, *Expositio in Hexaemeron* [*MPL*, CLXXVIII, pp. 771 f.]

---

[5] *De Gen. contr. Manich.*, I, 23 [*MPL*, XXXIV, pp. 190 ff.].

[6] Bk. XXII, ch. 30 [Ed. Welldon, II, p. 646].

[7] He was apparently fond of the idea of seven ages, for he repeats it in his *In Joannis evangelium*, Tr. IX, ch. ii, 6 and in Tr. XV, ch. iv, 9, without extended comment.

Hugo of Saint Victor, *De scripturis et scriptoribus sacris*, ch. xvii [*MPL*, CLXXV, p. 29].

The one original version of Saint Augustine's series of ages is to be found in a curious allegory by Philippe van Hareng. For him the first age is of gold, " more glorious and excellent " than the ages which were to follow. That golden age lasted until the time of Noah and was not simply the age of Adam and Eve before the Fall. The second age, of silver, is a decline which is remedied in the third age, of bronze, the age of the patriarchs. The age of David which in Augustine is the best, is in Philippe an age of discord between Gentiles and Jews. The discord is removed by the coming of Christ. Thus human history, whether Philippe was aware of it or not, became an undulation from periods of good to periods of evil and back.

In a second interpretation of the ages, the golden age is described as unique in its obedience to the " law of nature," which was apparently the seeing of God in the natural order much in the manner preached by Saint Bonaventura. The last age is that of Antichrist, in which the world grows old and dies. There is, it is perhaps needless to point out, no relation between Philippe's use of metals to name his ages and that of Hesiod.

> You looked, O king, and behold, a statue stood before you, whose aspect was truly terrifying. The head of this statue was of gold, its chest and arms of silver, its belly and loins of brass, its legs of iron, its feet partly of iron and partly of clay. As you looked a stone was cut out of the mountainside without hands and smote the statue on its feet of iron and clay and reduced it to ruins. Now this stone which smote the statue, as Daniel says [ch. ii], became a great mountain and filled the whole earth. Therefore the rock which was dislodged from the mountainside without hands is Christ, Who without carnal union was born from the sinning mass of mankind. Of this rock it is well said that it became a great mountain and filled the whole earth, because the Gospel, which the Lord Jesus established and gave to His disciples to preach, filled the whole earth, as He said to His disciples, " Go ye into all the earth and preach the gospel to every creature " [*Mark*, xvi, 15]. That mountain, however, was a little stone when God was known only in Judea, but this stone was made into a great mountainside when it was said, " From the rising of the sun unto the going down of the same the Lord's name is to be praised " [*Psalm*, cxiii], nor is anything hid from the heat thereof [*Psalm*, xix], that is, from the preaching of His Gospel, which was preached by the Apostles to the whole world. Thus did the stone become a great mountain and fill the whole earth, when, according to Isaiah the prophet [ch. ix, 6], He who was born unto us a child and was given to us for a son, when the star was pointing the way from Heaven, God on high appeared through the whole world. That stone, I say, that is, Christ, grew into a great mountain, because all nations, whom He had made, come together and adore Him and they glorify and praise His name to eternity.
>
> But now let us see what is the meaning of that statue which the rock shattered and reduced to ruins, for so wonderful a dream, so

unusual a vision, was in no way shown to the King of Babylon without the weight of a great inner meaning. Its head, he said, was of gold, its chest and arms of silver, its feet partly of iron, partly of clay. Thus the statue was divided into seven parts and is seen to have been put together out of five materials. If then we accept this statue as a symbol for this world, and if by the seven parts of the statue and by the five materials of which the statue consists we understand five or seven ages of the world, we shall have its probable sense and rational meaning. For those men who were in the first age of the world from Adam to Noah were as if they constituted the golden head of the statue, because just as the head is the first part of the body, so they were the beginning of the age to follow and of the human race, and as gold, because of its value, excells all metals, so that first age of the world was more glorious and excellent than the other ages to come.

But by silver, which is the next material after gold, is meant the second age of the world, which extended from Noah to Abraham. For just as silver is known to be much inferior to and worse than gold, so the second age is proved to be worse than and inferior to the first age of the world. Finally, because of the evil of this age, the Lord is related to have sent a Deluge over the earth.

By bronze, which we are accustomed to use sometimes as a symbol of patience and fortitude, we rightly understand the third age of the world from Abraham to Moses, because in that age men stood strong and patient in both adversity and prosperity, to wit, Abraham, Isaac, and Jacob, and several others who faithfully kept God's commandments in patience and fortitude of mind.

By iron we should understand the fourth age of the world, which is pointed out as having existed from the illustrious prophet, Moses, to David.

The fifth age, however, which lasted from the time of David to the advent of Christ, is properly understood to be symbolized by mud and clay, which, although it is conjoined with iron, yet also could not be united with it. For in that age which was before the advent of Christ, both Gentiles and Jews were mixed together, but as the clay in the statue could not be consolidated with the iron, so the Gentiles had no true concord whatsoever with the Jews.

Therefore in the sixth age the stone was dislodged from the mountain without the aid of human hands, that is, Christ was born of the Virgin Mary without the contact of a man, Who shattered the statue and reduced it to ruins, that is, the glory of this world, which is shown to be vile and contemptible. For when Christ said to His disciples, Blessed are the poor in spirit, for yours is the Kingdom of God [Matth. v, 3] He put the poor in spirit before gold and silver, bronze and iron, and all the riches of this world. Therefore it is well said that the rock shattered the statue on its feet of iron and clay, because Christ, who is the cornerstone, by preaching to the poor in spirit reduced the muddy and foul glory of this world to nothing and destroyed it. After this the rock grew to be a great mountain and filled the earth when Christ through the preaching of the Gospel spread to all throughout the world what God was.

We can also in this allegory understand in a spiritual sense the seven parts of the statue as the seven ages of the world. Clearly by the golden head of the statue we rightly understand the men of the first age of the world. For just as gold has none but its natural color, so the men of that first age had no law by which they might know God but the law of nature: "Thou shalt love the Lord thy God with all thy heart and thy neighbor as thyself." [*Deut.* vi, 5 and *Matth.* xxii, 37, 39]. . . . Since men's thoughts arise in their chests, it is not without cause that we understand men of the second age by the chest of the statue, whose depraved thoughts and evil deeds are said to have worried the God of majesty to the point that, if it were proper to say so, the Creator Himself was angry at His creatures and wiped out the whole race of mortals because of their iniquity by the outpouring waters of the Deluge, though a few survivors remained from whom He later restored the whole world. By the arms, in which the labor and fortitude of human endeavor are customarily expressed, may be meant the men of the third age which lasted from Abraham to Moses, who amid the adversities and prosperities of this world, persisted strong in their faith and in the keeping of God's commandments struggled greatly, as for instance that extraordinary patriarch, Abraham, who, as the Apostle says [*Hebr.* ii], desperately and faithfully believed in the spirit, and obedient to the commands of God's will, left his native land and also was prepared to give an obedience unheard of and contrary to the custom of anterior ages and generations when he was willing to sacrifice to God his son, in whom he had received the hope of new promise, giving us a perfect example of obedience. . . .

Now by the statue's bronze belly in which the human bowels are contained are symbolized the men of that age which went from Moses to the time of the Apostles, for just as below the belly are many things which are not open to human sight, so those things which were done in the time when the law was given in no way were clearly visible to our senses. Therefore since from the loins issues human progeny, the loins of the statue are justly interpreted as that age which is known to have existed in the time of the Apostles and the primitive Church. For the holy Apostles together with their mother, the Church, begot many sons of that time for God, through faith and the regeneration of holy baptism and the glorious preaching of the Gospel, which they had learned from God Himself. Wherefore also Paul said to certain men, "In Christ Jesus I have begotten you through the gospel" [*I Cor.*, iv, 15]. . . . And well do we understand by the loins of bronze the age of the apostles and doctors of the Church, because the metal bronze is particularly resounding. Therefore it is also said of the apostles, "Their line is gone out through all the earth and their words to the end of the world" [*Ps.* xix, 3].

By the iron legs of that statue that age is meant in which we are living, for just as iron breaks and shatters things, however strong, so the fervor of holy religion which in the Holy Church has grown more fully than usual by the grace of God, has joyfully shattered and destroyed the pleasures and carnal lusts of the declining world in the strength of the Holy Spirit.

But by the feet of iron and clay, which are the last part of our body, is rightly to be understood the last age, which is to come in the time of AntiChrist. In that age without any doubt, as the Lord says in the Gospel, there shall be great tribulation such as was not since the beginning of the world [*Matth.*, xxiv, 21] and, except that the Lord had shortened those days, no flesh should be saved; but for the elects' sake, whom He hath chosen, He hath shortened the days [*Mark*, xiii, 20]. Again, just as iron and clay cannot be welded together into one unit, so the men of that age will not be able to be held in the one lap of the Holy Church. For the followers of Anti-Christ will strive to affirm his depraved teaching and heresy, whereas the sons of the Holy Church will be the defenders of their mother and of the Catholic faith and evangelical teaching. Therefore, since different people feel different things and are drawn in opposite directions, just as iron cannot be consolidated with clay, so they will not be able to agree with one another. After this there will come to Judgment that stone which once was mysteriously cut out of the mountain, that is, Christ, Who once came forth from the shadowy density of the mountain of divinity and from His hidden dwelling place. But what will that stone do? It will shake and destroy the statue, that is, this world of ours, and by the wondrous power of its divinity, restore it to a better state. That this world must put off the state which it now has and receive a better state, the Lord makes manifest in the Gospel when He says, Heaven and earth shall pass away, but my words shall not pass away [*Matth.*, xxiv, 35] . . . Hence John the Apostle also says in the Apocalypse, " I saw a new heaven and a new earth " [*Rev.*, xxi, 1]. For the first heaven and the first earth are leaving us and the sea no longer exists . . .

[Philippe now proceeds to give another allegorical interpretation of the statue, this time as the Church, the head being Christ, the limbs being the faithful, the breast the Apostles, the arms the martyrs, the belly the confessors and doctors, the shins the celibates, the feet the laiety.] [8]

The undulatory course of progress as given in Saint Augustine and Philippe may be contrasted with the poetic account of history given in Prudentius who also uses the metaphor of individual life, with birth, growth, and eventual decay as the key to world history. While Prudentius, the most notable Christian poet of his age [d. 410 A. D.], satirizes primitivism, both chronological and cultural, and gives us one of the most striking expressions of the idea of progress in Latin literature, yet he does not deny the implications of his metaphor. For him the decay of senility has already begun. Since the passage in question was to play a part in the seventeenth century controversy over the same question, we quote the English version made by George Hakewill in his *Apologie of the Power and Providence of God in the Government of the World* [9] instead of making a new translation.

> If we must still embrace, and n'er refuse,
> What th' infant world in ruder times did use:
> Let us each age then step by step recall,

[8] *De somno regis Nabuchodosor* [*MPL*, CCIII, pp. 586 f.]. Cf. Philippe's *De silentio clericorum*, ch. xliv-xlvi, inc.

[9] 3d ed., 1635, p. 334.

And damne in order even to th' originall
What after by succeeding use was found.
In the first world no Rusticks ear'd the ground;
What meane the ploughes then? what the needless care
Of barrowes? akornes yield sufficient care.
Peece meale with wedges men did first woode rend:
Let axes then by th' forge again descend
Into that masse, backe to their metall drop;
Slain beasts cloathing did yield, and the cool grotte
A slender lodging: let's to our caves againe,
And of patcht skinns rough garments entertaine.
People once wilde, then tame (nature subdu'd)
Harshly againe let grumble, and renew'd
In savage manners, to their wont retire.
With Scythick piety their aged Sier
Let striplings tumble from the voting bridge
             Such once the custom was.
With slaughtered babes let Saturnes fanes abound
His cruell altars with sad vagits sound . . . .
W'are glad that Something spi'd
And brought to light at last which erst lay hid.
Man's life by slowe proceedings grows in sence,
And profiteth by long experience.
Such is the moving order of man's race,
So varieth Nature in her courses pace.
Infancie creepes: then childhoods feeble gate,
And reason staggers: next the synowy state
Of youth boyles in its bloud; then an age
Setled in full strength: last upon the stage
Appears declining old, for counsell better,
Clearer in judgement, but in body weaker.
Thus humane kind by differing seasons ranne
His changing course throughout: dull first beganne
And clogg' with earth, so crawl'd, and like a child
On all four did his milke-fed bowels weild
Next tender, docile Natur'd, and for arts
Now fit became, adorn'd with various parts.
Thence swolne in vice, so fervent years increased
Till be decocted strength grown firme he cased.
And now with clearer judgment 'tis high time
He know and favour things that are divine,
His thoughts in search of secrets wisely bend,
And now at length eternall life attend.[10]

The beginning of the arts: the Hebrew background.

Hebrew legend, like Greek,[11] recited the names of the reputed founders
of some of the principal arts; it did not, however, so far as the extant

---

[10] Tr. of *Contra Symmachum*, II, 277-297.

[11] See *PIA*, pp. 196-198, 200-202, 205, 209, 229, 374 f. This section borrows heavily
from notes by A. O. Lovejoy.

evidence goes, tell of any one pre-eminent culture-hero (or culture-villain) comparable to Prometheus, unless Adam himself was assigned a somewhat analogous role. The genealogy of the earlier generations of his descendants given in the continuation of the J-narrative in *Genesis*, iv, 16-26, contains what appears to be fragments of a list of the inventors or first practitioners of various crafts. Nothing is said of the invention of fire-making, by the Greeks usually conceived as the beginning of the technological progress of mankind. The order of the development of the arts is not traced in any intelligible way, and the entire passage is confused and contradictory. Cain's name probably etymologically means " smith," [12] and he may there-fore, in some older version, have been the first metal-worker, and it is possible that the primitivistic disapproval of this art was manifested by the tradition that he was also the first murderer. But nothing of this appears in the present recension. According to it, he built the first city [*Gen.*, iv, 17]—at a time when the descendants of Adam must have been few; but according to another passage [*Gen.*, iv, 2 and 12], he was a farmer before his crime and a " fugitive and a wanderer " after it. It is, however, possible that the text of verse 17—" And he builded a city "—is corrupt and that his son, Enoch, was represented as the first city-builder.[13] According to the implication of the present story, taken as a whole, Abel was the first shepherd, but if we follow *Genesis*, iv, 20-21, Jabal, of the sixth generation after Adam, was " the father of such as dwell in tents and keep cattle," i. e., the introducer of the culture of the nomadic shepherds, which is thus made of later origin than both agriculture and city-life; while his brother, Jubal, was the inventor of the first musical instruments, the lyre and the pipe. The inventor of metallurgy, " the father of every artificer in brass and iron," Tubal-cain, was of the same generation.[14] The passage cannot be said to be either clearly favorable or clearly adverse to technological primitivism; the introducers of the arts mentioned are not praised as culture-heroes, nor is the introduction of the arts mentioned deplored. Taken in connection with the rest of the larger story, however, this con-fused section could be read as implying a primitivistic moral: the original city-builder was also the original murderer, and the loss of the easy a-technic life of the first pair in Paradise was followed by a progressive development of the arts by their posterity.

There was another, possibly equally old or older, Hebrew legend which explicitly connected the origination of the arts with the degeneration of mankind. This is the story of the mating of the " sons of the gods " with the daughters of men. Of this *Genesis* contains only an obviously truncated fragment [*Gen.*, vi, 1-2, 4-5], which the redactor has not very skillfully

---

[12] Cf. Skinner, *A Critical and Exegetical Commentary on Genesis*, N. Y., 1910, p. 101, n. 1.

[13] See Budde, *Biblische Urgeschichte*, p. 123; Skinner, *op. cit.*, p. 16.

[14] For Tubal-cain as a sort of Hebrew Vulcan, see the *Story of Genesis and Exodus* [*ca.* 1250], *EETS*, London, 1865, p. 14

fitted into his main narrative as a prelude to the story of the Flood.[15] For
the tale in its entirety—and doubtless with some later additions—we must
turn to a passage of the Book of Enoch, which was to be an important
source of medieval cultural primitivism. The book—a Jewish writing of
which this portion appears to have been composed before 150 B. C.[16] but is
pretty certainly derived from much older sources—had an extensive vogue
to the end of the fourth century A. D., and was regarded by Tertullian and
other patristic writers as Scripture,[17] though after its condemnation by
Saint Augustine, it fell into disrepute and disuse in the Western church.
The story begins abruptly with a period of primeval innocence, lasting for
at least some generations—until "the children of men had multiplied"
[VI, 1]—during which the arts were unknown, the flesh of animals was
not eaten, and men and beasts lived in peace and concord [VII, 5], i. e.,
there was, as also apparently in the P-narrative in *Genesis*, no Fall of Adam.
The termination of this happy state was due to the sin of a large number
of angels,[18] in all two hundred, who "saw and lusted after . . . the beautiful and comely daughters of men," and took them to wife. The rest of the
myth is confused and is probably the result of a multiple syncretism. But
a vein of technological primitivism is manifest. The errant angels play
the same part as Prometheus in the Greek story; they taught men a number
of the practical arts, both natural and magical, which are both viewed in
the same light as unsuitable for mortals. It was in the acquisition of these
powers, not in the eating of a forbidden fruit, that the fall of mankind consisted. But only certain arts are specifically mentioned as thus unlawfully
imparted to man: metallurgy and its consequences, the manufacture of the
instruments of warfare and the ending of the primeval peace; the making of
cosmetics and paints and metal ornaments; the cutting of precious stones;
the knowledge of the movements of the heavenly bodies—and thereby of
astrology—and of the course of the seasons; something, apparently, of
gynecology; and the peculiarly depraving art of writing. As in the story
of the forbidden tree and in some versions of the Prometheus-myth, the
conception of the jealousy of the celestial beings, their unwillingness that
men should become as gods by sharing their knowledge, is apparently the

[15] This fragment says nothing of the introduction of the arts by these supernatural
philanderers. It includes [*Gen.*, v, 4] a vestige of an old legend of a race of giants
[*Nephelim*], who are not expressly said to be the offspring of these *mésalliances*, but
are described as "the mighty men which were of old, the men of renown"—possibly
a primeval race of "heroes," in the Greek sense, who were superior to the men of
later times.

[16] Cf. R. H. Charles in *The Apocrypha and Pseudepigrapha of the Old Testament*,
1913, Vol. II, p. 170.

[17] *Ibid.*, p. 163.

[18] The possible derivation of this myth from a mistranslation in some texts of the
Septuagint of *Gen.*, VI, 1-4, need not be considered here. Cf. Charles, *op. cit.*, II, p.
191. The mistranslation may equally well be due to the myth; but neither supposition is necessary.

source of the technological primitivism here; the loyal seraphim complain to the Most High that the rebel angels have "revealed the eternal secrets [preserved] in heaven, which men were striving to learn" [IX, 6]; and it is chiefly for this sin that Azãzẽl is condemned to an unending punishment not less severe than that of Prometheus.[19]   Aside, however, from the consequences of the communication of the arts to man, the unnatural union of the angels with mortal women resulted in other evils: the women gave birth to a race of "great giants whose height was three thousand ells"; these "consumed all the acquisitions[?] of men, and, when men could no longer sustain them, turned against them and devoured mankind"; whereupon men "began to sin against birds and beasts and reptiles and fish, and to devour one another's flesh and to drink the blood" [VII, 4-5].

The account of the introduction of the arts appears in *Enoch* in two partially inconsistent versions.

1. *I Enoch,* viii, 1-4

> Azãzẽl taught men to make swords, and knives, and shields, and breastplates, and made known to them the metals of the earth and the art of working them, and bracelets, and ornaments, and the use of antimony, and the beautifying of the eyelids, and all kinds of costly stones, and all coloring tinctures.   And there arose much godlessness, and they committed fornication, and they were led astray, and became corrupt in all their ways.   Senjãzã taught enchantments and root-cuttings, 'Armãrõs the resolving of enchantments, Barãqĩjãl [taught] astrology, Kõkabẽl the constellations, Ẽzẽqẽẽl the knowledge of the clouds, Araquiẽl the signs of the earth, Shamsiẽl the signs of the sun, and Sariẽl the course of the moon.   And as men perished, they cried, and their cry went up to heaven.[20]

2. *1 Enoch,* lxix, 3-13.

> These are the chiefs of the angels and their names, . . . The name of the first Jeqẽn: that is, the one who led astray all the sons of God, and brought them down to the earth, and led them astray through the daughters of men.   And the second was named Asbeẽl: he imparted to the holy sons of God evil counsel, and led them astray so that they defiled their bodies with the daughters of men.   And the third was named Gãdreẽl: he it is who showed the children of men all the blows of death, [and he led astray Eve][21] and showed [the weapons of death

---

[19] His sentence was to be bound hand and foot and cast into a desert place; to have "rough and jagged rocks" piled upon him and to abide thus in perpetual darkness until the day of the great judgment, when he was to be cast into the fire. Similar penalties were pronounced against the other rebel angels.

[20] Charles's translation, *op. cit.,* II, p. 192.   Cf. Commodianus's summary of the story in Latin verse, ca. 250 A. D., in his *Instructiones* [*MPL,* V, pp. 203 f. and Charles, *op. cit.,* p. 183] in which it is said of the rebel angels, " ab ipsis in terra artes prolatae fuere."

[21] This for obvious reasons may be supposed to be a redactor's interpolation.

to the sons of men], the shield and the coat of mail, and the sword for battle, and all the weapons of death to the children of men. And from his hand they have proceeded against those who dwell on the earth from that day and for evermore. And the fourth was named Pĕnĕmuĕ: he taught the children of men the bitter and the sweet, and he taught them all the secrets of their wisdom. And he instructed mankind in writing with ink and paper, and thereby many sinned from eternity to eternity and until this day. For men were not created for such a purpose, to give confirmation to their good faith with pen and ink. For men were created exactly like the angels, to the intent that they should continue pure and righteous, and death, which destroys everything, could not have taken hold of them; but through this their knowledge they are perishing, and through this power it is consuming me. And the fifth was named Kasdeja: This is he who showed the children of men all the wicked smitings of spirits and demons, and the smitings of the embryo in the womb, that it may pass away, and [the smitings of the soul] the bites of the serpent, and the smitings which befall through the noontide heat, the son of the serpent named Tabā'ĕt.[22]

The union of women and the fallen angels results in the corruption not only of mankind, but of the entire creation. The Deluge follows. But, unlike *Genesis*, the *Book of Enoch* predicts a future restoration of earth and of the virtuous remnant of mankind to a paradisaic state, after the final penal judgment has been pronounced upon evil-doers and the angels who have corrupted them. Unlike the Christian millenium, this second Earthly Paradise is to be a permanent one. In it the labors of the husbandman, orchardist, and vine-dresser will be happily practised. Nothing is said of the other arts, nor of urban life; the ideal is culturally semi-primitivistic.

The Lord said unto Michael: "Go, bind Semjājā and his associates who have united themselves with women so as to have defiled themselves with them in all their uncleanness. And when their sons have slain one another, and they have seen the destruction of their beloved ones, bind them fast for seventy generations in the valleys of the earth, till the day of their judgment and of their consummation, till the judgment that is for ever and ever is consummated. In those days they shall be led off to the abyss of fire: [and] to the torment and the prison in which they shall be confined forever. And whosoever shall be condemned and destroyed will from henceforth be bound together with them to the end of all generations. And destroy all the spirits of the reprobate and the children of the Watchers, because they have wronged mankind. Destroy all wrong from the face of the earth and let every evil work come to an end: and let the plant of righteousness and truth appear and it shall prove a blessing; the works of righteousness and truth shall be planted in truth and joy for evermore. . . .
And then shall the whole earth be tilled in righteousness and shall all be planted with trees and be full of blessing. And all

[22] Trans. by Charles, *op. cit.*, II, pp. 233 f.

desirable trees shall be planted on it, and they shall plant vines on it: and the vine which they plant thereon shall yield wine in abundance, and as for all the seed which is sown thereon each measure [of it] shall bear a thousand, and each measure of olives shall yield ten presses of oil. And cleanse thou the earth from all oppression, and from all unrighteousness, and from all sin, and from all godlessness: and all the uncleanness that is wrought upon the earth destroy from off the earth. And all the children of men shall become righteous, and all nations shall offer adoration and shall praise Me, and all shall worship Me. And the earth shall be cleansed from all defilement, and from all sin, and from all punishment, and from all torment, and I will never again send [them] upon it from generation to generation and forever.

And in those days I will open the store-chambers of blessing which are in the heaven, so as to send them down upon the earth over the work and labour of the children of men. And truth and peace shall be associated throughout all the days of the world and throughout all the generations of men.[23]

The same general feeling about the early steps in man's technological progress appears in the story of Babel [*Gen.*, xi, 1-9], which relates the consequences of the discovery of the art of making bricks and of constructing buildings out of them by the use of bituminous mortar [*Gen.* v, 3]. At this time, according to the narrative, all men were still "of one language and of one speech," and they all lived together as one community in the "plain of the land of Shinar." Having there learned, in this case without the aid of any magical fruit or of superhuman instructors, how to build edifices of brick—at first, evidently, ordinary houses—they presently were overcome by *hybris,* and proceeded to use this art in the service of their racial self-esteem by designing the first sky-scraper: "Come, let us build us a city with a tower whose top may reach unto heaven, and let us make a name for ourselves." The jealous deity, learning of this ambitious enterprise, descends to earth for the purpose of frustrating it: "This is what they have begun to do; and now nothing will be withholden from them which they purpose to do." The means which He adopts for keeping mankind in its place is the destruction of its unity and its power of co-operation, by dispersing it in separate nations "over the face of all the earth," and by a concomitant multiplication of languages. The passage is obviously in part both an aetiological and an etymological myth, an answer to the questions: why are there many peoples and languages instead of one only, and why is the great city of Babylon so called? What is significant is that the answer to both of these questions is found in that form of technological primitivism which is associated with the idea of the deity's fear of man's acquisition of too great power through practical knowledge.[24] There is an

---

[23] Charles, *op. cit.*, II, pp. 192-196.

[24] Gunkel in *Die Genesis,* pp. 92-97, and some other critics have sought to show that J here combines two inconsistent sources, a "tower-story" and a "city-story."

explicit suggestion—which can hardly, one would suppose, have escaped an ancient reader—of a sort of primitivistic cosmopolitanism: the race was originally one and of one speech and might have so remained; the existing multiplicity of nations and tongues is a punitive evil due to the presumptuousness of the men of a later, though a remote, age. There is, however, no hint that this evil is remediable.

Another tradition gives a different account of the rôle of the angels who descended to earth, and ascribes the introduction of the art of writing and the beginnings of astronomy and chronology not to the "errant sons of God," but to the virtuous patriarch, Enoch. In its present form, the version is probably derived from an older legend or body of legends of which Enoch was the hero. It is found with variations both in *I Enoch* and the *Book of Jubilees*. Here the angels are at first the benevolent instructors of mankind; from them and from revelations received in dreams Enoch acquired vast knowledge, including a prevision of all future history.[25] He was the first *savant*, the first author, and the first and greatest seer.

> In his [Jared's] days the angels of the Lord descended on the earth, those who are named the Watchers, that they should instruct the children of men, and that they should do judgment and uprightness on the earth . . .
>
> [And Jared's son Enoch] was the first among men that are born on earth who learned writing and knowledge and wisdom, and who wrote down the signs of heaven according to the order of their separate months. And he was the first to write a testimony, and he testified to the sons of men among the generations of the earth and made known to them the days of the years, and set in order the sabbaths of the years as we made them known to him. And what was and what will be he saw in a vision of his sleep, as it will happen to the children of men throughout their generations until the day of judgment; he saw and understood everything, and wrote his testimony, and placed the testimony on earth for all the children of men and for their generations . . . And he was moreover with the angels of God these six jubilees of years, and they showed him everything

Cassuto's argument in favor of the essential unity of the narrative [*La questione della Genesi*, 1934, pp. 359-365] seems to us convincing; and we have followed his rendering of verse 4, "a city *with* a tower," which is, as he shows, defensible on grammatical grounds (*Ib.*, p. 363). The only difficulty is found in the implication of the latter part of the verse, that one of the objects of the builders of the city and tower was to prevent the dispersion of men. This may be a redactor's gloss, or it may be construed as referring exclusively to the project of building the city, which would be a means of enabling a growing population to live as a compact unit. The etymological strain in the myth is the suggestion of a connection between the name "Babel" and the root *bbl*, "to confuse."

[25] The Enoch in question is not the son of Cain, but of the eighth generation from Adam; for the author of *Jubilees*—apparently attempting to combine the discordant genealogies of J [*Gen.*, iv, 16-26] and P [*Gen.*, v, 1-22]—introduces two Enochs, one the son of Cain, the other of Jared.

which is on earth and in the heavens the rule of the sun, and he wrote down everything.[26]

Here, however, the author abruptly and incongruously reverts briefly to the other story; Enoch " testified against the Watchers who had sinned with the daughters of men " [*Jub.*, iv, 22].[27] Enoch was finally " taken from amongst the children of men " and translated to the Garden of Eden " in majesty and honor " [*Ib.*, 23], where he apparently remains until the Day of Judgment. Here also a " new creation " is foreshadowed, when the " earth will be purified of all its guilt and its uncleanness " [*Ib.*, 26].

The author of the book was peculiarly preoccupied with questions of chronology, seeking to divide all history into year-weeks, i. e., periods of seven years, and of " jubilees," i. e., periods of forty-nine years. He presumably was a member of a learned priestly school to whose purpose it was to represent the astronomical and other knowledge which appeared to them valuable as having been imparted by superhuman agency to the antediluvian patriarch who " walked with God " [*Gen.*, v, 22].

In later passages of the Pentateuch no suggestion that the Deity looks askance at the practitioners of the arts is manifest. In *Exodus* Yahweh is represented as the patron and inspirer of the skilled craftsmen who fashioned the ornaments and furniture of the Tent in which the sacred objects were enshrined. It is, of course, the fine arts which are here in question, and these, as applied to religious ends. The passage is a portion of the J-document.

> Yahweh spoke unto Moses, saying, See, I have called by name Bezalel, the son of Uri, the son of Hur, of the tribe of Judah: and I have filled him with the spirit of God, in wisdom and in understanding and in knowledge, and in all manner of craftsmanship, to devise skillful works, to work in gold, and in silver and in cutting of stones for setting, and in carving of wood . . . And . . . in the minds of all that are wise I have put wisdom, that they may make all that I have commanded thee. [*Exodus*, xxxi, 1-6.]

Christian readers of the Hebrew accounts of the early history of mankind and of the Chosen People could, as the foregoing sections show, find in them equally authoritative support for cultural primitivism and anti-intellectualism and for the opposite view—a natural consequence of the conjunction in these histories of different legends. The weight of the texts inclined, on the whole, to the side of primitivism, though it is doubtful

---

[26] *Jubilees*, iv, 15-23. Tr. by R. H. Charles, *The Book of Jubilees*, 1917. Six jubilees would be 6.7.7 or 294 years.

[27] The same story of the sin of the angels and of the resultant corruption of mankind, followed by the Deluge, is given more at length—after *Gen.*, vi, 1-12, in *Jubilees* v, 1-4; here the giants are explicitly the offspring of these hybrid unions. Even here, moreover, there is no suggestion that, as in *I Enoch*, the wicked angels introduced the arts.

whether this was generally noted. What could not be found in them was any reasoned ethical and psychological argument for cultural primitivism such as was characteristic especially of Cynicism and Stoicism and of some passages of Plato, in classical antiquity.[28] There was, indeed, a broad implicit suggestion that before the arts were introduced—and certainly before the Fall—life was easier, happier, and more innocent. But the principal basis of the primitivistic strain in older Hebrew literature was the idea of the Deity as fearful of, and therefore hostile to, man's attainments in this field; the unhappy consequences of his acquisition of knowledge and of various arts were not usually represented as intrinsic or natural consequences, but as extraneous penalties imposed for self-protection by an anthropomorphic and jealous God. Such a conception of deity, though it did not disappear, was uncongenial to the theology both of later Judaism and of Christianity—doubly so after the latter had come under the influence of Greek, and in particular of Platonistic, philosophy.[29]

The beginning of the arts: in patristic writers.

Against this Hebrew background Christian writers were to set their philosophical meditations. We find Enoch credited with being the builder of the first city by Sulpicius Severus and the angels who begat the giants turn into the pagan demigods in Arnobius, while Tubal, as we have said, enters popular literature as a Hebrew Vulcan.[30] In Origen we find a defense of man's technological achievements which is based not upon these legends but upon a familiar pagan *topos*, the hostility of Nature to man. Celsus, the arch-enemy of the Alexandrine father had apparently been playing upon this theme, the most popular expression of which became the Latin slogan, *natura non mater sed noverca*, a slogan which was supposed to prove the superiority of the brutes over men. Origen, instead of justifying man's position as a necessary consequence of the Fall, argues that God did indeed create him in want, but at the same time endowed him with the power to remedy his deficiencies. Necessity, he maintains, is the mother of invention, and the brutes' lack of need is a defect, not an advantage. For feeling no lack, they invent nothing. It is clear that this innovation of Origen's, additional proof of his independence of thought, was as dangerous as his other innovations, for if one begins to praise the arts, one is tempted to praise their products, and thus to sink into a kind of worldliness antithetic to the main Christian tradition.

[28] See *PIA*, ch. III, IV, V, and X, especially pp. 118-123, 140-151, 163 ff.

[29] It is to be remembered that Plato in the *Timaeus*, 29E, declares that God, being "good," is incapable of "envy concerning anything, and, being devoid of envy, he desired that all should be so far as possible like himself"—a historically momentous negation of a deep-seated preconception in Greek popular religion, as well as in the early stories in *Genesis*.

[30] See Sulpicius Severus, *Chron.*, I, ii, 3; Arnobius *Adv. gent.*, II, 75.

Celsus, wishing to maintain that Providence created the things that grow on the earth not so much for us as for the wildest of the beasts, says, " We laboring and presisting in our labor, are fed in scarcity and with toil. But for them all things are grown unsown and unploughed." He does not see that God, wishing to exercise the human understanding in every respect, that it might not remain fallow and ignorant of the arts, created man in want, so that by his very want he might be forced to invent arts, some for food, others for shelter. For it was better for those who would not seek the divine mystery nor philosophy, to be in difficulty that they might use their understanding for the discovery of the arts, than that being in want of nothing, they should neglect their understanding. The lack of necessities of life at any rate was the foundation not only of the art of agriculture but also of viniculture, of horticulture, as well as of carpentry and metal-working, for they made the tools for the arts which help produce our food. The lack of shelter was the incentive to weaving, wool-carding, and spinning, as well as of house-building. And thus the understanding rose to the general principles of art. The lack of utilities also caused things produced in foreign parts to be conveyed by the arts of navigation and piloting to them who did not have them. So that even on that account one might admire the Providence who in comparison with the irrational animals made the rational in a state of need which was advantageous. For the irrational have their food all ready for them, but they have not even an impulse towards the arts. And they have also a natural covering. For they have hair or feathers, or scales, or shells. And let this be our defence against these allegations of Celsus, " We, laboring and perishing in our labor, are fed in scarcity and with toil. But for them all things are grown unsown and unploughed." [31]

The passage ends with arguments against the typical anti-intellectualism of the animalitarian. " We at any rate, though much weaker than the animals in body, and smaller than some to a great degree, are stronger than the beasts by our understanding." God has put them all at our disposal. We tame some and thus use their power. We eat others. " The Creator has made them all slaves of the rational animal and of his natural understanding."

Even Saint Augustine, whose sense of man's depravity was peculiarly sharp, could lose himself at certain moments in admiration of human technical achievements. Into that paean to God's goodness in the twenty second book of the *City of God*, which rings with a Senecan rhythm, he inserts a passage on the arts and sciences which seem more pagan in inspiration than Christian. He goes so far as to praise the theatre and war for the ingenuity which they exhibit. Saint Augustine recognizes that they have no ultimate value, that they are in themselves evidence only of human

[31] *Contra Celsum*, IV, lxxvi [Ed. Paul Koetschau, Leipzig, 1899. In *Opera*, I, pp. 346 ff.].

rather than divine skill, but that does not lead him to depreciate them or to maintain that God demands our renunciation of them.

> When we pass beyond the arts of living well and of reaching undying happiness—which are called virtues and are given to the Children of the Promise and the Kingdom by the grace of God alone, which is in Christ—has not human genius mastered and invented and applied a great many arts, some necessities, some luxuries, so that the outstanding excellence of the mind and reason, even when it seeks the superfluous, nay, the dangerous and harmful, bears witness to how great good there is in nature from which it derives the power to invent, to learn, or to apply?
>
> What wonderful, what stupendous achievements in clothing and building has human industry attained! What has it not perfected in agriculture, in navigation! With what variety has it designed and executed vases, statues, and pictures! What machinery, what spectacles has it contrived for the stage, marvelous to see, unbelievable to hear about! What and how many devices has it made for taking, killing, and taming the wild beasts!
>
> For the injury of men how many kinds of poison, of weapon, of armament has it invented, and for preserving and safeguarding his terrestrial welfare, how many medicaments and remedies! For the pleasure of the palate, how many sauces and appetizers has he found! For exposition and argumentation, what a number and variety of symbols among which words and letters have first place; for delighting the mind, what embellishments of eloquence, what wealth of varied sounds; for soothing the ears, what musical instruments, what varieties of song has it thought out!
>
> What skill in measurement and number, with what great sagacity has it comprehended the motion and order of the stars! Who could tell with how much thought about the universe it has been filled, particularly if we should wish not to make a brief summary of it but to give a detailed account? Finally, even in defending errors and falsehoods, who would have the powers which have made philosophers and heretics illustrious? [32]

Saint Augustine in this passage is not denying man's wickedness; he is merely praising his genius. He is praising it as a gift from God. A slight shift in emphasis would have made of it, taken in isolation, a document in support of anti-cultural-primitivism. For cultural primitivism by definition considers the arts and sciences as the source of evil; man would be better off without them; it is not a question of the use to which they are put.

The Legend of Saturn

Though, as has been suggested above, the Hebraic-Christian tradition had its culture heroes, many of the Latin fathers and their disciples seemed to have accepted the legend of King Saturn. This in part was probably due to the evil reputation which the Hebrew culture-heroes in the form of

---

[32] *City of God*, xxii, 24 [Ed. Welldon, II, pp. 625 ff.].

the fallen angels had acquired. Such writers as Cyprian and Commodianus considered them as demons, the former charging them with unfailing maleficence, the latter with the invention of the arts for which he had no high regard.[33] If a Christian writer wished to retain the legend of Saturn as a culture-hero, it was obvious that some device must be found for humanizing this ancient god. The device lay clearly in the Euhemeristic technique. Even Minucius Felix who spared no pains to bring discredit on most of the pagan myths, saw no reason to reject that of Saturn.[34] Euhemerism told him that Saturn was a primitive king, worthy of honor for his benefactions to mankind, but deified by his ignorant beneficiaries. Thus it was possible to explain polytheism without denying the existence of the more respectable gods. In doing this Minucius was forced into a kind of implicit anti-primitivism. For his doctrine presupposed that at some early period man was without the arts which he now possesses and that the inventors of them conferred a blessing upon their fellows.

> All the Greek and Roman writers of antiquity relate that Saturn was the prince of this horde of people and a man. Nepos and Cassius recognize this in their histories, and Thallus and Diodorus speak of it. And so this Saturn fled from Crete and came to Italy in fear of his cruel son, and, received in hospitality by Janus, he taught those untutored and rustic men many things, cultured Greek that he was, to write, to coin money, to make tools.[35]

Tertullian takes very much the same attitude towards Saturn as Minucius. He is not a god but a primitive king. Once his humanity is established, Tertullian is satisfied to grant him all that the Euhemerists have recorded of him. He invented writing and coinage.[36] Arnobius follows the same tradition as Tertullian and Minucius, but confuses, as some of the Greeks had done, Saturn with Cronus and Cronus with Chronus, Time.[37] It is this lead which Saint Augustine follows, and by showing that Saturn and Time are identical, also shows to his own satisfaction that he is not to be worshipped even as a culture-hero.

> What do they say of Saturn whom they worship? Is it not he who first came from Olympus,
>
>> " fleeing the weapons of Jove, an exile from his stolen realm. He brought together that ignorant race, scattered on the mountain tops, and gave them laws. And he wished the country to be called Latium, since he had lived safely in hiding [latuisset] in these parts." [Aeneid, VIII, 320 ff.]

[33] See *Quod idola dii non sint*, 6, 7 and *Instructiones*, I, iii, respectively. Cf. Theophilus, *Ad Autolycum*, II, 29, 30.

[34] See *Octavius*, ch. xx.

[35] *Octavius*, xxi, 4 [Ed. C. Halm, *CSEL*, vol. II, pp. 29 f.].

[36] *Apologeticus*, ch. x [Ed. Waltzing-Severyns, Paris 1929].

[37] *Adv. Gentes*, III, 29 [*CSEL*, IV, pp. 131 f.].

Was not his image made with covered head, as if to indicate that he was hiding? Did he not show the Italians how to tend their fields, as symbolized by his sickle? No, they say. For you shall see whether he was that man and the king of whom these things are related.

We interpret Saturn to be universal time, which his Greek name shows. For he is called *Chronus*, which by the addition of an aspirate, is the name of Time. Wherefore also in Latin is he called *Saturnus*, as if he were saturated with years. What now should be done with those who, trying to interpret in a better fashion the names and images of their gods, confess that their major god, father of the others, is time, I do not know. For what else do they mean than that all their gods are temporal, whose father they set up as time itself?

Their more recent Platonic philosophers, who have been living in Christian times, have been ashamed on this account. And they have tried to interpret the name *Saturn* otherwise, saying that he was called *Chronus*, as if it were understood to come from *satiety*, which is *choros* in Greek, and *thought* or *mind*, which is called *nous*. The Latin name also seems to suggest this, as if it had been in earlier times compounded out of both Latin and Greek, so that it was pronounced *Satur-nus*, as if it were *satur* [sated] and *nous*. For they saw how absurd it was, if Jupiter were held to be the son of time, he whom they either thought of, or wished others to think of, as eternal . . .[38]

Two definite traditions were thus fixed in the Christian mind by the end of the fourth century: (1) that Saturn was a primitive benefactor of his people who previous to his coming had been living in ignorance, (2) that he was simply the object of a superstitious cult, no different from the other gods. It is only the former of these traditions which interests us, for it kept alive the pagan notion that primitive man lived in conditions less desirable than those of civilization, and thus weakened the cultural primitivism which might have been the effect of the *Book of Enoch*. We cite below on a few documents to illustrate how this tradition was carried on.

1. *Paulus Diaconus* [8th century]

Janus, as some put it, was the first ruler of Italy and then came Saturn, fleeing from his son, Jupiter, from Greece to the city which was called Saturnia after him, whose ruins can still be perceived in Tuscany not far from the city. This land, because Saturn hid [*latuit*] in Italy, was called *Latium*. Now he showed the people who had been savages up to that time, how to build houses, cultivate the soil, plant vines, and to live in human ways, for before that time they had sustained life like half-wild beasts, living merely on acorns. And they dwelt either in caves or in shelters woven from leaves and twigs. He was also the first to strike bronze coins. Because of these benefactions, he was called a god by the untaught and rustic crowd.[39]

[38] *De consensu evangelistarum*, I, 23 [*MPL*, XXXIV, pp. 1057 f.].
[39] Preface to *Brev. ab urbe condit.* [Ed. H. Droysen, *MGH*, 1879, p. 6]

14

2. *Ps-Theodulus* [9th or 10th century]

An interesting attempt to allegorize the Saturn-Jupiter myth appears in the *Eclogue of Theodulus*.[40] This poem is a dialogue between Truth and Falsehood, in which Falsehood relates certain pagan myths to which Truth immediately gives a Christian interpretation. Thus the Legend of the Golden Age is accommodated to the story of the Earthly Paradise and the Fall of Man. According to legend, Theodulus had listened to disputes between heathens and Christians in Athens [41] and the *Eclogue* became a reconciliation of these debates. One of its important features for the historian is its anticipation of the famous *Ovide moralisé* of the early fourteenth century.

Falsehood

First Saturn came from Cretan shores, spreading [the blessings of] the Golden Age throughout all the earth. He had no father nor senior. A noble line of gods rejoiced in their sire.

Truth

The first man dwelt in a green garden, until at his wife's urging he drank the serpent's poison, mixing in his cup a draught of universal death. His offspring still feel the effects of their parents' sin.

Falsehood

Jupiter, not being able to stand the gleam of so much gold, cruelly expelled his father and took away his arms. A colorless silver image of the world succeeded and the court of the gods gave Jupiter the rule.

Truth

Ejected from his holy seat, the first made man went off in exile and his natural honor was turned to ashes. Yet, lest we be disgraced by the offshoots of the eternal apple, a flaming sword before the gate turns back all wishing to enter.[42]

3. *Baudry de Bourgueil* [11th century]

In Baudry de Bourgueil we find again an account of Saturn, the primitive king, which must have contributed to the perpetuation of the story. In this account there is less mention made of Saturn's technological gifts and more of the presumed etymological significance of his name.

The philosophers say that with his genitals, which had been cut off and thrown into the sea, he begot Venus, and myth relates how he devoured his children. This theme philosophy treats as follows.

Saturn is said to have been born of the aged Pollus, who, moreover, was the first king of Italy. By distributing generous quantities of

---

[40] For the date and what is known of the author, see J. Osternacher, *Theoduli eclogam etc.*, 1902.

[41] *Op. cit.*, p. 9.

[42] Ed. Osternacher, lines 37-52.

food to the people from the annual crop, he won a great name for himself among the common folk. Therefore he is called Saturn, because he "satisfied." Therefore also is he the husband of Ops, because he brought opulence. He is born of Pollus, because his largess made him powerful [*pollent*], or else because of his largess [*pollucibus*] [43] he was a man of great bounty.

His head is veiled, because all fruits are covered by the shade of leaves and, as a mother nurses her child, so Time devours whatever it seems to have begotten. This is Saturn: he eats what he begets. He bears a sickle, because time is cyclical, advancing to see, or returning to proceed, or else because fruits are cut off, under the image of a sickle, and are thrown into the sea, so to speak, in this way, since the strength of the fruit when it is cut off is thrown into the sea of the belly, which is the seat of lust. Thus Venus is said to have been born in the sea from the testicles of Saturn which were thrown into the sea.[44]

A criticism of hard primitivism

In at least one case, the desire of a Christian to depreciate pagan thought led to a criticism of a theory which might have been believed to be congenial to the saintly turn of mind. In a poem attributed to Antonius,[45] the *Carmen adversus gentes,* we find Diogenes the Cynic and the hard primitivists satirized as men who were ungrateful to God for His blessings.

The Physicists are called by the name of Nature; the ancient way of living was their delight, in its roughness and disorder. For one of them once carried a staff and an earthen vessel which he thought should be his sole possession, since it alone was useful, the one to be his support, the other his drinking cup. When he saw a farmer stand and drink from his cupped hands, he broke his earthern vessel, and when it was once cast aside, he said that superfluities should be eliminated. The rustic showed him that he could do away even with that. These men do not drink wine nor do they eat bread. They do

---

[43] This word does not occur in classical Latin, but its meaning is easily guessed.

[44] *Fragment on Mythology,* lines 1-24. In *Les Oeuvres poétiques de Baudri de Bourgueil,* Ed. Phyllis Abrahams, Paris, 1926, p. 274. There is a possibility that the interest in Saturn had a certain popularity since we know that the Saturnalia with its *libertas decembri* lasted well into the Middle Ages. Joannes Belethus [12th c.] in his *Rationale divinorum officiorum,* ch. 70 [*MPL,* CCII, p. 123], says with disapproval that "even bishops and archbishops sport in the cloisters with their subordinates" *ita ut etiam sese lusum pilae demittant.* "And this freedom is said to be the *libertas decembrica,* because once it used to be part of pagan custom that in this month slaves and serving maids and shepherds were given this kind of freedom, so to speak, and were put on an equal level with their masters, having a festival in common after the harvest. Although, to be sure, great churches, like that of Rheims, observe this custom of playing, yet it seems more praiseworthy not to play." For the pagan *libertas decembri,* which was a kind of return to the Age of Kronus, see *PIA,* p. 67.

[45] This poem is attributed to Saint Paulinus of Nola by O. Berdenhewer, following Muratori. See his *Patrologie,* 3d ed., Freibrug, 1910, p. 389.

not sleep on a bed nor keep off the cold with clothing.   Thankless to God, they spurn what He has provided.[46]

Progress as the realization of human potentialities

In the fifth century two men suggested that the development of history was the unfolding of a plan which was contained *in potentia* at the beginning of history.   As the relations between these two men were very close, it is probable that their theories were formed in common.

The first of these men, Prosper of Aquitania, a disciple of Saint Augustine, maintained that it is a rule of God to prepare future events by planting their seeds and letting them mature.   The seeds of God's plan contain their future entirely preformed within themselves.   History, therefore, is a steady growth and progress, but it is not the attainment of novelty. Nor could the perfection which growth implies be infinite; it is limited by the actuality resident *in potentia* in the germ.

> But of this preparation there is not a single uninterrupted advance, nor is there one measure.   For the works and gifts of grace are varied in many ways and with numberless differences and in each separate kind of benefaction there are different degrees and unequal quantities. For just as in the seeds of grasses and trees, which earth brings forth, there is no one species, nor one genus in them all, but each is produced in the form of its seed and in the quality of its stock, yet does not immediately receive its full beauty as soon as it is produced, but advances with sure and ordered increase until it reaches the perfect quantity of its condition by successive increments, so too the seeds of God's gifts and of the plant of virtue are not produced in the whole field of the human heart at once, because it is to be in the future, nor is maturity easily found in a seed, nor perfection in a beginning. Indeed, God, the powerful and merciful, frequently unfolds those wonderful effects of His work, and after a delay in carrying out His purposes, not expected by certain minds, He brings to fruition all at once what He was planning to produce.   In the loins of Abraham Levi was sanctified [*Heb.*, vii, 10] and at the same time as this the house of Aaron and the priestly order were blessed [*Gen.*, xiv, 19]. In Isaac's birth from a promised conception long delayed and against the hope [*Rom.*, iv, 8] of his sterile and elderly parents, the calling of all peoples and the form of Christ in its entirety is pre-established. Jacob, with no merit in his favor, selected before his birth, was chosen [*Malachi*, i, 2; *Rom.*, ix, 13].   To Jeremiah it was said, "Before I formed thee in the belly I knew thee; and before thou camest forth out of the womb, I sanctified thee" [*Jerem.*, i, 5].   John in the womb of his mother, Elizabeth, filled with the Holy Spirit, exulted [*Luke*, i, 44] and that none born of woman might be greater [*Matth.*, xi, 11] felt the beginnings of grace before those of nature.[46a]

According to Saint Leo the Great, man was made to be immortal, his earthly body animated by the celestial breath.   Yet even before the Fall, he

---

[46] *Carmen adv. gentes* [*MPL*, V, 263 ff.].
[46a] *De vocatione*, II, xi [*MPL*, LI, p. 695].

was not to remain quiescent, but to perfect his nature by continued observance of the law, so that he would seem not to have been made perfect *in actu*, but only *in potentia*. The reward of such perfection would appear to be immortality, not of his soul alone, but of his body and soul. Saint Leo's suggestion of development within Adam before the Fall is carried out in his advice to his own contemporaries. Here we see a picture of human education which, though its original is an individual, is based upon anti-primitivistic ways of thinking, not primitivistic. The goal of human development is not fixed; man has a road of unlimited extent to travel. Nor is this a matter of discouragement to the saint; he argues, like certain German romanticists, that endless striving for perfection is "true justice."

> Although, dearly beloved, at the approach of Easter the very return of the prescribed time speaks to you of the Lenten fast, the exhortation of our sermon must be added, which with the Lord's help may not be useless to the slothful nor burdensome to the pious. For since reason demands that our every observance of those days be increased, there is no one of you, I trust, who is not glad to bestir himself to the good work. For our nature, while it remains mortal, is mutable, and though it should be carried upward to the highest endeavor for the virtues, yet always, just as it has room to fall, has also room to grow. And this is the true justice of the perfect, that never do they suppose themselves to be perfect, lest ceasing from traveling along the not yet finished journey, they shall fall into the peril of deficiency there where they have left their striving for proficiency. Therefore, since none of us, dearly beloved, is so perfect and saintly that he cannot be more perfect and saintly, let us all together without distinction of rank or merit, run with pious eagerness from those things to which we have attained to those which we have not as yet grasped, and to the measure of our habit let us add something with needed increase. For he is shown to have been too little religious at some other time who in these days is not found to be more religious.[47]

Progress in John Scotus

Speculating upon another *praeparatio*, that made by John the Baptist, John Scotus lays the foundations for a theory of progress which, wittingly or unwittingly, looks backwards to Montanism and forward to Joachim of Florus.[48] There are, he maintains in his *Commentary on the Gospel according to John* [*MPL*, CXXII, p. 308] three *sacerdotia*, the first that of the Law, i. e., the Old Testament, which is "far removed from the vision of peace, because of its mysteries, obscure and very difficult to understand, and because of the thick mists of its teachings, greatly distant from the light of truth"; the second, that of the New Testament, "which began with

[47] *Sermons*, XL, ch. 1 [*MPL*, LIV, p. 268]. See Sermon XXIV, ch. 2 [*MPL*, LIV, p. 205] for the passage on Adam.

[48] This affiliation has also been noted by Henry Bett in his *Johannes Scotus Erigena*, Cambridge, 1925, p. 178.

the preaching of the Precursor and will terminate at the end of the world ";
the third " will be celebrated in the future life, in which there will be no
symbols, no obscurity of metaphor, but the clearest truth as a whole." Thus
the New Testament stands midway between the superseded religion of the
Synagogue and the celestial life. There are three " laws " which correspond
to these three *sacerdotia,* the law of nature, the written law, and the law
of grace.

> But if you ask the difference between these three laws, I mean the
> law of nature, and the written law, and that of grace, learn it in a
> few words. It is the law of nature which orders all men to love
> each other equally, that as they all have one and the same nature, so
> there may be one common love of all by all. It is the written law
> which forbids the law of nature to be broken, and distinguishes
> between virtues and vices and wears the likeness of the law of grace.
> I say that the written law is a support to the law of nature, so that,
> since the law of nature by itself alone has not proved strong enough to
> correct human nature, the force of the written law has repressed what
> was to be forbidden and taught what was to be fulfilled. To such a
> degree in fact has the law of nature been almost effaced in men that
> it neither knows its founder nor is able to make any distinction
> between virtues and vices. It is the law of grace which not only
> teaches men to love one another and distinguishes between virtues
> and vices, but even more than this—something which is possible only
> for divine grace—teaches us to die, if need be, for not only good men,
> but even for the wicked. Which law Christ fulfilled in Himself when
> He suffered not only for all men but even for all impious men.[49]

The three laws, it will be noticed, are set forth not only in order of their
inherent value, but also in chronological order. Human history is thus
presented as a process of threefold improvement, if not steady and continuous, being attributable to sudden acts on the part of God, at any rate
real and unmistakable. Nor must the fact that the last act of the drama
takes place in Heaven seem paradoxical. For John Scotus, as for many
medieval thinkers, the transition from terrestrial to celestial existence was
part of the natural history of mankind and, if a negation of some of our
experiences on earth, was nevertheless a continuation and intensification of
others. In fact, for him all things moved in a cycle, from a state of unity,
through diversity, and back into unity.[50] The two end terms are God, and
the intellectual model upon which this cycle is conceived is that of Plotinus
with his doctrine of emanations and return. The metaphysics of this process
do not concern us here. What is more important is to point out that the
process itself involved the complete disappearance of evil.

> Evil is in every respect opposed to the divine goodness. And so evil
> will be eliminated and will remain in nothing [lit., " in no-nature "],

[49] *MPL,* CXXII, p. 309, Comm. on St. John, fr. 1.
[50] A brief and convenient summary of Erigena's teaching is given in Bett,
op. cit., p. 83.

since the divine goodness will be at work and will appear in all.   And therefore our author [51] asserts that our nature is not fixed in evil and that it will not in the future be always held down by evil, but will return to the good, once all evil is ended.   For just as the shadow of the earth, which we call " night," is not extended infinitely into the regions of the air and the aether, but at a point not more than one hundred and twenty six thousand *stadia,* as natural scientists assert, since the sun's rays which are spread about the earth compress it on all sides, is drawn together like a cone, so that it entirely disappears, so evil, which like a shadow of our transgressions fills our nature, will be compressed by the abundance of the supernal and eternal goodness and entirely abolished, while the irrational impulses of the human soul are turned to rational impressions of the truth.   Then he un-hesitatingly asserts—and almost all the divine philosophers agree—that our nature will be always moved by and will seek nothing else but the highest good by which it began to be moved by its first princi-ple and towards which it will hasten its motion as towards its end.[52]

The Venerable Guibertus

Any Christian who reflected on the course of religious history must have been tempted to believe that, at least as far as the New Testament was concerned, the lot of human beings had improved.   He was not forced, however great the temptation, into believing in a third and final revelation, but he could scarcely maintain that the course of history had shown steady degeneration.   The notion of a *preparation* for Christianity was a common one and the question which had to be faced was that of why it was necessary. Why had not God simply given man a final and complete revelation of all religious truth at the outset?   Saint Augustine had popularized the analogy between the growth of humanity and that of a man.   Was it not probable that in religious matters, as in all others, man had to grow, that man in his early years on earth was incapable of understanding the truths of Christianity?

That was the lesson which the Venerable Guibertus drew from his study of history.   For him the Old Testament was prerequisite to an appreciation of the New.   The Jews, he maintains, were children who could be taught only as children are taught.   When they became ripe for it, God revealed the truth of Christianity.   Guibertus does not derive from this any general theory of history.   History interested him only in so far as it concerned the Hebraic-Christian tradition.   Within that tradition, there had been a steady improvement in intelligence, if not in other things.   As in Philo, who saw the story of *Genesis* as an allegory of the education of the *Nous,* so in this twelfth century figure, man learns bit by bit to reject material possessions and sensual pleasures and to replace them with heavenly felicity.

You have, I believe, several examples of a change in divine decisions, in which you can conjecture that God, even if immutable, has given

---

[51] He is speaking of Gregory Nazianzen.   See Bett, *op. cit.,* p. 161, n. 1.
[52] *De divisione naturae,* 5 [*MPL,* CXXII, p. 918].

diverse opinions to mutable man to apprise him of reforms. For just as you see little children taught in infancy by one set of lessons, in youth by other examples, and after they have grown up these are arranged in a more difficult way, while in the case of aged men the deepest subjects are treated, so understand that God has behaved in a similar fashion in regard to the progress of this world. For just as it is proper that a child be taught the rudiments of speech by the daily stories of the men and women who take care of him, and that as he grows older he is restrained from the freedom of infancy in a ·harsher school, that with increasing years he may be checked by its fellows, so that finally his youth is ruled spontaneously by its own impulsion, with birch discarded from love of virtue, so at first God taught the world with His own words and those of the angels, and as if by the form of their speech corrected the stuttering lips of the world, so that what is now manifest not even to the best of us was then clear to the most wicked and to the very beasts. A little later, as in the times of Noah or Abraham, it was proper to give physical punishment occasionally and there began to be a denoting of things by signs. Under Moses God forced man, as if he were a youth, to rise somewhat from his original baseness and to know certain things maturely. . . . Again, under the Redeemer's grace, He revealed to the weightier mind, as it were, capable of understanding His entire Divinity, the sterner elements of His inner counsel. For to them who minister unto their masters by love alone, their masters are accustomed to tell their secrets more easily. "Henceforth," He said [*John*, xv, 15], "I call you not servants; for the servant knoweth not what his lord doeth; but I have called you friends; for all things that I have of my Father I have made known unto you." In your law what rewards does God promise you? Possessions, full bellies, wives and sons, long life; and the punishments He threatens you with are but the opposites of these. Concerning eternal things, there is silence. Nothing is said of the rewards of heaven, the torments of hell. As a maid alone is tempted by a youth, burning with lust, and his indecent words are incomprehensible to her, so they [the Jews] were terrified away from vices by tortures or by death, and attracted to certain goods, not by feeling, not by admonition, but by the cajolement of such rewards . . ." [He cites the Bible in witness of God's treatment of the Jews.]

Many of the pagan philosophers despised the things promised you, and, like Diogenes, rejected possessions. And when the whole world was under their sway, like Octavianus Caesar, they held it of small value. What should I say to you? Is a law good, the rewards of which promise nothing stable? . . .[53]

There was thus in the development of Catholic thought a current of anti-primitivism running alongside of primitivistic currents. In all probability the strongest motivation was the revelation of the New Testament, which made it impossible for Christians to maintain that in all respects men should turn back to earlier times. It is true that man's greatest felicity on earth

[53] *Tractatus de incarnatione*, III, vi [*MPL*, CLVI, p. 519].

had been enjoyed by the primordial couple but the consequences of the Fall had involved the impossibility of returning to that state this side of Paradise. One might be a chronological primitivist in the sense of recognizing that the best period of history had been the earliest, but one could not fail to recognize that there had been a later period which had given men the chance to regain that happiness in the form of salvation. Had there been any agreement within the Church on the conditions of life before the Fall, it might have been possible to develop a theory of cultural primitivism which would have been a program for Christian living. But, as we have seen, the Bible itself gave no clear and unambiguous picture of such a life. The Christian community was free therefore to elaborate a diversity of theories about the best life. It made the most of it. From the solitary hermits whose life was an approximation to that of Diogenes to a man like Antonius with his satire of hard primitivism, there was room for every variety of opinion. All could with some justification claim to be good Christians. To maintain that Christian dogma was primitivistic, in any of the senses of that word, rather than anti-primitivistic is impossible.

JOACHIM OF FLORUS

The appearance of Christianity, a religion whose purpose was to super-sede more ancient faiths, was in itself evidence to some Christians that the best things were not necessarily the earliest, that at any rate after the Fall, human history might be supposed to be an ascent, not always uninterrupted, towards the realization of values until then unattained. Thus it was sug-gested by some of those writers who played with the idea of Adam as an infant that God intended the progressive education of mankind, that as men became more enlightened new truths would be revealed to them, until finally in the racial maturity they would know all the truth. Such sug-gestions are found in Theophilus, Clement of Alexandria, Lactantius in some passages, and Saint Ambrose, though they all differ in details and in the extent to which they develop the thesis.

One of the earliest and most influential statements of a Christian theory of progress, according to which there would be in the future, as there had been in the past, successive revelations, is found in Tertullian. In a passage in *De velandis virginibus* we find him maintaining that the series of divine revelations occur like the growing of a plant—the seed, first, then the shoot, the sapling, and so on. Religion, in other words, has been given us in embryo, then in the Law and the Prophets, then in the Gospels, and now through the Holy Spirit.

> Finally Ecclesiastes says, " There is a time for everything." Watch that creature little by little attain fruition. At first it is a seed, and from the shoot the sapling bursts forth. The branches and leaves push out and the whole tree comes into its own. Then the swelling bud and the flower is loosed from the bud and from the flower the fruit is born. This, crude and somewhat shapeless, little by little developing its growth, perfects the suavity of its flavor. So too for justice—for God is the God of Justice and of creation—first in the rough, when nature feared God. Then through the Law and the Prophets it moved into infancy. Then in the Gospels it burst into youth. Now through the Paraclete it has attained maturity. For he will be the only master to be proclaimed and revered by Christ. For he does not speak in his own person, but what has been commanded by Christ. He alone is the forerunner, because he alone is after Christ. Who have received him prefer truth to custom. Those who have heard him prophesy now, not in the past, veiled virgins.[1]

The metaphor of the growing plant is somewhat transformed in a pas-sage of *Adversus Marcionem*, but there too Tertullian is careful to point out that the appearance of novelty does not imply a break with the past; the novelties of the new religion are a development of things contained in

---

[1] *De velandis virginibus*, ch. 1 [*MPL*, II, p. 890].

the old. Though the Gospel is different from the Old Testament, yet it is the realization of that which was contained in the Old Testament, not something utterly new and different added to it.

You have erred also about that expression of the Lord, in which He seems to distinguish between new and old things. You are puffed up by the old bottles and befuddled with the new wine, and so you have sewn upon the old, that is, the earlier, gospel a patch of heretical novelty. I should like to learn in what respect the Creator has spoken otherwise. When through Jeremiah He taught us, "Break up your fallow ground," does He not turn us away from old things? When He decreed through Isaiah, "Old things are passed away; behold, all things are become new," [2] is He not turning towards new things? Once we believed that this disposition of early things had rather been promised by the Creator to be exhibited by Christ, under the authority of one and the same God to Whom belong both the old and the new. For he does not put new wine into old bottles who does not own the bottles, and no one sets a new piece into an old garment unless he owns the old garment. He does not do anything, if it is not to be done, who does not possess the wherewithal to do it, if it is to be done. And so, if He made the comparison in this matter, in order to show that He was separating the novelty of the gospel from the antiquity of the law, He was also showing that that too was His from which He was making a separation. The separation was not to be marked as that of things foreign to each other, because no one joins his own possessions to things foreign to them to enable himself to separate them from the foreign things. A separation operates through the union by which it is made. Hence what He separated, He also showed to have been one, and thus they would have been if He had not separated them. Nevertheless, if we admit that separation, we admit that it has come about by reformation, by amplification, by progress. Just as the fruit is separated from the seed, although the fruit is from the seed, so also the gospel is separated from the law, although it is borne forward out of the law, a thing other than that, but not foreign to it, different but not contrary.[3]

The expression of Tertullian which speaks of the present era as that of the Holy Spirit is similar to the heresy of Montanus, which was defined as follows: "The Paraclete had said more things in Montanus than Christ had revealed in the Gospels, and not only more, but greater and better." [4] The Montanist movement, which is known mainly through the works of its enemies, was at best a doctrine that certain individuals, then living, had received the gifts of prophecy from the Holy Spirit. Among these were, of

[2] The Latin corresponds to II *Corinthians*, v, 17; the passage referred to in *Isaiah* would seem to be *Isaiah*, xliii, 18, "Remember ye not the former things, neither consider the things of old."

[3] *Adv. Marcionem*, IV, 11 [Ed. Kroymann, *CSEL*, vol. 47, pp. 451 f.] There is a play upon the word *novamen* in the quotation from Jeremiah which is not fully conveyed in the English rendering. The Vulgate reads *novale*.

[4] Ps-Tertullian, *Adversus omnes haereses*, VII [Ed. Kroymann, p. 224].

course, the founder of the doctrine, Montanus, and his associates, Priscilla and Maximilla. If it was believed that these men and women were genuine prophets, a corollary of the belief was the presence in them of the Paraclete. But if they were divinely inspired, then one must believe that the age of revelation was not ended a'nd that in so far as the new prophecies were in conflict with the old, the old had been superseded. Apparently the idea that a new age, the Age of the Paraclete, had set in was advanced to explain the prophetic gifts of the leaders of the new movement and not to elaborate a new theory of history.[5] Yet a new theory of history was included in the teachings of Montanus and it was perhaps inevitable that the third age would be considered as the culmination of Christianity, which relegated the second age, that of Christ, to a simple transitional period between the first and the last.

It was clear to many Christians that if one were to return to prophecy, to use the phrase of Professor Rufus Jones, one must abandon the idea of religion's being the prerogative of an organized church. Authority would be transferred from the priesthood to the individual men and women to whom God had vouchsafed the truth through His Holy Spirit. The heretical aspects of the doctrine then lay more in its theory of prophecy than in its theory of history and it is quite possible that the Church could have accepted the latter, if it had not been used to substantiate the former. But the Montanist could not very well give up the former, since it was rooted in the Biblical text [*Acts*, ii, 17] which announced that in the " last days " the Spirit would be poured forth upon all flesh and that both men and women would prophesy. A third century document, which has been called " the literary gem of Montanism," [6] the *Passion of Saint Perpetua*, makes it clear that it is an essential tenet of the group to believe in the continuance of revelation and of a new age.

One of the characteristics of the new age is the general participation in knowledge of all men and women. The human race will then become *Spiritual*, as distinguished from corporeal, the flesh presumably being thought of as actually disappearing. It was that side of Montanism which appealed most strongly to Tertullian. He was in fact willing to go to the length of denying that the Church has the " power of binding and loosing," asserting that Peter as an individual alone had this power and that it could as well belong to all individuals who have become spiritual men.[7] It is clear that such ideas made an organized church, the church of the bishops, as it was sometimes called, unnecessary.

The errors of Montanus, then, lay only partly in the doctrine of the

---

[5] A sympathetic exposition of Montanism is given by Rufus M. Jones in his *Studies in Mystical Religion*, 1909, ch. III. Jones deals with the movement almost exclusively as centering about the idea of a " return to prophecy." For the documents, see Munter and Bonwetsch, *Gesch. des Montanismus*.

[6] Jones, *op. cit.*, p. 43.

[7] *De pudicitia*, ch. xxi.

three ages. But neither that doctrine, nor the error associated with it, died out. The most important revival of the former occurs in the works of Erigena, which has been discussed elsewhere in this volume.[8] His three *sacerdotia*, that of the Law, that of the New Testament, and that of the Celestial Life, correspond to the three ages of the Father, the Son, and the Holy Spirit, and the characteristics of each age may be presumed to be similar to those preached by Montanus. But the most influential of these revivals was that of Joachim of Florus.[9]

Of Joachim's dates we know for certain merely that he died in 1202 and was probably born in 1132. He was educated in Calabria where he may very well have been acquainted with eastern legends and doctrine, though it seems unlikely that any Montanist MSS or even versions of Erigena should have fallen into his hands. The transmittal of heretical and erroneous ideas through the Middle Ages is in the very nature of the case impossible to trace. But we do know now that Joachim's main tenets were not original with him and that similar notions—such as those of Almaric of Bena— [10] were current during and immediately after his lifetime.

The outstanding contribution of Joachim to anti-primitivistic thought in the Middle Ages is the doctrine of the Three Ages, according to which history repeats the order of the procession of the three persons of the Trinity.

> When we wish to expound something figuratively in the Scriptures, it should first appear to us as if there were a procession of the Holy Spirit from the Father, according to which the first period of history would be considered as that of the Father, the second that of the Spirit, then, as if there were a procession of the Holy Spirit from the Son, according to which the second period must be considered to be that of the Son, the third that of the Holy Spirit.[11]

The characteristics of each age, in so far as they are found in secular, as distinguished from ecclesiastical, history are as follows: in the first age men lived according to the flesh; in the second, " between " the flesh and the

---

[8] See essay on antiprimitivism, under *Progress in John Scotus*, p. 201.

[9] Out of the mass of literature produced about this semi-legendary figure, perhaps the best English study is that of Henry Bett, *Joachim of Flora*, 1913. In French Renan's study of the MS material in Paris still remains of great value—*Nouvelles études d'histoire religieuse*, 1899, pp. 217 ff. This was first published as *Joachim de Flore et l'évangile éternel*, in the *Revue des Deux Mondes* in 1866, though begun in 1852. Herbert Grundmann, *Studien über Joachim von Flora*, has done pioneer work in the writer's biography. Eugène Anitchkof in his *Joachim de Flore et les milieux courtois*, 1931, has revealed many details about his influence hitherto unnoticed. Finally, Buonaiuti has begun a re-edition of Joachim's works which will make a first hand study of his doctrines more successful than has been possible previously. We use his edition where feasible. For a brief account based on Salimbene, see G. G. Coulton, *From St. Francis to Dante*, 1907, ch. 13.

[10] See Betts, *op. cit.*, p. 56 f.

[11] *Super quatuor Evangelia* [Ed. Buonaiuti, Rome, 1930, vol. I, pp. 22 f.].

spirit; in the third, they will live according to the spirit alone.   The terms used are Pauline, and Joachim is thinking obviously of the possibility of men's becoming purely spiritual, *i. e., pneumatic,* in Paul's sense of the word.   It will be noticed in the following passage that the *fructificatio* of an age dates from a time much later than its *initiatio,* so that within an age there is definite progress.   The metaphors used clearly suggest Tertullian who probably echoed a Montanist source.

> Now there was one period in which men lived according to the flesh, that is, up to the time of Christ.   It was initiated by Adam.   There was a second period in which men lived between the flesh and the spirit, which was initiated by Elisha, the prophet, or by Uzziah, king of Judah.   There is a third, in which men live according to the spirit, which will last until the end of the world.   It was initiated in the days of the blessed Benedict.   And so the fructification of the peculiarities of the first period, or to speak more truly, of the first condition, lasted from Abraham up to Zacharias, the father of John the Baptist. Its initiation dates from Adam.   The fructification of the third age dates from that generation which was the twenty second after Saint Benedict.[12]

That there will be no further progress after the third age is clear from the following passage.

> We say that in this age is the termination of the process of perfection. At that time will be verified the charge of Paul to those already reborn in Christ [I *Cor.,* ii, 14], when he calls those men " animal " and says to those who have not the need of solid food, the animal man " receiveth not the things of the Spirit of God."[13]   The conclusion, therefore, is that we must understand the end of our perfection to have been placed in the third heaven, in the heaven of spiritual intelligence, which follows from both testaments.[14]

The changes which occur in human life during the three ages are paralleled by changes within the Church: during the first, we have the prominence of the laiety; in the second we find the clerics; in the third, the monks.   Just what this prominence consists in is not very clear, but it is possible that Joachim was thinking of social domination, and thus predicting that in the Age of the Holy Spirit, the monks would rule the world.   Details will be given below.

> Because in the first age the order of the laiety stood out, in the second the order of the clerics, in the third, the beginnings of which are making themselves felt, nay, even some outstanding mysteries, the order of monks ought to appear.   Particularly, however, since the advent of Eli, who was the first in Israel to show that spiritual life of which we are speaking, can that order, which is partly of the flesh

---

[12] *Concordia,* fol. 8b, in Anitchkof, *op. cit.,* p. 177, n. 1.

[13] The King James Version reads " natural " where we read " animal "; the Greek " psychic." Tertullian retains " psychic."

[14] *Concordia,* fol. 6d, in Anitchkof, p. 176, n. 1.

and partly of the spirit, say not undeservedly of that which is wholly spiritual, "He who cometh after me was made before me, and I baptise you in water, but he shall baptize you with the Holy Ghost and with fire." [15] [*Math.* iii, 11; *Mark,* i, 8; *Luke,* iii, 16; *John,* i, 33.]

Within the Church there are three ages to be distinguished.

> There must be distinguished three periods, as if by stretches of three days, in the generations of the Church. The first ran from Zacharias, the father of John, who had the covenant of Abraham, up to the blessed Pope Sylvester, fourteen generations; [the second], from the blessed Pope Sylvester to Pope Zachary, fourteen generations; and [the third] from him to the present, fourteen generations. [16]

The development of each age is marked by certain subordinate stages, so that history is thoroughly permeated with change, going from immaturity to maturity. Thus even the four Gospels represent four stages in the life of Christ. [17]

> According now to the spiritual interpretation, we may assign the Four Gospels themselves to four periods. For in the Gospel of Matthew, which begins with Abraham, we take up the whole divine account of the Old Testament, which announced that the Saviour of the world would be born of the seed of David and Abraham, according to the flesh. In the Gospel of Luke, which concerns the boyhood and education of Christ up to His twelfth year, we find the doctrine of Mother Church which, beginning with John the Baptist, as if by intervals of time, comes step by step down to these our times, according to that verse of Daniel, "Many shall run to and fro, and knowledge shall be increased" [*Dan.,* xii, 4]. In the Gospel of Mark, in which Christ's manhood, that is, the time of His preaching, is related, His spiritual doctrine, of which the Apostle says, "We speak wisdom among them that are perfect" [I *Cor.,* ii, 6]. That is, the spiritual doctrine beginning at the time in which Elias will come and continuing until the end of terrestrial history. In the Gospel of John we find that ineffable wisdom which will exist in the future. [18]

This passage clearly adds a fourth period to the three which Joachim usually propounds. But in another passage of the same work we find him speaking of seven periods. These periods, however, divide the history of the Church, all of which of course occurs after the Age of the Father. They are symbolised by the seven seals which were progressively broken in the

---

[15] *Super quatuor Evangelia,* Ed. Buonaiuti, vol. I, p. 155.

[16] *Super quatuor Evangelia,* Ed. Buonaiuti, vol. I, p. 106. Pope Zachary is conjecture, the grounds for which can be found in Buonaiuti's footnote.

[17] Tertullian, too, in some of his moods, likes to emphasize the omnipresence of change. See the opening three chapters of *De pallio,* but note that Tertullian expressly points out in Chapter IV that change may occur without improvement.

[18] *Super quatuor Evangelia,* Ed. Buonaiuti, vol. I, pp. 6 f.

Book of Revelations. The passage which we quote begins after an exposition of the meaning of the healing of the nobleman's son.

That the boy's father asks the hour when he began to mend and they answer that at the seventh hour the fever left him and the father knows this to be the very hour when Jesus said to him, " Go thy way; thy son liveth " [*John*, iv, 46-53] means, as we have said above, that at the opening of the seventh seal this must be fulfilled. For just as by the sixth hour is meant the sixth period of the Church, so by the seventh is meant the seventh period, with this exception . . . in no way will that seventh period be distinct from the sixth as the five preceding periods are distinct, but will be a twofold period, having within itself both periods similarly, side by side, and interconnected. In a double manner there will be shown in it that which pertains to the labor of the sixth and in a double manner that which pertains to the repose of the seventh. And therefore this is said here of the seventh hour, that it must be understood to be not after the sixth period but contained within it, so that when it is said, " Yesterday, at the seventh hour," in no wise does the eighth day on which this is said refer to the Day of Judgment which will follow long after, but, as I should say, to an intercalary day. For in two ways will the sixth day occur, and in two ways must the Sabbath be interpreted, by the occurrence of causes of very great mysteries. Thence it is that one evangelist says that after six days the Lord will be transfigured before three disciples; the second says after about eight days, doubtless because one expected that sixth period without the interpolation, the other noted the duality of the period with the interpolation of [a day of] rest, which is the necessary inference, since he does not say, " After eight days," but, " After about eight days." This very difference is found not only in the lesser periods, but also in the greater ages. Since the sixth age began with the Lord's passion, so the seventh began with the following Sabbath, although in another sense the sixth age began with the birth of Christ. Because in fact those two ages proceed synchronously and what belonged to the sixth appeared from the time of the Lord's passion up to the time of Constantine; since the great battle which took place between the King of the North and the King of the South was fought in that period. From the time of Constantine, or rather from the death of Julian, up to the opening of the sixth seal, there appeared what belonged to the seventh. And, again, from the beginning of that sixth age up to the end of this sixth age, there reappears what belongs to the sixth, that is, when at the end of time and years the King of the North will return and will prepare a multitude much greater than before, and will fight more desperately against the King of the South [*Dan.*, xi, 13]. And so at last, when the battle is over, the sixth age will end and the seventh will continue to the end of the world.[19]

One of the more curious features of the Joachimite outline of history is the progressively more youthful nature of the leaders of civilization. The

[19] *Super quatuor Evangelia*, Ed. Buonaiuti, vol. I, p. 307.

leaders of the first age were old men, of the second youths, of the third children. Here we have an echo of that type of pious anti-intellectualism according to which the very young are wiser than the old for the very reason that they have no experience of this world.

> Perhaps it is pertinent and not external to the cause of the mystery that the Church on the Feast of the Innocents permits a child to be seated on the episcopal throne and to enjoy to some degree the office of priest. This is so no doubt because as in the first age it was granted to the aged to have children of the promise in the order of fleshly marriage. In the second, at the time of Christ, it was granted to youths who were reborn from the water and the Holy Spirit to have them in the clerical order. So in the third, which will be the last, which was initiated in the days of Saint Benedict, as we have clearly pointed out in our *Concordia*, it will be given and already is given to children to have spiritual sons, seeing that most of them, divinely inspired, precede their elders in the Kingdom of God. And of these, the first is symbolized by Abraham and those who like him begot in old age. The second is symbolized by David, who was thirty when he began to reign, and in Ezechiel and John the Baptist and the like, who were of the same age when they began to preach. The third is symbolized by Joseph, Samuel, Solomon, Daniel, John the Evangelist, the blessed Benedict and the like, who from the very time of their boyhood, having an aged heart, were made the masters of the elders and the fathers, so to speak, of their parents.[20]

The wisdom of the child is not unlike the inborn wisdom of the saint, who requires no learning to be wise. So the spiritual man of the Third Age will be a man who is full of grace, who will know without having passed through the hands of the Doctors. Such men by implication would have no need of the " Church of the Bishops."

> " And on the third day," says the Evangelist [*John*, ii, 1], " there was a marriage in Cana of Galilee; and the mother of Jesus was there and both Jesus was called, and his disciples, to the marriage." Wherefore does the Evangelist, about to say, " There was a marriage in Cana of Galilee," preface it with " the third day?" What is that third day? According to the meaning which is gathered from a complete reading of the entire Gospel, the third day means the third period of the Church, in which peace was given to the Church of God that she might be permitted to contemplate her King and unite with Him to Whom she had been betrothed already, by Him Who said to her, " I have espoused you to one husband, that I may present you as a chaste virgin to Christ " [II *Cor.*, xi, 2]. Finally in the same third period the water of the letter was changed into the wine of spiritual intelligence, because when the Doctors were multiplied in the Church of God, light began to arise from darkness and the icy coldness of the law to be converted into the soothing warmth of love. In truth, according to this interpretation, which applies absolutely to the whole

---

[20] *Super quatuor Evangelia*, Ed. Buonaiuti, vol. I, p. 91 f.

15

Church, the third day either signifies the time which is called the time of grace, which is the third period from the time before the law, or it signifies the third age which was to begin with the coming of Elias. Moreover, this time, which is called the time of grace, was preceded by the writing of the Old Testament and that time which will be the time of greater grace, since He has given us grace for grace, is preceded by the writing of the New Testament. And thus once the letter of the law was turned into wine and more strongly, when that time comes, the water of the Gospel-reading will be turned into wine, as the Apostle says, " When that which is perfect is come, then that which is in part shall be done away with " [I *Cor.*, xiii, 10]. Therefore both in the first and in the second meaning it is the Spirit which vivifies, the Spirit which does mighty works and prodigies.[21]

These childlike individuals will be the monks, who, says Joachim, arose in the eastern church, just as the priests arose in the western. The new age, which is almost to dawn, is thus a derivative from the eastern form of monasticism.

According to this interpretation, Mary does not symbolize the universal church, nor the host of the monastic profession in general, but a certain special church of the same monastic profession, to which it was given by the Lord, as its more special function, to elect celibacy and to love life.[22] And this is particularly true in what concerns the pregnancy of both Mary and Elizabeth. Understand in the same way the mystery of Mary pregnant and the birth of Christ. Note this with care, prudent reader, if you wish to cross the seas of such great mysteries without difficulty. Consequently, let us now treat of the second interpretation, of which we began to speak a little above. Just as Elisabeth signifies the primitive Church, whose husband was the apostolic order, so Mary designates the chaste and virginal Church whose husband is a certain order of the spiritual fathers. But if among the Gentiles and in this second period of the age there is a successive order of prelates which Zacharias signifies, how is there among the Gentiles and in this second period of the age a virginal Church which Mary signifies? It should be known that because of this and similar mysteries, God wished there to be a double Church, that is, an eastern and a western, so that, by sending Peter as supreme pontiff to the western Church, He might confirm in it the ecclesiastical or sacerdotal order which John signifies, and by sending John the evangelist, the mirror of chastity, to the eastern Church, He might confirm in it the virginal and chaste religion which Mary signifies. Just as the office of preaching is known to have arisen in Rome, so the doctrine of monastic and hermitical profession is known to have arisen in the eastern Church.[23]

All men in the Age of the Monks will live an apostolic life, bound

[21] *Super quatuor Evangelia*, Ed. Buonaiuti, vol. I, p. 191.
[22] There is a play upon words in the Latin which cannot be reroduced in English without forcing usage. The text reads, *celibem eligere et diligere vitam.*
[23] *Super quatuor Evangelia*, Ed. Buonaiuti, vol. I, pp. 32 f.

together in the unity of charity and sharing all things.[24] There will be no practical life, no trades, no crafts, no labor. Man will spend his time in beatific ecstacy. This does not mean that this material globe will disappear and that life will continue in Heaven, but rather that this globe will become "spiritualized" and Heaven will descend upon earth. It was probably this aspect of his teachings which so captivated his contemporaries and spread his doctrines so far.

For we find throughout Europe in the early thirteenth century not only doctrines of three dispensations like that of Joachim, but also the rise of mystical groups of men and women who look to a reign of love and believe in the apostolic life. They hold also in general to the idea that each individual is as sure a source of religious truth as the hierarchy is, thus nullifying the need of a priesthood. We have only to mention the ideas of Almaric of Bena, already cited, of the Ortlibenses, the Carthari, and the Brethren of the Free Spirit.[25] Regardless of details, and in details there were important differences to be noted even in the fragments of the doctrines now left to us, these movements had the greatest importance in the subsequent history of Christianity and therefore of Western Europe. They popularized the idea that history might move from worse to better, which was essential if men were to believe in progress; they also popularized the idea of individual interpretation of religious truths, which was essential if Protestantism in some of its forms was to survive. The Church saw the danger and attempted their extermination.

A little over fifty years after Joachim's death, there appeared in Paris *The Eternal Gospel*, a book sometimes attributed to Joachim but shown by Renan, with as much plausibility as such demonstrations can have, to be a simple compilation of Joachim's other writings [26] and no new composition. Another publication, the *Liber Introductorius in Evangelium aeternum*, possibly by Brother Gherardo of Borgo San Donnino,[27] was frequently confused with this compilation, and was used by the Church as evidence of the heretical tendencies of Joachitism. It was apparently a violently anti-papal document, full of hatred for the upper clergy, preaching the date of the Second Coming as 1260, a date at which Anti-Christ would hold the sea of Saint Peter, hailing Saint Francis at the initiator of new age and Joachim as his John the Baptist. Because of this confusion and the willingness of the "spiritual Franciscans," in whose interests the book was composed, to accept it as the heart of the Joachite doctrine, Joachim became identified with an heretical movement which seriously shook the Church in the thirteenth century.[28]

[24] See Anitchkof, *op. cit.*, pp. 323 ff.

[25] Bett, *op. cit.*, p. 59, even speaks of a Jewish doctrine of the same sort which dates from the tenth century and is thus earlier than Joachim.

[26] See *Nouvelles études, etc.*, pp. 262 ff.

[27] *Ib.*, esp. pp. 265 ff.

[28] The story of the quarrel between Dominicans and the two wings of the Fran-

The doctrine of the Eternal Gospel was condemned in 1255— just five years before the prophesied beginning of the new era—and the book was ordered burned. This action did not apparently succeed in entirely stamping out Joachitism, for after another five years the doctrines were again examined and again condemned. But in spite of suppression, the ideas implicated in it remained as a guiding force among the spiritual Franciscans. Thus Angelo Clareno, who was excommunicated in 1317, and his Fratricelli, are certainly descendants of the Joachites. Olivi, the leader of the Provençal spirituals, admitted his connection with Joachitism. Arnold of Villanova, who died in the early years of the fourteenth century, the Béguines and their analogues, Ubertino, Segarelli, Dolcino of Novara, and others, carried on certain echoes of the doctrine into later centuries.

ciscan order does not concern us here. A brief account of it can be found in Bett, *op. cit.*, ch. iv, p. 67.

INDEX OF TEXTS

The following Index lists all texts of patristic and medieval authors translated, summarized, or referred to. In general when a reference is made to a foot-note, the passage cited is not translated. Editions used are given on the pages indicated. Only the page on which a passage begins is given.

217

INDEX OF NAMES AND SUBJECTS

[Only the page on which a subject begins is given in this index. Passing references to a subject or person are not listed.]